MW01038474

# HAUNTED
# GREENWICH
# VILLAGE

# HAUNTED GREENWICH VILLAGE

## Bohemian Banshees, Spooky Sites, and Gonzo Ghost Walks

### Retold by Tom Ogden

Guilford, Connecticut

To buy books in quantity for corporate use
or incentives, call **(800) 962-0973**
or e-mail **premiums@GlobePequot.com**.

Copyright © 2012 by Tom Ogden

ALL RIGHTS RESERVED. No part of this book may be reproduced or transmitted in any form by any means, electronic or mechanical, including photocopying and recording, or by any information storage and retrieval system, except as may be expressly permitted in writing from the publisher. Requests for permission should be addressed to Globe Pequot Press, Attn: Rights and Permissions Department, PO Box 480, Guilford, CT 06437.

Maps by Alena Pearce © Morris Book Publishing, LLC
Text design: Sheryl P. Kober
Project editor: Meredith Dias
Layout: Sue Murray

Library of Congress Cataloging-in-Publication Data

Ogden, Tom.
  Haunted Greenwich Village : bohemian banshees, spooky sites, and gonzo ghost walks / retold by Tom Ogden.
    p. cm.
  ISBN 978-0-7627-7038-0
  1. Haunted places—New York—New York. 2. Greenwich Village (New York, N.Y.) I. Title.
  BF1472.U60425 2012
  133.109747'1—dc23

                                                    2012003159

Printed in the United States of America

10 9 8 7 6 5 4 3 2 1

*For Middy Streeter, Paula Grande,*
*and their daughter, Youjing*

# CONTENTS

# Contents

# PREFACE

Before we start our survey of all the ghosts that infest Greenwich Village, perhaps a short history of the district might be in order.

The island of Manhattan (named for the Manhatta branch of the Lenape tribe that occupied it) was most probably first spotted by Europeans in 1524 when Florentine explorer Giovanni da Verrazzano sailed by New York Harbor. It was first mapped in 1609 by English navigator Henry Hudson while sailing for the Dutch East India Company. He and the crew of the *Half Moon* (*Halve Maen*) explored the bay and then sailed up the river on the west side of the island (today the Hudson River) all the way to present-day Albany.

Hudson did not discover a Northwest Passage to the Orient, which was the primary goal of his voyage, but he did return home with a boatload of beaver pelts, which set off a series of fur-trading expeditions over the next decade. To exploit trade with the Native Americans, the Dutch West India Company was established in 1621. The operation was a private concern, but it had full authority to act on behalf of the Dutch government in the territories that were being called New Netherland.

In 1624 the Dutch West India Company set up a permanent fur-trading settlement on Governor's Island. Other trading posts soon followed. In 1625, to protect the colonists and to guard the entrance to the Hudson River, the company built Fort Amsterdam at the southern tip of Manhattan Island. As a result 1625 is recognized as the official date for the founding of New Amsterdam, or, as it is now known, New York City.

Peter Minuit replaced Willem Verhulst as director-general of New Amsterdam in 1626, and it was that year that the legendary purchase of the 22.7-square-mile, 13.4-mile-long island was made from the Manhatta for goods worth about sixty guilders or, according to an 1846 historian, the equivalent of twenty-four dollars. (The mythic tale of the purchase usually has Minuit personally maneuvering the exchange. He was no doubt intimately involved in the negotiations, but no actual deed or bill of sale exists listing either his name or how much money was involved in the trade.)

For the first few years, most of the European inhabitants populated only the harbor end of the island. Before long, settlers began to move northward and clear parcels of land for farming. In the 1630s, Dutch farmers and freed Africans cultivated pastures near present-day Gansevoort Street and called the area Noortwyck, or Northern District.

At the time of the Dutch purchase of the island, the land that would one day be Washington Square was a small marsh with a stream running through it known as Minetta Creek, or Minetta Brook. The Native American village of Sapokanikan (meaning "Tobacco Field") lay close by. By the middle of the 1600s, the Dutch had taken over the property and driven out the native inhabitants.

A little-known experiment in emancipation took place soon after. The Dutch farmers who had tracts along the Minetta freed some of their slaves and gave them small plots on either side of the creek. This was done in the hopes that the new landowners would act as a sort of "human shield," if need be, between the Dutch and the restless Lenape whom they had displaced. The catch was that a percentage of freedmen's profits had to go to the Dutch West India Company, and any new children they conceived would be born as slaves. From 1643 to 1664 the acreage making up today's Washington Square Park was informally known as "The Land of the Blacks."

In 1664 English ships appeared in the harbor off New Amsterdam demanding the keys to the city. The colonists were assured that if they surrendered peacefully they would be allowed to keep their property as long as they swore allegiance to the British crown. Dutch Director-General Peter Stuyvesant found no colonists willing to defend the city, so he was forced to surrender. Upon taking control, the British changed New Amsterdam's name to New York.

As the eighteenth century approached, much of the farmland north of the city was subdivided and sold for real estate to meet the needs of a burgeoning population. Carriage paths and horse trails became lanes, then roads. Around 1673 the new hamlet became known as Groenwijck, meaning "Green District."

The community was officially recognized by the name Greenwich Village in 1712. (The earliest surviving mention of "Grin'wich" is in a 1713 Common Council record book.) The town's borders were roughly from what are now Houston Street to Fourteenth Street and from the Hudson River to the current Sixth Avenue (also known as Avenue of the Americas). Well into the early 1800s, however, Greenwich Village was sparsely settled and was separated from New York City by a canal that ran along the route of present-day Canal Street, with two main crossings: Greenwich Road (today's Greenwich Street), which was almost unusable when it rained, and a stone bridge at Broadway.

The Commissioner's Plan of 1811, passed by the New York State Legislature, laid out a grid pattern for the streets of Manhattan to facilitate further development on the island.

Technically the proposal was enacted for the areas north of Fourteenth Street, but it was decided to follow the design all the way to the southern end of the island wherever possible. An exemption was made for the area west of Greenwich and Sixth Avenues, which explains why much of what is now the Greenwich Village Historic District was allowed to keep its labyrinth of narrow, curved lanes. Broadway defies the island's boxlike checkerboard of streets, cutting diagonally from the southeast to the northwest, because it was originally a Manhatta footpath known as the Wickquasgeck Trail.

In April 1797 the Common Council of New York bought the fields east of Minetta Creek and turned them into a public cemetery and potter's field. Recent discoveries suggest that the north side of the graveyard, especially along Waverly Place, was a more formal burial ground used mostly by German immigrants. The south side was for the indigent and those who were unclaimed or unknown. The cemetery was closed in 1825, but none of the graves were relocated. It's estimated that as few as five hundred to as many as twenty thousand people are still laid to rest under Washington Square Park.

In 1826 the city purchased the land immediately to the west of Minetta Creek. It was combined with the former cemetery, and the whole lot was leveled, graded, and turned into a 9.75-acre public square called the Washington Military Parade Ground. Used by the state militia, it was also open to local volunteer militias as well. Now and then a cannon or some other piece of heavy artillery fell through the unpacked earth into a sunken grave, but it was a small price to pay for such a splendid exercise yard.

Over the next two decades, the property surrounding the rectangular plot of land became very fashionable.

Between 1829 and 1833 a series of Greek Revival attached homes were built along the north side of the square. The block of townhouses, now landmarked, is referred to as "The Row." The buildings were constructed of red brick in Flemish bond, and their doorways are framed by Ionic or Doric columns, topped by marble pediments. In 1849 and 1850 the parade ground was transformed into a fenced public park with walking paths, and in 1852 a large, central fountain was added.

In 1871 Washington Square Park became part of the New York City Department of Parks. The grounds are bordered on the west by MacDougal Street, to the east by University Place, on the south by West Fourth Street, and on the north by Waverly Place.

In the fifty-five years since the parade ground was established, however, the neighborhood had changed considerably. Though the north side of the park remained desirable to the well-to-do, period houses along the rest of the perimeter were mostly replaced with high-rises, lower-rent housing, and office buildings. In turn, many of these structures have since been replaced or renovated, many by New York University.

In the early part of the twentieth century, the Village became a haven for the avant-garde, the unorthodox, and the downright odd. The Beat Generation emerged in the 1950s, along with a nascent jazz scene. Off Broadway theater and intimate music clubs began to thrive. "Beatniks" led to "hippies," and in the 1960s Greenwich Village was the site of antiwar protests. And on June 28, 1969, the West Village saw the unofficial beginning of the Gay Rights movement when a police raid on a gay bar, the Stonewall Inn, sparked violent street demonstrations. Gentrification of the

Village over the next few decades ended years of reasonably priced housing, and many artists who had been surviving on God's good graces were forced to move out.

Originally Greenwich Village only stretched from the Hudson to Sixth Avenue or slightly beyond, but after the creation of Washington Square, Broadway became accepted as the eastern boundary of the Village. Some felt the Village's new border went as far as Bowery.

In the 1970s many of the bohemian elements that characterize the Village started to take hold in the blocks of the Lower East Side between Broadway and the East River. This area includes the neighborhood known as Alphabet City (so called because Avenues A, B, C, and D run through it) and NoHo (short for North of Houston; bordered by Broadway, Bowery, Astor Place, and, of course, Houston Street). Taken together, the district between Houston and Fourteenth, from Broadway to the East River, is referred to as the East Village. The quarter has now become upscale, too, as housing was upgraded and trendy shops moved in.

The year 2012 marks the three-hundredth anniversary of the official founding of Greenwich Village. Despite its growth and many changes over the centuries, the entire district—but especially the West Village—still has the feel of an enclave, whose independent spirit is fiercely protected and preserved by its residents.

# ACKNOWLEDGMENTS

While writing this book, I had the luxury of a longer deadline than usual. Unfortunately, in my case, that also allowed me to procrastinate even more than I normally do. Thank you to my fellow authors Michael Kurland and Dustin Stinett for keeping me focused on filling the empty pages. Thanks, too, to David Shine, Joan Lawton, and Linda Robertson for their help as I worried, whined, and obsessed over the tiniest details.

Thank you to the Streeter family, my East Village connection, for all of their help throughout this entire "Haunted" series. Roberta Belulovich at the Merchant's House Museum was delightful to talk to and very helpful during my fact-checking. Thanks also go to Father Albert Wagaman for his insight into church architecture and religious terminology.

Thanks, too, to my agent, Jack Scovil, and to Gary M. Krebs, who first brought me to the attention of Globe Pequot Press.

As always, my special thanks and appreciation go out to everyone at GPP: my editor, Erin Turner; my former editor, Meredith Rufino, who first suggested *Haunted Greenwich Village;* project editor Meredith Dias; copy editor Tom Holton; and Bret Kerr for his amazing cover design.

# INTRODUCTION

I've always been drawn to Greenwich Village—a tangle of short, winding lanes and picturesque brownstones, all peopled by a cast of characters straight out of Central Casting. Somehow I knew that many of the pubs, taverns, hotels, churches, and historic houses would turn out to be haunted. Imagine my surprise to discover that these few square miles have, perhaps, more ghosts per capita than any other comparable city district anywhere on the face of the planet!

Fortunately this book gave me the opportunity to seek them out.

Some of the Greenwich Village phantoms, such as Peter Stuyvesant, who materializes in St. Mark's Church in-the-Bowery, date back to the city's earliest days, when it was the Dutch colony of New Amsterdam. Several spooks come from the time of the American Revolution: Thomas Paine, Aaron Burr, and Alexander Hamilton to name just a few. Two famous spectres whose time on earth straddled two centuries are Mark Twain and Harry Houdini. Two others who came to fame in the 1900s shared a first name but little else. In fact, they could not have been more different: Charlie "Bird" Parker and Charles "Lucky" Luciano.

Some of the Village ghosts hang out in public areas, such as Washington Square Park and the Lexington Avenue subway line. A few like the limelight and have come back to take a bow at one of the quarter's many Off Broadway theaters. There are at least two hotels whose tenants have never checked out. (One of the inns houses ghosts that were survivors of the *Titanic*!) There are also a couple of fire stations with resident spirits. And speaking of "spirits," Greenwich

Village also seems to have more than its share of haunted taverns. Maybe the pubs' late-night apparitions, such as poet and taproom regular Dylan Thomas, never heard the bartenders shout out last call.

Most of the haunted places found in Greenwich Village don't have famous phantoms, however, and the venues are mostly nondescript from the outside. It's not until their residents think they're safe behind closed doors that the spirits come out to play.

I've separated this book into three sections. Part One details some of the hauntings that take place in and immediately around Washington Square Park because it's the primary landmark of the Village. With its distinctive Memorial Arch, Washington Square has to be considered "Ground Zero" in any discussion of Greenwich Village ghosts.

Part Two takes us over into the West Village. Streets around Washington Square are laid out more or less in a grid fashion. Roads in the West Village are more helter-skelter, following old footpaths and horse trails, resulting in a maze of intersecting lanes. The nineteenth-century townhouses, taverns, and hotels that line them make perfect hiding places for an abundance of banshees.

At one time, the blocks between Broadway and the East River were simply considered parts of the Lower East Side, the Bowery, and Alphabet City, but these blocks have merged to form its own identity—the East Village—since gentrification moved into the area in the 1980s and 1990s. This is the neighborhood we'll visit in Part Three. And trust me, like the rest of Greenwich Village, it's not lacking for apparitions and other paranormal activity.

After the ghost stories, there are three appendices in the back of the book. The first one is a bibliographic resource for some of the books, articles, videos, and websites I consulted while writing this book. The second appendix lists the addresses and contact information for all of the major sites mentioned throughout the stories in case you want to visit them. And finally—new for this series—a third appendix offers three suggested walking tours of the haunted sites found in Greenwich Village, one aligned with each of the sections of the book. Any one of these walks should take about a half day to complete, depending upon how much time you spend inside the places that can be entered. But if you're hardy and adventurous enough, you might be able to combine them into one long, very full day of ghost hunting.

Whether you let your fingers or your feet do the walking, I hope you enjoy all of the tales of terror in *Haunted Greenwich Village.*

## Part One

# GREENWICH VILLAGE—THE HISTORIC CENTER

The words "Greenwich Village" instantly conjure up the archetypal image of a hip, bohemian enclave, filled with the eccentric, the artistic, and the unconventional. But it's also a neighborhood filled with ghosts. And why not? Much of the area was once a forbidding marshland, and for about a quarter of a century Washington Square Park served as the pauper's graveyard. And then there were the executions from the Hangman's Elm!

Today "the Village" stretches from the Hudson to the East River, but its historic center is bounded by Sixth Avenue to the west, Broadway to the east, Fourteenth Street to the north, and Houston Street on the south. How many hundreds (or even thousands) of Big Apple apparitions must live within its borders?

# Chapter 1
# Ghost Central Station

## Washington Square
## Waverly Place, West Fourth Street,
## University Place, and MacDougal Street

*Up to twenty thousand people were buried under the commons now known as Washington Square, and many of their spirits walk the grounds. As, too, do the ghosts of those executed on the property, "celebrity" apparitions, and even a phantom dog. But perhaps first among equals are the spectres that proclaim Greenwich Village an independent republic from the top of the Memorial Arch.*

Cold wasn't the word for it. Jeff could almost feel little crystal flakes forming on his breath as he exhaled. At first he thought his entire face was freezing over, but then he realized the stinging tightness around his eyes and lips was caused by having spent the last couple of hours in an overheated room with no humidity. *Oh, well,* he thought. *You know what they say: Out of the frying pan, into the refrigerator.*

It was his own fault. He hadn't expected the sudden drop in temperature, and his winter coat was at the cleaners. He was stuck with a flight jacket, more appropriate for autumn than midwinter. He could have gotten away with it if he'd worn layers, but he knew he was going to be indoors most of the night and didn't want to roast. No, he'd have to make do.

Jeff and his girlfriend, Melissa, had spent the evening uptown helping her BFF mark one of those milestone birthdays. All birthdays seemed to be milestones for women, he laughed to himself, but this was a real one: The Big 3-OH! Jeff had passed that point of no return a few years before, rather uneventfully as he recalled, but he did remember thinking at the time that he could no longer pretend to be young. At thirty, like it or not, you are absolutely, unforgivingly, an adult.

Perhaps that fact weighed more on women, Jeff mused. Which was why he had put up no argument when Melissa discreetly told him she wanted to stay a bit longer with Melodie and that he could run along. She'd see him tomorrow. Yada yada. He could take a hint. The rest of their night would be girl talk with (knowing those two) lots of laughs and tears over several bottles of Chardonnay.

Now, tucking his fingertips under his arms, Jeff picked up his pace. The walk was longer than he had thought it would be. There was a subway stop within a half block of Melodie's place on Fifty-seventh, and he had run down into the station without thinking. It was the N heading downtown, which in normal weather would have been fine. But it had let him off on Eighth on the east side of Washington Square, so he now had to cross through the park to get to his apartment over on Sullivan. If he had just paid a little more attention, he could have transferred at Herald Square and taken the F down to Fourth Street.

He was about halfway through the park when a sudden gust of wind whipped around and smacked him full in the face. Where had that come from? Jeff pulled the knit cap all the way down over his ears.

His eyes strayed over to the Memorial Arch. No matter how often he passed it, he couldn't get over how amazing it looked, especially since it had been restored. And at this time of night, in this frigid weather, with all the tourists, students, office workers, street performers, and skateboarders gone, there were no distractions. He could simply stand and take in the marvel. It stood there silently, solid, a thing of beauty.

Jeff was about to lower his head and force himself onward when something caught his eye. There! Standing on the top of the grand arch was one . . . no, two . . . no, a whole group of people. They were huddled together, and bundled up in long, old-fashioned, fur-collared coats, wearing gloves and mufflers, they almost looked like Christmas carolers out of a Dickens novel.

They seemed to be hollering to Jeff, though he couldn't hear a sound, and were wildly gesturing for him to come closer. Did they want him to join them?

Jeff knew there was a spiral stairway inside the west leg of the arch, installed so that workmen could access the roof. In fact, for a day or two back when the structure was refurbished in 2004, people were allowed to climb the steps to view the interior brickwork.

Did he dare go up? He looked around. There were no patrol cars in sight. What the hell! What's the worst that could happen?

Jeff set off at a trot, quickly reaching the bottom of the structure. He walked over to the west leg, expecting to find the entryway to the staircase wide open, but no . . . The door was sealed tight, as usual.

So how did they get to the top? Jeff circled both legs to see if there was another way up, but the only entrance, open or shut, was the one on the west leg.

Puzzled, he walked about a hundred feet toward the fountain located in the center of the park, then turned back to look at the memorial. He was far enough away that he could see the top of the arch, or at least anyone who was standing up there. But now there were no signs of life. The silent revelers were no longer there.

All at once the sounds of the city began to pound in Jeff's ears. It was only then that he realized everything around him had been deathly quiet for some time—ever since that strange blast of air had caught him in the face. He glanced at his watch. The whole experience had taken less than five minutes.

Who had the people been? Where did they go? Had he even seen them at all? Jeff hunched his shoulders and drew in his jacket more tightly as he began walking the last few blocks to his apartment. The mystery could wait. For now, he had to get out of the cold.

Jeff didn't know that the folks he saw on top of the arch weren't flesh and blood, and he was far from the first person to have spotted the spectres. One or more phantoms have been cavorting there for more than a quarter century.

The Memorial Arch, located at the north edge of the park, where Fifth Avenue dead-ends at Waverly Place, is undoubtedly the most conspicuous landmark in Washington Square Park. The original arch was erected in 1889 for a three-day festival commemorating the centennial of George Washington's inauguration. Designed by famed New York architect Stanford White (of McKim, Mead, and White), it was built in wood and festooned with papier-mâché wreaths, garlands, and electrical lights. The $2,700 temporary structure stood about one hundred feet north of the park spanning Fifth

Avenue and was so popular that local residents immediately commissioned White to fabricate a permanent Tuckahoe marble edifice in the nearby park.

Ground was broken on May 30, 1890, but construction was soon delayed when workers hit a layer of human bones ten feet down. Once the skeletal remains were cleared away, the project resumed. The seventy-seven-foot-tall, $134,000 Beaux Arts Memorial Arch was dedicated on May 4, 1895. White had provided the basic design, and David H. King Jr., who had built the pedestal for the Statue of Liberty, oversaw construction. Most of the ornamentation, including the distinctive spandrel panels covered with rosettes on the underside of the arch, was by Frederick William MacMonnies. The marble eagles on the north and south sides of the arch were by Philip Martiny. Two statues were later added to the north side of the arch's legs. The figure on the easternmost leg, designed by Hermon Atkins MacNeil, depicts Washington as Commander-in-Chief, accompanied by Fame and Valor. Alexander Stirling Calder's Washington as Statesman, accompanied by Wisdom and Justice, flanks the other leg. Both statues were carved from Dover marble and were added in 1916 and 1918, respectively.

On the night of January 23, 1917, French artist Marcel Duchamp, American painter John Sloan, Sloan's art student and Texas-born poet Gertrude Drick, and Provincetown Playhouse actors Alan Russell Mann (also known as Forrest Mann), Charles Ellis, and Betty Turner slipped through the unattended iron door on the west leg of the Washington Square Arch and climbed the stairway to the top. It was Drick who had found out about the maintenance staircase and instigated the whole thing.

Drick was quite a character. Slender and bob-haired in the flapper style, she was prone to bouts of melancholy. Among other idiosyncrasies, to introduce herself she carried black-bordered name cards with a single word, WOE, engraved on them. When anyone asked why she wanted people to call her that, Drick would reply, "Because Woe is me."

On January 22 Woodrow Wilson spoke before the US Senate, recommending that all countries should avoid foreign alliances and entanglements. (America would not enter World War I until April 6.) Drick—who had long before decided that Greenwich Village, populated as it was by eccentric artists, should be recognized as its own nation—took the president's speech as a call to action. She decided she would declare the Village's sovereignty from the top of the Memorial Arch.

She already knew about the "secret" door and stairwell. She rounded up a bunch of Chinese lanterns, red balloons, food, and lots of liquor. She also filled hot water bottles to sit on, knowing it would be cold that night. Somehow she managed to get all the odds and ends up to the roof of the arch. She then convinced her convivial friends to meet her there that night. As they arrived, no doubt already a few sheets to the wind, Drick handed each person a cap pistol. When everyone was assembled, Drick dramatically read her proclamation, a Declaration of Independence for the Republic of Greenwich Village. The cap pistols were fired in jubilation, a bonfire was lit, toasts were made, and for the next several hours, as the old saying goes, a good time was had by all. The next morning, as people crossed through Washington Square, the only trace of the previous evening's celebration was a ring of red balloons tied to the low wall encircling the top of the arch.

There is some debate as to what night the incident took place. Many books of ghost tales and website listings of paranormal hauntings give the date as New Year's Eve or just after midnight on January 1, 1917. That has a nice ring to it, story-wise, but most Greenwich Village historians say the event really happened on January 23. Regardless, the revolutionaries' ghosts have been spied standing on top of the arch, waving to those passing below, on various dates throughout the year, starting in the 1980s or early 1990s.

Marcel Duchamp and his companions seem to limit their activities to the roof of the arch, but other denizens of the dark ramble through the park more freely. Many of the apparitions are thought to be the spirits of people whose bodies still lie buried underground from the square's days as a cemetery for the poor. Do their ghosts show up because they wish to be remembered, or are they upset by all the living who defile their graves by walking on them?

Other phantoms roam the square as well. It's easy to identify some of them: They are Manhatta who had been chased off their land, recognizable by their tribal clothing. They couldn't return to the banks of the Minetta while they were alive, so perhaps their spectres have returned to claim the park as their Happy Hunting Ground.

Rumors persist that a large tree in the northwest corner of Washington Square was originally known as the Hangman's Elm. Supposedly executions were held there from the time of the American Revolution up to when burials in the graveyard were discontinued. The problem with the old wives' tale is that, at the time the hangings were supposedly taking place, the tree was on private property west of Minetta Creek, not on the cemetery grounds.

Only one hanging in the graveyard has ever been documented, and stories differ as to the site of the gallows. Some say it was where the fountain is now located; others say it was where the Arch stands. As for the Hangman's Elm, the branch from which the noose was allegedly strung cracked and had to be removed in 1992. The tree itself survives—one of the oldest in New York City—and from time to time people passing under it swear that they see the shadowy form of a corpse hanging from one of its limbs. Other phantoms that converge around the tree are thought to be the lost souls of innocent prisoners who had been put to death.

Other sightings have included the ghosts of Edgar Allan Poe, who lived in the Village for a time, and folk singer Woody Guthrie, who stayed with the Almanac Singers at 647 Hudson Street in the early 1940s and also at 74 Charles Street.

No doubt the cutest apparition is that of Fala, the beloved Scottish terrier of President Franklin Roosevelt. In 1952 Robert Moses, then Parks Commissioner, announced plans to extend the four lanes of Fifth Avenue through Washington Square Park in an attempt to revitalize the south side of the quadrant. Neighborhood activists, including West Village resident Eleanor Roosevelt—who had kept a house at 29 Washington Square West from 1942 to 1949—rose up against the proposal, and it was successfully nipped in the bud. Despite objections, however, cars continued to be allowed to drive in a single lane under and through the Memorial Arch until the end of the decade.

During Eleanor Roosevelt's time in the Village, Fala was no doubt a welcome visitor in her home. The canine died in 1952 and is buried next to FDR in Hyde Park. But Fala apparently enjoyed playing in Washington Square Park enough to make it a private dog run for the rest of eternity.

Today as one stares up at the Memorial Arch, wades in the park's new fountain, or strolls peacefully through the plaza, listening to a street musician, stopping to watch street mimes, or checking out the players at one of the permanent outdoor chess tables, it's hard to believe that it wasn't until 1959 that Washington Square was permanently closed to automobile traffic. Or that it's been the site of massive political rallies, protest marches, and union demonstrations.

Or that it's filled with ghosts.

# Chapter 2

# The Spindrift Spectres

## The Mark Twain House
## 14 West Tenth Street

*The apartment building may be nondescript, but a dark aura exists inside. Mark Twain, who lived there one winter, may have returned. And he's not alone. According to author Jan Bryant Bartell, he was one of twenty-two spirits who were in residence when she stayed there in the 1960s.*

"No, we're not haunted. I don't care what you saw on *Ghost Hunters*. That's a TV show. This is the real world."

Bradley bit his lip. He'd already been reprimanded once. Never be sarcastic to people who call to ask about the spirit. They don't know any better. Just state the facts.

"Yes, Samuel Clemens, or rather Mark Twain, lived here for almost thirty years back in the 1800s. But I've worked at the museum for several years, and I've never seen any ghosts all the time I've been here."

Bradley put down the phone. He'd been on staff at the Mark Twain House and Museum in Hartford, Connecticut, for almost five years and considered himself somewhat of an unofficial Twain scholar. He thought he knew everything there was to know about the celebrated author, humorist, lecturer, and world traveler, but all this spook nonsense was new to him.

Back in 2009 The Atlantic Paranormal Society, also known as TAPS, investigated the mansion where Samuel Clemens, his wife Olivia, and their three daughters lived from 1874 to 1891 for the SyFy Channel's popular show *Ghost Hunters.* Bradley had no idea why. He was never able to find out who had told the program that the spectre of a young woman in a long white dress, perhaps one of Twain's daughters, was drifting around the house. According to the TV show, the apparition was supposedly caught tugging at visitors, giggling and whispering, and would sometimes press her face up against the windows. Ever since the episode first aired— and it seemed to be in continuous reruns—Bradley had been fielding several calls a month about it.

He hated bursting anyone's bubble. *Any* interest in Mark Twain was a good thing as far as he was concerned. But it was a shame it had to come about because of some silly fairy tale.

Not that Twain hadn't written a few of his own. In 1903 he published one of his most delightful though least known works, "A Ghost Story," in *Sketches New and Old.* In the yarn, a man is awakened in his hotel room to discover that invisible hands are pulling the blanket off the bed. Some sort of entity then passes through the door into the corridor without opening the latch. Before long, the man's room is filled with the sounds of footsteps and rattling chains, luminous faces floating in the dark, and droplets of liquid—was it blood?—falling from the ceiling. And then, to the boarder's surprise, the ghost of the Cardiff Giant materializes. (The Cardiff Giant was supposedly the petrified body of a humongous man that was dug up on a farm in Albany, New York. It was a complete hoax. Nevertheless, the fossilized figure was put on exhibition, and at the same time a plaster replica claiming to be the "only genuine" article was showcased in Manhattan.) When the ghost in Twain's story finds out that the relic on display in New York City is only a copy and not his actual remains, he slumps away in embarrassment.

Twain had a lot to draw on when writing about the Spirit World. He lived during the height of the Spiritualism movement, and he attended a number of séances—many of which he described in comic detail in the constant flow of articles he sent to newspapers and magazines.

But, Bradley assured himself, Twain didn't believe in ghosts or spirits. Or, if he did, he never said so publicly, despite having had a personal encounter that was impossible to explain in any other way. During a large reception, the writer had momentarily spied a female acquaintance on the other side of the room. When he caught up with her later that night at dinner, he apologized for not having spoken to her earlier. To his surprise, she claimed she had not been at the party. Her train was late, and she was still traveling when the afternoon gathering was going on. She told Twain that the whole time she was on the train she could think of nothing except the party: It was so clear in her mind, it was almost as if she were actually there.

Bradley knew that paranormal investigators like those *Ghost Hunters* people would claim the woman Twain had seen at the party was actually a "spirit double" as a result of astral projection. During an out-of-body experience, also known as an OBE or bilocation, an "astral body" separates from and leaves a person's physical body. Most times, the spirit hovers nearby, but sometimes it travels far afield. The doppelgänger may look translucent like a ghost or (as happened in Twain's case) completely solid.

Bradley had been so fascinated by Twain's spectral encounter that he read up on the phenomenon. It seems there are several different types of astral projection. The stories most often reported come from those who have had near-death experiences. Survivors tell of feeling their spirits temporarily leave their bodies. Often, they can still see their separate, physical forms. They may also be greeted by the apparitions of loved ones or be drawn toward the clichéd "tunnel of light." But then, sensing it's not yet their time to Cross Over, their spirits return to their mortal selves.

Other astral projections are "crisis apparitions," in which a person's spirit is released at a time of great trauma, illness, or imminent death. The astral body travels, sometimes over great distances, to visit another individual, usually a loved one. (Because it's so difficult to pinpoint the precise moment of death, there's sometimes a debate among psychic researchers as to whether a crisis apparition is a spirit double, meaning the person is still alive, or whether the individual is already dead and the astral body is a ghost.)

Bradley was secretly pleased when he found out Twain's type of encounter was the rarest of all in the OBE files. His was an "arrival case," in which the astral body of an individual who is in transit shows up at a destination before the actual person does. In such instances, the spectre is usually seen wearing the same clothing as the traveler has on, and many times the apparition looks so real that people talk to it. Sometimes the phantom answers back! As was the case in Mark Twain's brush with the supernatural, by the time the flesh-and-blood person turns up in an arrival case, the astral double is always long gone.

The museum shop was about to close, and Bradley had started to cash out the register when the phone caught him by surprise. It was very seldom anyone called that late in the day. He was unprepared for the urgency of the voice at the other end of the line.

"Hello, is this the Mark Twain House? My name is Jessica. I think I just saw his ghost!"

Bradley wanted to brush the woman off, but remembering his boss's admonition and realizing that the caller was deadly serious, he responded as matter-of-factly as possible, "Excuse me? Where are you calling from?"

"I'm in Manhattan, and I saw him last night—well, obviously not *him*, but his spirit—down at his old house in Greenwich Village."

Bradley was vaguely familiar with the place. Although the building at 14 West Tenth Street is sometimes called the "Mark Twain House" for convenience sake, Clemens never owned it, nor did he do any of his major writing there. The row house was constructed as a private home around 1855 and was later split into apartments. Bradley wasn't sure what state the classic brownstone was in when Twain and his wife lived there during the winter of 1900–01, but regardless, its connection to the author was minimal at best.

Nonetheless, Bradley decided to hear the young woman out. She was clearly shaken by whatever had occurred. Jessica had been visiting a friend and was climbing the stairwell to her flat when she noticed an elderly man gently ambling, almost floating, down the steps toward her. His appearance—the wild shock of white hair and bushy moustache—was unmistakable.

Jessica knew from her friend that Twain had once lived in the building, but that was more than a hundred years ago. The woman had only seen the author in photos, of course, and, yes, at some point she had seen Hal Holbrook's definitive portrayal of the writer on stage, but this was no actor in makeup. This guy, whoever he was, was the real deal.

Jessica was at once bewildered and amused. Did the man live in the building? But then, as she was about to greet the stranger, the man started to fade, like a lightbulb slowly being dimmed, until finally he completely vanished.

Unsure what to do, Jessica stood there on the staircase, frozen in place, for several minutes. Finally she made her way up to her friend's apartment.

Before long Jessica learned that she wasn't the only one who had run into the apparition. It had been going on for years. Back in the 1930s the spectre turned up in a ground-floor apartment and scared a woman and her daughter half to death. When the mother demanded the intruder tell her who he was, the spirit said his name was Samuel Clemens and that he was there to complete some unfinished business in the house. And with that, the phantom had disappeared in front of their eyes as well.

Bradley thanked Jessica for the information but told her, honestly, that he wasn't familiar with any stories of Twain's apparition showing up at his former home in the Village. As far as he knew, Samuel Clemens had been resting in peace next to his wife in Woodlawn Cemetery in Elmira, New York, since 1910.

After the phone call was over, though, Bradley got curious. Normally he would have completely dismissed what Jessica had told him, but she had been so sure. Was it possible the house on Tenth Street was really haunted?

A weekend of Internet and library research followed, and Bradley found out that word on Twain hauntings in Manhattan was decidedly mixed. Most ghost books and paranormal websites said the world-famous author shows up in his former Greenwich Village residence. Other sources, including Dennis Hauck's authoritative *Haunted Places: The National*

*Directory*, insisted that Twain's spectre has never darkened its door.

But everyone agreed that *something* haunts the place. Even those who doubt the existence of ghosts admit that there is an aura of dread and despair that seems to hang over the building. And one woman, Jannis Bryant Bartell, wrote in detail about the terrifying experiences she endured during the years she and her husband Fred lived at the address.

Jan, as she liked to call herself, was born in New York City in 1921. She was an author, poet, and actress. Fred was a combat veteran from World War II. Both suffered from depression. Today, the husband's condition would probably be diagnosed as post-traumatic stress disorder, or PTSD. They moved into their apartment at 14 West Tenth Street around 1961. They were on the top floor, where the servants' quarters had been located back when the building was a single-family mansion.

Jan had always believed she had psychic abilities, and she began to experience paranormal activity in the flat soon after becoming a tenant. It was being caused, she felt, by the unhappy spirits of twenty-two people who had died in the building over the preceding century. Among them was a tortured child whose parents had forced the youngster to walk in circles around a chair for hours at a time while being tethered to it by a rope. Eventually, they let the child starve to death.

The Bartells' hauntings started with the sound of disembodied footsteps in the apartment and hallways, even when Jan was sure no one else was in the building. She could also hear the sound of rustling clothing, and when crashing noises were investigated, it turned out that nothing was out of place. Jan would feel the silken touch of invisible fingers on her skin, and unfamiliar perfume fragrances would waft through the air.

At one point a cleaning woman swore she had seen a spectral woman dressed all in white sweep by her into the next room. When she went to look for her, no one could be found. And Bartell herself saw large black shadows creep across the walls.

Bartell could feel the apparitions' presences even if they didn't materialize. She would regularly wake up between 2:30 and 3:00 in the morning and immediately be aware that an unseen someone was standing close to the bed watching her. Her dogs often stared pointedly into empty space, and one of them began to act up so much that Bartell believed the spirits had driven the canine insane.

Needless to say, Jan's spectral encounters with the Great Beyond weren't particularly agreeable, and she soon started to fear the phantoms—even the seemingly benign ones like Twain, whom she had run into on the stairway. (It was Bartell who first told the two women on the ground level about the author's return.) At one point Jan called in ghost hunter Hans Holzer, hoping he could rid the place of its bogies, but his attempts were unsuccessful.

In 1973 the Bartells moved to a house in New Rochelle, fifteen miles outside the city, but Jan apparently thought a few of the spirits followed her. She died on June 18, 1973. According to police, it was a suicide, but a year after her death, a book she had written about the hauntings in the Greenwich Village apartment was published. It was entitled *Spindrift: Spray from a Psychic Sea.* An addendum to the book said that Jan Bartell had died of a heart attack.

The house's notoriety did not end with the Bartells' departure. Joel B. Steinberg, a criminal defense attorney who resided there with his family, was convicted of manslaughter in the November 2, 1987, beating death of his six-year-old adopted daughter Lisa. Newspapers at the time dubbed the apartment building "The House of Terror." Steinberg was paroled in 2004. As a side note, the Steinbergs lived in the same rooms once occupied by Mark and Olivia Twain.

Whatever ghostly activity may or may not take place in the old Mark Twain House, another haunting is said to occur almost next door at 18 West Tenth Street. The building was once the home of a well-to-do sugar refiner, Moses Lazarus. His daughter Emma and her family were living there in 1883 when she wrote the poem "The New Colossus." The sonnet, best known from its inscription on a brass plaque added to the pedestal of the Statue of Liberty in 1903, begins:

> Give me your tired, your poor,
> Your huddled masses yearning to breathe free

Emma died at the age of thirty-eight, just four years after the poem was written. During her brief lifetime she was deeply concerned with Zionist and immigration issues. It's said that whenever either topic is hotly debated or passionately discussed in her former house, the presence of her spirit can be felt in the room.

# Chapter 3

# The Ascension
## of John LaFarge

### Episcopal Church of the Ascension
### Fifth Avenue and West Tenth Street

*The spirit of American artist John LaFarge is not only attached to the mural he painted for the Episcopal Church of the Ascension in Greenwich Village. He also seems to be fond of his old studio on West Tenth Street—even though he's gone to meet the Master Painter in the Sky.*

Jeremy stood in front of the altar. He knew he wasn't supposed to be sightseeing. But he didn't want to come in on Sunday and have to pretend to be there for the service. On weekdays the church was open for just an hour, from noon to one, and that was supposed to be for private meditation rather than tourism. But he couldn't help himself. Jeremy had to see *The Ascension*!

The previous fall he had started classes at the Art Students League of New York on West Fifty-seventh Street near Central Park South. He was talented enough, fortunately—and had a good enough portfolio—that he could have had his pick of schools in the city, but he didn't want what most of them had to offer. He wasn't interested in graphics, or web design, or fashion, or media, or interior decorating, or, indeed, any degree.

All he wanted to do was paint. Or sculpt. Or make collages. Or . . . Okay, if he had to be honest, Jeremy wasn't sure what medium he'd wind up working in. For now, he wanted to try them all. What was important was to get hands-on experience working on the actual craft of creating art. The Art Students League seemed ideal for that. It had about eighty current instructors and had a list of former members and guest lecturers that read like a Who's Who of the art world from the past 125 years. Surely he could find the guidance he needed there.

It was during a discussion of stained glass—a form of art Jeremy had never considered—that the name John LaFarge first came up. LaFarge was born to wealthy French parents in New York City in 1835. His maternal grandfather taught him to paint when he was six. He learned English watercolors at Columbia Grammar School, then studied at Mount St. Mary's University and St. John's College. Along the way, he was also schooled by French landscape painter and Hudson River School artist Régis François Gignoux. Then, during a visit to Paris in 1856, LaFarge spent several weeks at the studio of Thomas Couture. After returning to the States, LaFarge decided in 1859 to dedicate his life to painting.

He moved to Newport, Rhode Island, to learn at the hands of William Morris Hunt. He married in 1860, and he and his wife Margaret Perry would have ten children.

Although he was working primarily in oils during this period, LaFarge was also fascinated with block engravings. Between 1859 and 1870 he illustrated Robert Browning's two-volume *Men and Women* and Alfred, Lord Tennyson's 1864 poem "Enoch Arden."

LaFarge become famous for the 1877 painting he produced for the interior of Boston's Trinity Church. Many art historians consider it to be the first great American mural. About the same time, LaFarge was beginning to experiment with stained glass, finding new ways to infuse color into the translucent panes, including layering glass. In the process, he created opalescent glass, now generally referred to as American stained glass, which he patented in 1880. LaFarge would go on to create four stained-glass windows for Trinity Church, which were installed between 1883 and 1902.

His work would be influenced by travels to Japan in 1886 and the South Seas in 1890 and 1891. In his later years LaFarge also began writing, producing half a dozen or more books containing his essays and letters on Japanese, Polynesian, and Christian art. He was granted membership in all of the major American art societies and was awarded the Cross of the Legion of Honor by the French government. LaFarge continued to work into his seventies, turning out four lunettes in the Minnesota State Capitol building at the age of seventy-one, as well as painting the mural *Ancient Lawgivers* in the lobby of the Baltimore Court House in 1907 when he was seventy-two. He died three years later and was buried in Green-Wood Cemetery in Brooklyn.

LaFarge was a lifelong Roman Catholic, but, along with architects Ralph Adams Cram and Richard Upjohn, he was honored for his services with a feast day, December 16, on the liturgical calendar of the Episcopal Church in America. (The Episcopal Church doesn't canonize saints. In its eyes, all baptized Christians are saints of God. Rather, it recognizes men and women who have been exemplars of the Christian faith.)

*Wow!* Jeremy thought. *LaFarge wasn't just a painter. They made him a saint!* This was a Renaissance man he had to check out! When he discovered some of LaFarge's masterpieces were in an Episcopal church down in the Village, he *had* to see them.

The next day, precisely at noon, Jeremy entered the Church of the Ascension in New York City, often known simply as Ascension, at the corner of Tenth Street and Fifth Avenue. Other than the sexton who opened the door, Jeremy noticed he was alone in the chapel.

The Church of the Ascension had been founded on Canal Street in 1827, when New York City (almost unbelievably) had only about two hundred thousand inhabitants. Its first building was in Greek Revival, fronted by a six-pillar colonnade topped by an entablature and pediment.

Unfortunately the church was destroyed by fire in 1839, but that didn't deter the congregation. They moved north to the current Fifth Avenue location and constructed a new house of worship, designed by British architect Richard Upjohn. It was the first church to be built on the avenue, which at the time ended at Twenty-third Street and was still unpaved.

The new Gothic Revival edifice, fronted by a massive square tower, was consecrated on November 5, 1829. Early parishioners included the Astors and the Belmonts, and it was the site of several society weddings, including the 1844 nuptials of President John Tyler and Julia Gardiner. In 1881, in another marriage with names straight out of the Social Register—even though the first actual Social Register wasn't published until 1886—August Belmont Jr. wed Bessie Hamilton Morgan.

The church's interior was renovated by McKim, Mead, and White under lead architect Stanford White between 1885 and 1889. The rector during this refurbishment was Reverend E. Winchester Donald, who believed that great art reflected the glory of God. A major donation from Julia and Serena Rhinelander allowed him to transform the sanctuary from its stern, barren look into a thing of beauty. Central to his plan was the commission of a monumental mural by John LaFarge to place above the altar.

LaFarge's spectacular *The Ascension of Our Lord* depicted Jesus Christ in flowing robes surrounded by a host of angels as He rose toward Heaven bathed in a golden glow of light. Onlookers, no doubt His disciples among them, watched the Ascension in wonder from down below. The artist completed the work in 1888, and it was hung and dedicated soon after.

So there Jeremy was, standing in front of the first pew of the church. He had already scrutinized the four amazing stained-glass windows by LaFarge in the church. One, *The Good Shepherd,* dating from 1910, was placed among four panes by other artists along the north wall. For LaFarge aficionados, the south wall was an embarrassment of riches, with three of the five windows by him: *Nicodemus Coming to Jesus by Night* from 1886; *Mary Magdalene, Joanna, and Mary the Mother of James at the Sepulchre,* installed in 1890; and *The Presentation of Christ in the Temple,* given in memory of Francis Leland and his wife sometime after 1885.

The windows were splendid, but Jeremy realized he didn't know enough about glass yet to fully appreciate them. He'd come back another time. Oils he understood.

Jeremy gazed up at the immense mural. He could admire the painting from where he stood, but what he *wished* he could do was get really close to examine it. He'd love to be able to put his face right up to the canvas to look at the fine technique, analyze the individual brushstrokes. But that was impossible. Even if he walked into the chancel and leaned against the main altar, the bottom edge of the mural would still be ten or fifteen feet above his head.

Besides, he didn't want to walk into the apse without permission. Jeremy hadn't been into a church in years, so he didn't know the rules. Was he allowed to go up those little steps? Was that considered blasphemous? Or, at the very least, would it get him thrown out? After all, he was supposed to be sitting in the pews in quiet contemplation, not looking at pretty pictures on the wall.

He glanced around to see if the sexton who had unlocked the church was still around. No, he wasn't. But, Jeremy was surprised to discover, he was no longer the chapel's sole visitor. He hadn't heard anyone else come in, but there, standing silently at the far end of the first pew, was a pale man, probably in his late sixties. He wore round wire-rimmed glasses and had a full moustache and a bald pate fringed with hair. Jeremy couldn't place the style of the man's clothes. He was no expert, but even he knew the guy's suit was at least fifty years out of fashion. At first, the man stood there in rapt attention, his eyes never moving from *The Ascension*. But then, as if the stranger slowly seemed to become aware of Jeremy's presence, he turned to look at the young student and nodded, a faint smile on his lips . . . and vanished.

There are those who say LaFarge's apparition used to show up quite regularly in the Church of the Ascension to check up on his mural. There have been few if any sightings in the past forty years. But there's one early visitation by LaFarge that's hard to explain away.

On November 14, 1910, *The Ascension* fell from the wall. Fortunately there was no major damage to the altarpieces or to the work itself. Some suggested that the many coats of lead-based white paint the artist had used to create its luminescent effect made the canvas too heavy to be held in place. A stronger stretcher was made, the painting was remounted, and the mural was put back on the wall.

It was the timing that made the event so significant. According to Oliver LaFarge, the artist's grandson, the mural dropped from its perch at the exact same moment John LaFarge died.

It was shortly thereafter that the painter's apparition supposedly started visiting the church. More often, the phantom chose to show up around the corner at 51 West Tenth Street where LaFarge kept his studio.

The Tenth Street Studio Building, constructed in 1858, was a first of its kind. It was financed by James Boorman Johnston (whose brother John Taylor Johnston would become the founding president of the Metropolitan Museum of Art), and it was designed by Richard Morris Hunt, who was the first US architect to have been trained at L'Ecole des Beaux-Arts in Paris. The three-story, redbrick, Neo-Grec structure was one hundred feet wide and contained twenty-five studios surrounding a two-story court with a domed skylight. The individual rooms varied in size from fifteen-by-twenty to twenty-by-thirty feet.

The artists who were fortunate enough to obtain a lease— there was a long waiting list—used their studios to work, teach, show their art, and entertain. Some lived in them, though the studios were never designed as apartment space. Among the artists who set up shop in the Tenth Street Studio Building were Winslow Homer, second-generation Hudson River School painters Frederic E. Church and Albert Bierstadt, William Merritt Chase, and, of course, John LaFarge, who kept a studio there for fifty-two years.

In the second half of the nineteenth century, before museums and galleries were plentiful in Manhattan, the atrium of the Studio Building doubled as an exhibition space. The center lost its key role in the New York art scene as other institutions opened, and its importance waned further when Chase gave up his studio in 1895.

In 1920 a consortium of artists bought the Studio Building. By 1956 the real estate had become too valuable to prevent its sale to developers. The entire structure was torn down, and an apartment building with an entrance at 45 West Tenth Street was put up in its place.

Before it was razed several artists reported seeing, hearing, or being touched by John LaFarge's spirit at the Tenth Street Studio Building. Among them was artist Feodor Rimsky. He and his wife lived in Studio 22, which had been LaFarge's workspace. One night in the fall of 1944, the couple came home from the opera to find their door unlocked and a light on in the library. They found someone sitting at the desk, and when they approached the stranger, he disappeared right in front of their eyes. It wasn't until a former tenant showed Rimsky a photograph of LaFarge that the artist realized he had seen a ghost.

On another evening, artist William Weber was visiting Rimsky and his wife with three other guests. That time, it was Weber alone who saw LaFarge as the phantom strolled through the salon.

Three other hauntings by LaFarge revolve around illustrator John Alan Maxwell. In the spring of 1948, Maxwell was taking an afternoon nap on his couch. He woke to discover an unknown woman standing over him in the darkened room, straightening the sheet he had pulled over himself. Hovering behind her was a gentleman whom Maxwell also didn't recognize. When Maxwell tried to punch the man, both intruders instantly dissolved. Maxwell later realized the spectral pair had been John and Mary LaFarge.

On separate occasions, two female friends of Maxwell also ran into the spectres. One of the ladies encountered John LaFarge as she was leaving a party at Maxwell's studio. The other saw an otherworldly woman dressed in nineteenth-century attire hover in the hallway before she evaporated into thin air. These last two sightings were typical of most people's brush with LaFarge in the building.

Sometimes LaFarge didn't materialize, but he still liked to make his presence known. It was said that for many years crystal portraits, painted by LaFarge's icy touch, would appear in the frosty windowpanes of the Studio Building each winter.

Today the apartment building on the site of the Tenth Street Studio Building is a co-op, the lone one on the block. In October 2010 actress Julia Roberts purchased a penthouse there with a rooftop terrace. There have been no reports of the current building being haunted.

Pity.

# Chapter 4

# That Old College Spirit

## Brittany Residence Hall
## 55 East Tenth Street

*The Brittany Residence Hall, one of New York University's dormitories, was once the Brittany Hotel. It was constructed in 1929, and the university bought the building thirty-eight years later. It's supposed to be student housing only, but apparently some of the former, now-ghostly tenants liked their rooms so much they never moved out.*

Karen walked into Brittany Hall with her daughter Amber, unsure how she felt about the girl's wanting to move into the dorm. But she knew better than to fight her about it. Once Amber got her mind set on something, well, one way or another it was going to happen.

Amber idolized her mother and wanted to follow in her footsteps. That included having the same college experience: the same university, the same major, and—as Karen was loath to find out—the same dorm.

It wasn't as if Karen could give Amber a good reason not to live in Brittany Hall. At least, not one she was ready to share. After all, Karen *had* stayed there when she was a freshman—freshwoman?—at NYU back in the 1980s. The university had done its best to modernize the rooms and other facilities since then, but even when Karen was a student it was obvious the place had once been a hotel. The layout of the rooms, the old iron radiators, the style of the elevator in the hallway: Everything smacked of a 1920s-era hotel-turned-apartment building.

Karen had not made it through the whole first year at Brittany, though she'd never told Amber. In the middle of the second semester, just before spring break, Karen burst into her RA's, insisting she had to change rooms. Or more than rooms. Buildings. Eventually she had to take her story to the Office of Residential Life and Housing Services before anyone would listen.

Brittany Hall was haunted!

While her claims were met with skepticism and initially dismissed, when it became obvious that Karen was ready to transfer to another university, the housing department finally relented. (And if they had been honest with Karen, she would have found out it wasn't the first time the board had heard similar rumors.)

Karen was able to finagle a move to Rubin Hall, which was located across from the Church of the Ascension, about two blocks away from Brittany. She wasn't sure why there had been a vacancy midsemester. But she didn't care. All she knew was she wasn't going to spend another night in Brittany. Not after the incident.

Not after being attacked by a ghost.

On the night in question, her roommate was already passed out when Karen came in a few minutes after midnight. She quietly undressed, slipped under a sheet and thin blanket and, thankfully, fell quickly asleep. How many minutes went by before it began? Karen began to toss and turn, then struggle, as she realized something was pressing against her, forcing her down. She couldn't breathe! She awoke with a start, gasping, the nightmare still swirling in her mind. As she sat up slowly, steadying herself with both hands, she discovered it hadn't been a dream at all. Something was still holding down her legs!

She looked to the end of the bed. Standing there was a dim figure, one of its hands clasped around each of her ankles. Was it a man? A woman? She couldn't tell. Despite light peeking around the window shade, it was too dark for Karen to make out any of the intruder's features. It was only after her roommate snapped on the light switch that Karen was aware she was screaming. And except for the two students, there was no one else in the room.

Karen had enrolled at NYU because to her, having grown up in the city, the university *was* New York. In 1830 Albert Gallatin, secretary of the treasury under Thomas Jefferson and James Madison, convened a conference in Manhattan to convince New Yorkers that they should found a local university. Admission would be based on ability, not on wealth, social status, or other connections—unless, Karen wryly noted to herself, you were a woman. Females were not admitted until the late 1800s.

When the school received its charter in April 1831, it was incorporated as the University of the City of New York, but from the start everyone referred to it as New York University. The name was officially changed in 1896. Its first classes were held in 1832 in rented rooms at Clinton Hall, near City Hall in lower Manhattan. Before long, a campus was established in the Washington Square area.

The university consists of eighteen colleges with undergraduate and graduate degree programs spread over six campuses in Manhattan and Brooklyn, as well as satellite sites abroad. The Washington Square campus is considered to be NYU's home base—so much so that until 2008 almost all of its graduations were held in the park. To this day, most of its buildings abut the eastern and southern edges of the square.

With approximately 12,500 students, meeting the need for living accommodations has always been a challenge, especially when campus housing is guaranteed to first-year enrollees. NYU currently has more than twenty residence halls at its disposal, although some of them are outside Greenwich Village. Many of the dorms are former apartment buildings or hotels and have been converted for student occupancy, just like Brittany Hall.

The dorm had once been the Brittany Hotel. It was built, according to most sources, in 1929 by Henry Mandell, who at the time was a noted developer in and around New York City. The sixteen-story hotel occupied an L-shaped lot with 160 feet of frontage on Tenth Street. There were shops on ground level on the Broadway side. The hotel had a grand lobby and a doorman. For most of its years of operation, the Brittany Hotel had 245 rooms, and at one point before Prohibition was lifted, a speakeasy operated out of one of the penthouses. Among the more celebrated guests who stayed at the Brittany Hotel were journalist Walter Winchell, the Grateful Dead's Jerry Garcia, and actor Al Pacino.

When NYU acquired the hotel in 1967, there were about forty long-term tenants living in the building with rent-controlled rooms. Most of the them agreed to move, but three elderly women were determined to stay, and rather than be evicted, they initiated what turned into a four-year court battle with the university—during which time the school converted all of the other rooms and opened the new dorm to students. With a guarantee of subsidized housing elsewhere, the three holdouts finally relented, and the situation was resolved to everyone's satisfaction. In fact, it was ancient history by the time Karen moved into the dorm.

Amber looked over at her mother, trying to read her expression. She expected to see some telltale nostalgia. But, no, instead there seemed to a look of—well, if Amber had to put a word to it—apprehension. What could she be worried about? Hadn't her mom told her she loved her time at NYU?

Karen had never gone back inside the dorm since she moved out all those years ago. But it was part of Amber's orientation tour of the campus, so there they were at Brittany. The Resident Assistant who was showing the pair around told Karen and Amber that she had stayed at Brittany herself as a first-year student and was very proud of the building. "We have about 575 students in the dorm. There are fifteen of us RAs, and on the first floor you'll find the offices of the Residence Hall Director, the Assistant Director, and the Resource Manager. Let's check the place out."

Their guide ushered Karen and Amber into room after room: the television and game lounge, a piano room, a dance studio, even a darkroom for kids interested in photography. There was a penthouse study lounge for individual and group studies. And they got to peek into a couple of vacant dorm rooms so that, as the RA lightheartedly explained, "you have an idea of how much space you won't have and how much stuff to leave home.

"And now let's go into the Rhodes Room. This is where we hold a lot of our activities and special events. That's funny . . ."

The three came to a dead stop as they began to enter the room. The RA was stunned to see, standing there all by himself at the far end of the chamber, a rather rotund man wearing a hat with a large plume and holding a rapier in his right hand. Suddenly, he bent slightly at the knees and thrust the épée forward. Advance and recover. The man ignored the others as he lunged and parried, sword-fighting an invisible foe. To the RA's amazement, there was no sound. Not a swish of the blade or the clump of his foot as the swordsman stomped his appel before each attack. Nothing.

Flustered at first by the unexpected stranger, the RA immediately regained her composure. She knew the room was often used for evening programs, so maybe "the Musketeer"— at least, that's what he looked like to her—was rehearsing for a theatrical production of some sort. *It would have been nice,* she thought to herself, *if someone had told me about it in advance.*

"Excuse me, sir. I don't want to interrupt, but I am showing one of our new students . . ."

Karen and Amber looked at each other warily. What was going on? Who was the RA talking to? As far as they could tell, except for the three of them, the room was empty.

The RA's eyes widened, and she pressed a hand over her mouth in horror. The swordsman raised his weapon to his forehead, bowed to his imaginary opponent, and then instantly disappeared.

A sudden panic seized Karen. Twenty years of trying to rationally explain away what had happened to her all those years ago evaporated in a flash. As the RA continued to stare at the vacant space, Karen gently took her daughter's arm, leading her out of the room.

"Amber, honey. There's something I have to tell you."

The story of a mysterious apparition pressing down on a female student's ankles and clamping her feet to the bed is simply one of many ghost legends that have surfaced over the past fifty years. It's believed that all of the dorm's ghosts date back to the residence hall's time as the Brittany Hotel.

Take the duelist. His identity is unknown, but he definitely was never a student living in the dorm. Whenever the Spanish spectre shows up, Sir Eduardo, as he's been nicknamed, is always spotted working on his fencing skills in the Rhodes Room.

Other paranormal activity in Brittany Hall? Students have reported unexplained music, lights that flicker on and off by themselves, and other lights with no known source shining in the rooms and halls. Disembodied footsteps echo down the corridors. Other times, people are aware of an unseen presence watching them.

One of those spirits who is "felt" but never materializes has acquired the sobriquet Molly. Her light steps reverberate through the building, especially on the sixteenth floor, but for some reason she chooses to remain out of sight. Tradition has it that she tragically fell to her death down an elevator shaft.

Skeptics explain away most of these occurrences as having been caused by bad wiring or thin walls in an old building, but some ghost investigators have theorized that the goings-on are from long-dormant spirits who have been awakened by the emotional stress and anxieties of the current young residents. If that's the case, why is Brittany Hall the only NYU dorm that's haunted? And why have former students posted messages on paranormal-related websites saying that Room 306 is particularly active?

Don't let the old wives' tales spook you if you plan to enroll at NYU. Brittany Hall is perfectly safe for students and visitors alike. But there may be a few more "residents" than the college catalog lets on.

Chapter 5

# The Triangle Terror

## Brown Building of Science
## 23-39 Washington Place

*The Brown Building of Science off Washington Square was once the Asch Building, where 146 workers lost their lives in the infamous 1911 Triangle Shirtwaist Factory fire. Though the building has been completely redone and now houses NYU's chemistry and biology labs, students there are sometimes overwhelmed by a desperate need to leave the premises.*

Elizabeth leaned back from the eyepiece. What *was* it today? Normally she couldn't wait to get back to the lab to pick up where she'd left off the day before, but today she just couldn't concentrate.

Perhaps it was the long spring break. She was doing postdoctoral work and had independent access to the genetics lab, so she didn't have to go on vacation when most of NYU shut down the week before. But she knew that many of the support offices would be closed. Most of the professors she regularly conferred with would be out of town. And with all of the students gone, the ninth floor of the Brown Building where her workspace was located would seem like a ghost town.

So in the end she relented and gave herself an enforced holiday. Her big breakthrough in biochemical research would have to come another day. Her Nobel Prize would have to wait. She'd come back refreshed on March 25.

When she returned to her lab that morning, she quickly fell back into her old rhythms. She was reviewing the findings of colleagues who had painstakingly sequenced the genes of a tiny aquatic animal known as the sea squirt. If the average person thinks about the tube-shaped creatures at all, it's when they become a nuisance by latching onto boat hulls or pier pilings. But scientists have long been fascinated with the physical structure of the adult sea squirt, specifically its flexible spinal column. It's been theorized that understanding the animal's genetic structure could one day have huge implications for spinal cord pathology and regenerative medicine.

For an article to be accepted by a major journal for publication, it has to be checked and double-checked by peers. So here Elizabeth was, comparing the paper's contents to what she saw in the slides mounted under the microscope in front of her.

Elizabeth was detail-oriented, so the analysis of the thesis suited her perfectly. It was tedious work, but for Elizabeth the hours always seemed to fly by.

Until today.

For some reason, as the four o'clock hour approached, Elizabeth became aware that she was fidgeting in her chair. She was never this restless. But today there was some quiet unease that kept niggling at the back of her mind. Something didn't feel right.

As the clock passed 4:30, the odd, unsettling sensation began to grow. Soon Elizabeth could think of nothing else. Small beads of sweat broke out on her forehead, and her fingers started to tremble as she tried to focus the lens on the scope.

Was she having a—what do they call it?—a panic attack? No, she couldn't be, she told herself. Nevertheless, having graduated in pre-med, she recognized the signs. And she knew what she had to do. Stop! Breathe. Relax. Breathe again. Be calm. Everything would be all right. The room was empty. She was alone. There was nothing and nobody around that could harm her.

"No!"

Elizabeth was startled to realize the scream had come from her. It was a wake-up call. As the shout echoed into silence and an absolute stillness returned to the room, she knew she had to move. She had to get out of there! And if she didn't, she would die!

Elizabeth grabbed her backpack and ran. She raced to the elevator and slammed her fist against the call button. Hurry up, dammit! What was taking so long? She couldn't wait! Her eyes now wide in terror, she ran to the stairwell emergency exit. She took a deep breath and, with all her might, lunged forward, throwing the door open so hard that it crashed against the frame. Elizabeth looked down, flight after flight. It was only nine stories. She could make it!

Afterward, she didn't remember the scramble down the stairs. As she broke out onto the street, her lungs unconsciously sucked in a long, healing gasp of air. Panting, Elizabeth bent forward and rested her hands against her knees. Passersby barely took notice. What was another out-of-breath New Yorker?

Elizabeth stood there, wobbling slightly, as she slowly regained her composure. She leaned back against the side of the building, completely oblivious to the brass plaque mounted on the wall directly above her head. Perhaps if she had read it, she might have had some clue as to what had possessed her up there on the ninth floor. But as it was, she simply felt glad to be alive. And free.

Elizabeth wasn't the first to be overtaken by an inexplicable and uncontrollable need to exit the Brown Building. She probably won't be the last. The building, you see, was the site of perhaps the most horrendous workplace fire in the first half of twentieth-century America.

Named for its owner, real-estate investor Joseph J. Asch, the ten-story, gray stone and brick Asch Building was designed in a Neo-Renaissance style by New York architect John Woolly. It was put up on the northwest corner of Washington Place and Greene Street a block east of Washington Square Park, on the site of the house where author Henry James was born. Construction began in 1900, and at the time of its completion in 1901, the Asch Building was considered a skyscraper and had cost about $400,000. Leasing the eighth, ninth, and tenth floors was the Triangle Shirtwaist Factory.

As its name implies, the company specialized in making shirtwaists—tailored, lightweight, buttoned-front women's blouses to be worn with skirts. The style, mimicking a gentleman's shirt, was considered bold yet fashionable by the independent breed of "new women" at the turn of the twentieth century. The shirtwaists were so popular that the factory operated six days a week, often with a twelve-hour shift, to fill orders. At peak production, the company produced about two thousand "waists" a day, grossing the company more than a million dollars a year.

In the first decades of the 1900s, Manhattan was a major center for clothes manufacturing in the United States, employing more than eighty thousand people, in large part because there was a ready source of cheap, available labor. Most of the factory workers were women—Eastern Europeans, Jews, Italians, and Russians—many of them newly arrived immigrants in the country. Many spoke no (or very limited) English, so even though the work was grueling and paid just six dollars a week, the girls were thankful to have the job, any job.

Many garment manufacturers' facilities were sweatshop factories crammed into small apartments in Lower East Side tenement buildings, with little air circulation and poor lighting. Larger businesses established themselves in buildings clustered around the east and south sides of Washington Square.

At the Triangle Shirtwaist Factory, about 180 to 200 women worked on the eighth floor, 250 on the ninth floor, and 70 on the top floor. In addition, there were about 30 men, either cloth cutters, machinists, or supervisors, working mainly on the lower two floors. The offices of the company's two owners, Isaac Harris and Max Blanck, were on the tenth floor.

The workrooms were overcrowded, filled with row after row of sewing machines and tables to cut the fabric. Despite the tall windows, ventilation was poor, and the machinery was extremely dangerous. Although there was an elevator up to the factory, it was reserved for deliveries and shipments. Workers had to trudge up the staircases, and there were only two entrances: One was on Washington Place, and the other, which most of the women used, faced Greene Street.

Conditions in the workspace were so bad that in 1909 the International Ladies' Garment Workers' Union (or ILGWU) called for action against Triangle. When an actual strike took place that autumn, more than twenty thousand workers from factories all over the city—four-fifths of them women—walked off the job. The settlement resulted in a very modest pay increase, but nothing was done to correct the safety hazards.

Like many factories of the time, the Triangle facility was ill prepared for fire. Asch considered the building to be fireproof, so he never spent the $5,000 it would have cost to install a sprinkler system. Harris and Blanck didn't bother either. Instead there were always pails of water at the ready, but not enough to combat a major blaze. There were fire hoses attached to the wall, but they turned out to be inoperative. Fire drills weren't required by law, so despite their recommendation by the fire department, none were ever carried out. The fire escape on the north, rear side of the building only reached down to the second story. Smoking was prohibited in the rooms because of all the highly flammable materials, but the rule wasn't enforced. All in all, it was a recipe for disaster.

And, indeed, disaster did strike at 4:45 p.m. on March 25, 1911. Fire broke out in the trash bin at the end of the first cutter's table on the eighth floor. (It was later determined that the cause was a discarded cigarette stub.) The water from the emergency buckets was immediately poured onto the rapidly growing blaze, but it wasn't enough to douse the flames. The fire leapt up to the string of shirtwaist patterns hanging over the tables as well as onto the piles of thin cloth lying by the machines waiting to be assembled. Lubricating oil stationed around the room further fueled the flames. Within minutes, the entire floor was engulfed in the conflagration, and it quickly spread upward to the ninth and tenth floors.

The executives on the tenth floor fled to the roof. Fortunately for them, the New York University Law School occupied the building next door. Students saw what was happening, and they laid two ladders from roof to roof across the narrow alley—little more than an airshaft—that separated the two structures. This allowed about a dozen souls to be rescued.

On the two floors below, the panicked employees by and large had to fend for themselves, and they tried to escape by any means possible. Amazingly, about two hundred people were able to get down the narrow staircase to Greene Street and spilled out onto the sidewalk. Somehow the elevator managed to make two or three trips, rescuing about 150 more people, until returning to the upper levels became impossible. One hardy woman survived because she wrapped her hands in a fur muff and slid down the elevator cable.

Two-thirds of the deaths occurred on the ninth floor. Survivors claimed that on that fateful day, the exit to the Washington Place staircase was locked when the blaze broke out, even though Section 80 of the New York Labor Laws made it illegal for any factory doors to be "locked, bolted, or fastened during working hours." The workers said management routinely locked the door at quitting time to force people to leave through the Greene Street exit so a watchman could inspect the ladies' handbags for theft.

Unfortunately the Greene Street staircase was on the side of the building most engulfed in fire. Some people on the ninth floor forced themselves through the curtain of flames and were among those who got out. But most of the workers never even made it to the door. The majority were overcome by the thick, noxious smoke and burned alive. Several were found in the crush of bodies in front of the locked door on the Washington Place side of the room.

Those who poured out onto the fire escape didn't realize it was a road to nowhere. Not that it mattered. As it turned out, the metal frame wasn't strong enough to hold the combined weight of all the people who crowded onto it. The scaffolding collapsed and fell to the pavement, killing everyone on it.

As a last resort, people began jumping from the windows. Many were already on fire and, knowing the end was certain, were choosing the less painful of two deaths. Some girls leapt together, embracing each other arm in arm. For most, their deaths were immediate upon impact. No one who jumped from the building survived.

The first of eight fire wagons from the nearby stations arrived within two minutes of the initial alarm. The firemen's attempts to rescue people through the windows failed. Such tall buildings were new to the New York skyline, and the fire ladders could get no farther than the sixth story. The safety nets were also inadequate for people falling from such great heights. They broke right through them.

Firefighters burst into the building and scrambled up the stairs to the factory. Within twenty-eight minutes—a mere 1,680 seconds—the fire was brought under control. But it was too late for the 146 people who had already died. Ninety percent of the dead were women between the ages of thirteen and twenty-three.

The bodies were removed to a temporary morgue set up on Charities Pier on the East River at Twenty-sixth Street so that relatives and friends could come identify them. Even the corpses that were burned beyond recognition were put on display. It was a gruesome scene. According to some newspaper accounts, a hundred thousand people turned up to inspect the remains. No doubt most of those who filed past came out of morbid curiosity.

Eight months later Harris and Blanck were put on trial for manslaughter in the first and second degree. The district attorney limited the case to the death of one woman, Margaret Schwartz, alleging she died from asphyxiation because she couldn't get through the locked door on the ninth floor.

After a heated trial and 155 witnesses, the all-male jury found the owners not guilty due to conflicting evidence and, in large part, because of the very specific charge given by Judge Thomas C. T. Cain: In order to find the men culpable, the jury had to conclude that the door was actually locked, that both owners knew the door was locked, and that the locked door was the direct cause of Schwartz's death beyond a reasonable doubt.

(One jury member later revealed that he believed the door was locked, but it hadn't been proven that the owners knew about it. It's worth noting that two years later Blanck was fined $20 for locking the doors at another one of his clothing factories.)

Some good did come out of the catastrophe. The public was so outraged that eight new safety laws were passed in Manhattan in the immediate aftermath. A New York State Factory Investigation Committee was formed to hold hearings and inspect businesses, and of the first seventy-four places it checked, seventy-one were cited. Within three years twenty additional workplace safety laws were enacted by the state legislature. Members of the garment workers' union marched to rally support and commemorate the dead. By 1915 union membership in the city had increased eightfold.

The Asch Building, built as a flameproof structure, survived the Triangle fire and was completely restored. In 1918 NYU rented the ninth floor, and the following year it leased the tenth floor. At some point, real-estate mogul Frederick

Brown bought the building, and in 1929 he donated the entire structure to the school. New York University subsequently renamed it the Brown Building of Science (or simply the Brown Building) in his honor. The entire interior space has since been completely renovated.

The building, listed on the National Register of Historic Places, was named a National Historic Landmark in 1991. Since 2003 it has also been a New York City Landmark. Two plaques posted on the wall outside the Brown Building—one from the ILGWU and the other from the New York Landmarks Preservation Foundation and the National Register—memorialize the tragedy and those who lost their lives.

Today the Brown Building houses chemistry and biology laboratories for both students and researchers. The entire ninth floor is taken up by NYU's Center for Developmental Genetics. And it also may house a few spirits.

Almost since the day the building was reopened to occupants after the 1911 fire, there have been individuals who have suddenly become overwhelmed by an irrational, unstoppable urge to flee the premises.

Not everyone who's affected feels compelled to leave the place. Instead they become aware of a dark aura or negative energy in the room, or they sense a feeling of helplessness and despair. Some have felt an unexplainable stuffiness or experienced claustrophobia.

Other paranormal activity has been reported in and around the building as well. Some folks have heard disembodied screams. And the scent of smoke and (on a few occasions) burnt flesh has been detected, especially on March 25, the anniversary of the fire.

Sightings of apparitions are very rare, but they're not unheard-of. A banshee has been spotted running down the hallway on the upper floors, and sometimes she appears in one of the ladies' bathrooms. A few people have seen a group of female phantoms marching back and forth in front of the building. The spectres are thought to be the shades of some of the union workers who picketed the Triangle Shirtwaist Factory in 1909, returning to show their solidarity for eternity.

# Chapter 6

# The Phantom
of the Firehouse

## The former Fire Patrol No. 2
## 84 West Third Street

*Fire patrolmen at the former station on West Third concluded long ago that they had a resident ghost: a middle-aged former colleague known as "Schwartz." The facility closed in 2006 and has been renovated into a private residence, but could Schwartz still be there behind the former firehouse walls?*

Gail couldn't believe it. Anderson Cooper was going to be her neighbor? How cool was that?

Of course she didn't know whether he was actually going to live there. He purchased the former firehouse at 84 West Third Street in September 2009, and it was still undergoing renovation. Meanwhile, Cooper had a home in Westhampton Beach out on Long Island and a penthouse up on West Thirty-eighth. So how often he would show up in his Village townhouse was anybody's guess.

Gail had been aware of the baby-faced, silver-haired television personality ever since he hosted *The Mole* on ABC, but she became a real fan once he moved over to CNN. After his years of reporting straight news, she remembered thinking "It's about time!" when he finally got his own show, *Anderson Cooper 360°*. And now, to everything else on his plate, he was adding *Anderson*, a

daytime syndicated talk show. Where did he get the time
. . . *and* the energy?

Gail had run into him once, quite literally, uptown. She
was leaving Central Park at Columbus Circle, turned a corner next to Time Warner Center, and—bam!—there he was:
the closely cropped, perfectly coiffed hair; those piercing
blue eyes. She smiled at the memory. Yes, Gail decided,
it would be very nice to see him walking down her block
every so often.

She just wondered if he knew the building he bought
was haunted.

She'd known about the ghost for years, and she heard
about it firsthand. Gail would pass the old Fire Patrol No. 2
every morning as she walked over to Sixth Avenue to catch
the bus to work. And sometimes the station's oversized front
door would be open as she strolled to the West Village to meet
up with friends. She'd always exchange a few words with any
of the crew that was hanging out front, and one October, the
week before Halloween, she overheard an earful:

"Nah, I don't think we'll be puttin' up any decorations.
We already got our own spook, don't we?"

Well, that was enough for her to want to learn the whole
story. She wasn't shocked to discover that many of the guys
admitted to having seen, heard, or felt a ghost. It was finding out that the fire station she'd been walking by all these
months, the fire truck she'd seen the men polishing, and
all the folks at the firehouse weren't really part of the New
York Fire Department. Instead Fire Patrol No. 2 was a branch
of an independent organization set up and financed by the
insurance industry!

*What's the difference?* Gail wondered at first. *Isn't a firefighter a firefighter?* Well, as it turned out, not exactly.

The origins of the Fire Department of New York (FDNY) date back to 1648 when the Dutch colonists passed the first fire ordinances for the city. Funded by fines on dirty chimneys, a group of eight wardens was established as a fire watch. Another group of men known as "prowlers" patrolled the streets from 9 p.m. to dawn. The men carried water to the scene of a fire by hand in leather pails, so they became known as the "Bucket Brigade."

The first two fire trucks—hand-drawn wheeled pumpers imported from London—were introduced in 1736. The New York General Assembly formally created a volunteer department the following year, but it was not incorporated until 1738. Initially just thirty firemen were appointed, and in lieu of compensation they were exempted from jury duty and military service.

In 1865 the state ended the all-volunteer organization and created a Metropolitan Fire Department with paid, professional firefighters. Five years later the city took over and created the "Fire Department City of New York." Eventually the fire companies of all five boroughs would become part of the FDNY, consisting of more than 11,000 firefighters, 2,800 EMTs, and 1,200 civilians, all under the command of the Fire Commissioner.

Gail had always assumed that her local fire station was part of the FDNY, but the Fire Patrol was a separate organization. It had its start back in 1803 when a group of volunteers got together to form the Mutual Assistance and Bag Corporation. The mission of firefighters everywhere is simple: to extinguish flames and save lives. The Mutual Assistance association realized it was also important to try to remove or, if that wasn't possible, preserve the contents of the buildings from both fire and water damage. From the very beginning, the Mutual Assistance Corporation worked hand in hand with the regular fire department.

Needless to say, the fire insurance industry took a huge interest in the upstart venture. They knew that the more material goods that could be saved or salvaged in the event of fire, the less they would have to pay out in claims. In 1839 the New York Board of Fire Underwriters, made up of insurance companies certified to write policies within the state, formed its own firefighting group, the New York Fire Patrol. Its mission was to be on the lookout for conflagrations in commercial structures and, if one were discovered, to secure property inside the building while the city's firemen fought the inferno. The Fire Patrol would also respond to high-loss residential fires, but their chief concern was business establishments.

During a blaze, the Patrol operated under the command of the FDNY, and there was always some overlap in the two groups' duties. The Fire Patrol would also assist in getting people out of the buildings, for example. And after 1867, when the Patrol received its state charter, they were also authorized to help extinguish flames.

The prime responsibility of the patrolmen would be, first, to save anything that could be easily removed from the burning edifice, then to cover the rest with fire-resistant tarps known as canvas salvage covers to minimize damage from water and falling ash. While firefighters doused the flames, the Fire Patrol would pump out excess water that could cause secondary damage. After the fire was contained, the Fire Patrol stayed on the scene to get rid of the last of the water, safeguard utilities, secure sprinkler systems, and cover broken windows and doors to protect the building from the elements, theft, and vandalism.

As 2000 approached, the New York Fire Patrol was responding to about ten thousand calls a year. Its motto was "Always Ready." Although FDNY firefighters' helmets vary in color, members of the Fire Patrol could always be identified by their signature red hats. Their work prevented the loss of millions of dollars of inventory and irretrievable computer data and saved priceless works of art from galleries and museums. Also to its credit, even though the Fire Patrol was funded by the insurance industry, it never failed to respond if a building was uninsured.

The Fire Patrol was essentially a salvage corps, but its members put themselves at tremendous risk, and over the years thirty-two of them made the ultimate sacrifice. On September 11, 2001, eighteen patrolmen responded to the attack on the Twin Towers; one, Keith Roma of Fire Patrol No. 2, did not survive. A bronze plaque commemorating his service was placed on the outside wall of the fire station. (It joined three other plaques in the firehouse honoring earlier fallen comrades from the Patrol.) Four former patrolmen who had transferred to the FDNY also lost their lives in the 9/11 tragedy, as did firefighters who were relatives of Patrol members.

At the end of the 1930s, the Fire Patrol had about four hundred men and ten firehouses scattered through the boroughs. But as the twentieth century waned, the Fire Underwriters began to question the cost-effectiveness of operating its own fire agency. As costs to maintain the Fire Patrol continued to rise, the ninety-six insurance providers making up the Board began to balk. Before long, most of the firehouses were closed. By the end of 2005, there were only ninety-eight Fire Patrol members and three houses left: Patrol No. 1 in Midtown, Patrol No. 3 in Cobble Hill, Brooklyn, and Patrol No. 2 in Greenwich Village.

On January 31, 2006, the Board of Fire Underwriters voted to close the remaining stations by the end of the year. Despite several appeals, on October 15 the New York Fire Patrol was officially disbanded. It was the last insurance-funded salvage unit to operate in America.

(Keith Roma's father, Arnie, is spearheading an effort to reestablish the Fire Patrol, separate from the insurance industry. He also rescued the four memorial plaques, which had been removed and almost discarded when the firehouse went on sale.)

So the "firemen" that Gail had been flirting with all those months—and, if she had to be honest, fantasizing about as calendar models—weren't exactly what she thought they were. But no matter. They were heroes just the same. And it's little wonder she couldn't tell the difference between the two squads if she went by appearances. The Fire Patrol's station looked just like a regulation FDNY firehouse.

The four-story, redbrick headquarters for Fire Patrol No. 2 was built in 1906, designed in a Beaux-Arts style by architect Franklin Baylis. The structure was 8,240 square feet, not including a two-story former stable in the rear. The first floor was naturally used to house the fire truck and heavy equipment, and a watch booth was located in the northeast corner of the room. The bunkhouse took up the second story, the third floor was the locker room, and the top floor contained a workout room and storage space.

The wide arched entrance to the garage's single bay was topped by a keystone bearing a statue of the helmeted head of Mercury, the Roman god of speed. (Because Mercury's name comes from the Latin *merx,* from which we get the words "merchant" and "merchandise," he is also considered to be the god of commerce and trade—a perfect match for a fire agency dedicated to protecting business property.) There was a standard doorway on one side of the garage door and a tall, narrow window on the other side.

The first floor of the firehouse's façade was further decorated with limestone. The phrase FIRE PATROL, along with a bold "2" on either side of the words, was set in relief in a narrow strip along the front wall between the first and second floors. At some point, an American flag was mounted on a pole directly above that. At the top of the building, dead center, was a cornice bearing the date 1906 flanked by herald-style trumpets made of terra-cotta.

Inside the building, the floor of the ground level was made of brick, set in a herringbone pattern. The walls were decorated with glass tiles, including murals that depicted the history of the Patrol. There was a traditional brass fire pole as well as a spiral staircase, and wide ceiling beams were used to spread out canvas and hang hoses to dry.

Gail didn't know how much of the building Anderson Cooper was going to change. She had read in the papers that he paid $4.3 million for the firehouse and had hired noted architect Cary Tamarkin to redesign the interior. As for its exterior, so far the work looked to her to be more restoration than renovation, which was welcome news to preservationists: The structure had already been nominated to be placed on the National Register of Historic Places.

For instance, Gail could see that the years and layers of bright red paint had been removed from the front of the firehouse, revealing the original brick surfacing. Cooper planned to keep the spiral stairs and possibly the pole as well. And he had told Arnie Roma that he would be honored to return the service plaques to the building's outer wall as soon as the other work was complete.

But with all the changes, will the firehouse phantom stick around?

The ghost, who's been there as long as anyone can remember, is a former patrolman about forty years old, with a mustache and graying hair. All of his clothing dates to the 1930s. He's sometimes seen in full firefighting gear, but more often he's more casually dressed in pants and a red wool double-breasted shirt. Often he also wears a helmet or is spied in the act of putting it on.

According to a psychic who was brought in to identify him, the guy's name is Schwartz. He supposedly hanged himself on the fourth floor after he discovered that his wife was being unfaithful. This occurred sometime in the decade before World War II—which would explain why his attire dated from that period.

Schwartz has never been hostile or put anyone in danger, but he sure likes to let his presence be known. His full-form apparition has been seen on all four floors of the station as well as walking on the spiral staircase. He's also appeared down in the basement, where one patrolman saw the spectre of a grown man slide out of a coal chute that's too narrow for an adult to fit through. In 1992 another fireman awoke in his bed on the second floor to see Schwartz standing directly over him, staring down at his face. Anytime anyone gazed back at the ghost, he vanished.

Even when Schwartz didn't materialize, his footsteps were heard all over the station, as was his rapping on walls, windowsills, and railings. Many times, as people descended the spiral stairs, invisible fingers would tap them reassuringly on the back on the hand—especially if they were rushing to answer a fire call. And then there was the time that folks on the ground floor heard a loud scraping sound coming from the fourth story. When they investigated, they discovered that somehow a 150-pound dolly had moved from one end of the room to the other on its own accord. That shouldn't have been so surprising: Schwartz's presence is most strongly felt on the fourth floor where he died and, apparently, where he now lives.

It remains to be seen whether Schwartz stays on now that all of his buddies have gone. Perhaps Anderson Cooper, or some other owner in the future, will let people know.

Another haunted venue, the so-called Edgar Allan Poe House, was located at 85 West Third Street directly across the street from Fire Patrol No. 2. The three-story building was nicknamed for the famous poet and American master of horror who lived there from 1844 to early 1846. At the time, the lane was known as Amity Street. During his stay, Poe wrote "The Cask of Amontillado" and revised and published his most celebrated poem, "The Raven."

New York University acquired the property, and in 2000 made plans to tear it down along with other buildings to build residence halls and expand its School of Law. Preservationists stepped in, and the following year an agreement was reached by which the school could dismantle the Poe House if it used the bricks to incorporate a re-creation of the façade within the new structure. What is now being called the Poe House is part of a larger building, Furman Hall, and its entrance is about half a block from where it used to be. A brass plate on the outside of the reconstructed outer wall identifies the site's connection to the famed writer.

There have been no reports of ghostly activity since the home was razed and "relocated." It was not Poe who haunted the original house, however. It was the female spirit of a mentally ill woman whose family had kept her confined in the attic. After her death, heavy pounding and the sound of unintelligible babbling used to be heard coming from the empty garret.

Poe lived for a time in several other places in Manhattan as well, including a house at 130 Greenwich Street (in April 1844), a room in a farmhouse on what is now Eighty-fourth Street between Broadway and Amsterdam (June 1844), a residence at 195 Broadway (in May 1845), and a room on East Forty-seventh Street near the river. His last home was a still-standing cottage on East Knightsbridge Road and the Grand Concourse in the Bronx. He lived there with his wife from May 1846 until her death from tuberculosis in January 1847. None of the premises are considered to be haunted.

Poe's spectre does show up elsewhere in the city. He's been spotted walking through Washington Square Park, and there's also a rumor that he's the spirit who haunts a cellar and empties bottles of wine at 47 Bond Street. The ground level of the building currently houses Il Buco restaurant. The reason why the ghost is thought to be Poe is unknown.

Poe's spirit also used to haunt NYU's Gothic Tower, which stood on campus at the eastern edge of Washington Square from 1837 to 1894. In addition to classrooms, the "tower" held a lecture hall that hosted a number of luminaries from the fields of art, literature, and science. Poe wasn't the sole guest speaker to return to its lectern from the Other Side. Samuel Morse and Walt Whitman came back as well. The ghost-free Silver Center for Arts and Sciences is now located on the site.

Fire Patrol No. 2 isn't the only firehouse in Greenwich Village to be haunted. So is Fire Company No. 33 (technically Engine Company No. 33, Ladder Company 9). Located at 44 Great Jones Street, it's part of the Fire Department of New York. The company, founded in 1865, was originally on Mercer Street. In 1899 it moved into its current facility on Great Jones Street, which is another name for the two blocks of Third Street between Broadway and Bowery.

The Great Jones Street firehouse was designed by Ernest Flagg and W. B. Chambers in a Beaux-Arts style, similar to that of Fire Station No. 2. It has two truck bays and is made of red brick with limestone trimming. The structure was designated a New York City Landmark in 1968 and was added to the National Register of Historic Places four years later.

Ten of the station's fourteen firefighters who responded to the September 11 terrorist attacks died in the rescue operations. Some of "New York's Bravest" think that the Great Jones Street firehouse is haunted by one of their own, whose time at the station predates that terrible event. One fireman believes he has captured a hazy image of the ghost on his cell-phone camera.

If phantom firemen are your thing, Fire Station No. 2 and Fire Company No. 33 are very close to each other, about five blocks apart. Why not visit them both? And while you're at it, keep an ear out for any unusual sounds coming from the old Poe House. You might score a trifecta!

Chapter 7

# Aaron Burr Returns

## D'Agostino Residence Hall
## 110 West Third Street

*The spirit of a famous early American politician haunts a block of Third Street by parking his horse and carriage directly in front of NYU's D'Agostino Residence Hall. Along with his daughter, who disappeared at sea, he disrupts a restaurant about four blocks away in the West Village.*

"Hey, Sarah, did you by any chance see the old dude sitting in the carriage out front? That makes three times this week. I think we might have a sugar daddy on our hands. I wonder who he's hooking up with?"

And so, with an innocent remark made in jest to her roommate, Tiffany set in motion a round of inquiries that would result in her coming to an inescapable conclusion: She had come face to face with a ghost.

She and Sarah shared an apartment in Filomen D'Agostino Hall, located on West Third at the intersection with MacDougal Street. The fifteen-story building is part of New York University and is across the street from its Law School. There were seven types of furnished units in the building for them to choose from, all of them with air-conditioning, wall-to-wall carpeting, wireless Internet, and one to three bedrooms. The girls, who had known each other since junior high school, opted for what the school calls an O-type room. They shared a kitchen and bath, but they got to have separate bedrooms.

Tiffany and Sarah were thick as thieves, and they loved trading gossip about the other people on their floor, especially if new guys were coming to see any of the coeds. So it was natural Tiffany wanted to dish the dirt about the odd man she'd seen hanging around outside the building.

"No, I haven't seen him. What's he look like?"

"Well, first of all he's *ancient*. He must be at least fifty." And with that, Tiffany was off. She conceded the guy might have been handsome at one time, but the years had made his face thin and pale. He had prominent cheekbones, a nondescript nose, intense dark eyes, arched eyebrows, and a high forehead. His hair was peppered, more silver than black, with a, receding hairline that gave the stranger a distinct widow's peak. He also kept unfashionably wide sideburns trimmed well below the earlobes.

And, speaking of unfashionable, the unknown visitor was wearing a deep burgundy jacket with high lapels and pantaloon sleeves, unbuttoned to reveal a gold-trimmed brocade vest. An ascot poured out from inside the man's white, ruffled, high-collared shirt, and he had on tight white trousers, almost like riding breeches—highly undignified for someone his age, Tiffany thought—tucked into knee-length, black leather boots.

"Well, it has to be a costume of some sort, don't ya think?" Sarah offered. "I mean, unless he's in a play or something, why would anyone dress like that? Especially if he's trying to pick up one of the girls in the dorm."

The only practical explanation occurred to them simultaneously. Obviously the coach was one of the ones that carry lovers around Central Park. The thought hadn't occurred to Tiffany because, as far as she knew, city laws forbade the carriages south of Thirty-fourth Street. The man riding in the coach must have been the driver. He probably figured if he parked near NYU, sooner or later some guy would come up with the romantic idea of treating his girlfriend to a carriage ride around Washington Square.

When the horse and carriage didn't appear for the next couple of days, Tiffany got curious and started asking around. Had any of the other students in the hall seen the guy? Yes, some of them had, and, like Tiffany, they had always spotted him late at night. But he wasn't always in his coach. Just as often, he'd be strolling up and down Third Street. Other times he'd be standing at the corner of Sullivan Street, impatiently staring off into the distance.

It was during a casual conversation with one of her advisors that Tiffany heard the impossible. The man she had been asking about was well known to all the instructors who'd been at NYU for any length of time. In fact, he was familiar to local denizens before D'Agostino was put up. Folks lounging in Cafe Bizarre, the popular bohemian hangout that stood at 106 West Third Street from the 1950s to 1984, used to see the lonely figure standing on the street corner all the time, and occasionally he'd turn up inside the coffeehouse.

According to Tiffany's professor, there was a reason the curious-looking person was dressed like he stepped out of the nineteenth century. "I know it's going to be hard for you to believe, Tiffany," he warned her in advance. "But according to the legend that's been going around as long as I've been here, that man you ran into comes from the 1800s. It's the ghost of Aaron Burr."

Tiffany was speechless. Aaron Burr? It couldn't be. She wasn't the kind of person who sees ghosts.

Yet when she did a little more investigating, she found out that the notorious politician's spectre has been spotted in the neighborhood ever since his death back in 1836, and sightings have been documented with some regularity since the 1950s.

Aaron Burr was born in 1756. He served in the Continental Army during the American Revolution before moving into law and politics. He was twice elected to the New York State Assembly and acted as the state's attorney general for three years. He was then elected to the US Senate before becoming vice president under Thomas Jefferson. Despite his service to the country, Burr is mostly remembered today as the man who killed Alexander Hamilton in an infamous 1804 duel and for standing trial for treason in 1807.

Burr was admitted to the New York bar in 1782. That same year he married Theodosia Bartow Prevost, the widow of a British army officer. In 1783 she gave birth to Burr's only child, a daughter whom they also named Theodosia. By then the Burrs were living in the Wall Street area of New York City. An adept trial lawyer, Burr prospered, and his holdings soon included stables at several spots in Greenwich Village. But tragedy struck when Burr's wife died of stomach cancer in 1794.

Burr was always reputed to be quite a dandy and a ladies man, but he believed in a woman's right to an education, and his daughter was trained in music, language, and literature. She married well in 1801, to Joseph Alston, a well-heeled planter from South Carolina. They spent their honeymoon in Niagara Falls, one of the first couples of note to do so. Their son, Aaron Burr Alston, was born the next year.

Burr ran for president in 1800. When votes were counted in the Electoral College, Jefferson and Burr had tied for first place. The election was thrown into the House of Representatives, and after thirty-six ballots Jefferson was named president. Burr, in second place, was made vice president. Although they were from the same party, the two didn't see eye to eye, so Burr chose not to run for reelection. Instead, in 1804, he ran for governor of New York. He lost.

Both of the losses were due in part to machinations behind the scenes by Burr's bitter rival, Alexander Hamilton, the first US secretary of the treasury and the founder of the Federalist Party. The two had traded insults back and forth for years, but in the summer of 1804 Burr finally decided that his adversary had badmouthed his reputation once too often. He challenged Hamilton to a duel. The fatal appointment took place on the morning of July 11 across the river from Manhattan in Weehawken, New Jersey. Hamilton was mortally wounded and died back in the city the following day.

Duels of honor were common at that time, even though they were illegal in both New York and New Jersey. They were seldom prosecuted, and Burr was never brought to trial. After finishing out his term as vice president in 1805, he moved west, leasing land in what is now Louisiana. Foreseeing war with Spain (which would not take place until 1836), Burr armed members of his expedition. Jefferson, who had recently acquired the region as part of the Louisiana Purchase, perceived Burr's actions as treasonous and sought his arrest. Burr surrendered peacefully, and the charges were so spurious that it took arraignments by four grand juries to indict him. In the trial, which took place in August 1807, Burr was found not guilty on all counts.

His political standing was irrevocably tarnished, however, and Burr never sought office again. Deeply in debt and somewhat a social pariah because of the trial, Burr fled to

Europe for four years. Time heals many wounds, and with the help of friends he returned to New York City in 1812.

Sadly, Burr suffered a double loss that year. His ten-year-old namesake grandson died of a fever. Then, that winter, his daughter Theodosia was lost at sea somewhere off the coast of the Carolinas, a victim of shipwreck or piracy.

Burr practiced law in New York for the remainder of his life. He remarried in 1833—at the age of seventy-seven—to fifty-eight-year-old Eliza Jumel, a wealthy widow. They moved into her home, what's known today as the Morris-Jumel Mansion, in Washington Heights.

The house was built in 1765 for Colonel Roger Morris, who had come to the colonies as a captain to fight for the British in the French and Indian Wars. A Tory sympathizer, Morris left the country during the Revolutionary War, allowing George Washington, then later the British, to use the home as a headquarters. After the war the property changed hands several times, eventually winding up with Stephen Jumel, a French wine merchant. Jumel took Eliza Brown, twenty years his junior, as a mistress, but he later married her when he thought she was about to die. He passed away instead, in May 1832, after falling from a mound of hay onto a pitchfork. Eliza Jumel and Burr wed the following year.

Eliza's decision to marry Burr was no doubt influenced by the prestige of having a former vice president as a husband. Was she aware, though, that Burr was practically penniless? No one knows, but she kicked him out after four months. Jumel accused Burr of adultery, which was grounds for divorce. The next year Burr suffered a stroke, which left him practically paralyzed. He granted the divorce on his deathbed, and it was finalized on the day he died—September 14, 1836. Burr was buried in Princeton, New Jersey.

For her part, Jumel became somewhat of a recluse. She remained in the house until her death at the age of ninety-one. She is buried in Trinity Cemetery at 155th Street and Broadway.

As Tiffany found out, Burr apparently hasn't stayed in Princeton. His wandering spirit is seen to this day, both on foot and in his carriage, staking claim to the block-long stretch of Third Street between MacDougal and Sullivan Streets. One of Burr's former stables used to extend along the whole block until the 1830s.

Burr may turn up nearby at another of his former carriage houses as well. The building is now the One If By Land, Two If By Sea restaurant, located at 17 Barrow Street. Burr seems to be a little more animated there. His spectre has been blamed for hurling and smashing plates, grabbing things from tables, and pulling chairs out from under people. Burr's daughter Theodosia also sometimes gets into the act, tugging at (and sometimes successfully removing) the earrings of female diners. It's comforting to know that Burr and his daughter have been reunited in the Afterlife. They're sometimes seen sitting together in the restaurant on the second floor by the windows.

Finally, the Morris-Jumel Mansion is also haunted—by *several* phantoms. Miles north of Greenwich Village, it's the oldest surviving house in Manhattan. Eliza Jumel is seen most often, wearing a purple dress. She's also heard tapping on the walls and windowpanes, and people outside the building see her peering out through the third-story windows. In 1964 a group of students from a local school were horsing around outside the home when a woman appeared on the balcony and yelled at them to quiet down. The problem was, the place was locked up at the time, and no one was inside.

The students later identified the person who scolded them as Eliza Jumel from a painting of her they saw hanging on the second floor of the mansion.

Four other ghosts have materialized inside the house, including Stephen Jumel, a Hessian soldier from the Revolutionary War era whom legend says fell on his bayonet as he was walking down the stairs, and a servant girl who leapt to her death from the balcony after a romance went sour. The fourth phantom is an unidentified soldier, whom some think may be Aaron Burr, though why he would appear in uniform or bother to return to the site of an unhappy marriage is unknown. The Morris-Jumel Mansion can be toured, but the museum staff dismisses all of the ghost stories. But be careful if you decide to visit. If your guide shows up in a period plum-colored dress, you might be meeting Eliza herself!

Part Two

# HUGGING THE HUDSON— THE WEST VILLAGE

More than any other section of Greenwich Village, the West Village is known for its free-spirited, nonconformist residents. The quarter is filled with boutiques, artists' studios, nightclubs, coffeehouses, and performance spaces. For all intents and purposes, the modern gay rights movement began there with the Stonewall riots in 1969. Add a few ghosts into the neighborhood's mix, and Little Bohemia (as the area has been called since the 1920s) is more than a little exciting and well worth exploring.

The West Village is bordered by Fourteenth Street to the north, Houston Street to the south, and the Hudson River to the west. At one time the district's eastern boundary was generally accepted to be Seventh Avenue, but many now push it all the way to Sixth Avenue (the Avenue of the Americas). Let's visit with a dozen or so of the many apparitions that call this part of the Village home.

# Chapter 8

# Stage Fright

## Cherry Lane Theatre
## 38 Commerce Street

*Little theaters, many of them haunted, have long dotted the landscape of Greenwich Village. Some, like the Provincetown Playhouse, are now gone. A few, like the Little Thimble Theatre, are all but forgotten. But others, like the Cherry Lane Theatre, persevere.*

Commerce is an odd little street. Now allowing only one-way traffic, it extends for two blocks southwest from Seventh Avenue, then takes a ninety-degree bend to the northwest before continuing one block to intersect with Barrow Street. It's a perfect example of the kind of quirky, oddly angled lanes that were originally walkways, trails, and horse paths in the early days of the West Village.

At the beginning of the nineteenth century, the land on which Commerce Street lies was part of the Gomez Farm. In 1817 a small silo was built on the south side of the lane very close to where it curved. In 1836 the storage tower was replaced by a three-floor, redbrick brewery, with large arched double doors facing the street. The place later served as a tobacco warehouse and then a box factory.

Although there were already other acting troupes in the Village at the time, in 1924 a small group of performers and writers decided to make the then-empty building at 38 Commerce Street their home. The company hired scenic designer Cleon Throckmorton to transform it into the Cherry Lane Theatre.

The theater's name has confused many people from the very beginning. First of all, it's not located on Cherry Lane. It couldn't be. There's never been a street named Cherry Lane in Greenwich Village, nor has Commerce Street (where it *is* located) ever been lined with cherry trees. According to Terry Miller, author of *Greenwich Village and How It Got That Way*, the theater's founders at first named it "Cheery Lane" as a play-on-words, comparing itself to "Dreary Lane," the unflattering nickname acquired by London's Theatre Royal, Drury Lane. The story goes that a journalist mistakenly reported the name of the Village playhouse as "Cherry Lane," and it simply stuck.

The 179-seat Cherry Lane Theatre is still around today. It has had a number of different owners since it first came on the scene, but it remains New York's oldest continuously operating Off Broadway theater.

And one of its most haunted.

Two hazy male phantoms are regularly seen there, both separately and together. One appears at the top of the lobby staircase dressed all in white. Another manifests itself in the backstage hallway near the dressing rooms. The spectres' faces have always been obscured, so no one can be certain who they are. For some reason, legend has it that one of them is Aaron Burr, Thomas Paine, or perhaps Washington Irving. Other than the fact that Burr and Paine lived in Greenwich Village and Irving often stayed with his sister at 11 Commerce Street, no direct association has ever been established between any of the men and the Cherry Lane Theatre (or either of the structures that predated it on the property). Nevertheless, the rumors persist.

(Interestingly, the Drury Lane theater in London is also haunted. People say it's the most haunted theater in England—perhaps in the world. Among its many spooks are actors Charles Macklin, Charles Kean, and Dan Leno, actress Sarah Siddons, the celebrated clown Joseph Grimaldi, King Charles II, and a mysterious Man in Gray.)

The company that founded the Cherry Lane Theatre was nominally headed by Edna St. Vincent Millay. Born in Rockland, Maine, in 1892, Millay was one of the best-known American poets of the twentieth century, having won the Pulitzer Prize for poetry in 1923 for her fourth collection, *The Harp Weaver*. But during her lifetime, she was almost as famous, or perhaps infamous, for her feminism, bohemian lifestyle, and being openly bisexual.

Millay's early poems were published in magazines while she was in her teens. She caught the eye of the poetry world in 1912 when "Renascence," a piece she had entered in an important contest sponsored by *The Lyric Year* magazine placed fourth—even though most people agreed her entry was the best in competition. Millay's recitation of the poem at a subsequent social gathering so impressed Caroline B. Down, the executive secretary of the YWCA training school in New York City, that she offered to pay Millay's tuition to Vassar. Millay enrolled in 1913.

Five years later Millay moved to Manhattan, settling into a nine-foot-wide garret room in Greenwich Village. Her sister, Norma Millay Ellis, married to artist Charles Ellis, lived nearby at 139 Waverly Place. Millay would go on to live in several different spots in the Village.

In 1918 Millay auditioned to become an actress with the Provincetown Players, and she was accepted into the company, which included her sister Norma. Before long, Edna was writing plays for the Provincetown Playhouse as well as acting in its productions.

By the time Millay became involved, the Provincetown Playhouse was already well established. Its history dated back to the summer of 1915 when a group of actors and playwrights vacationing in Provincetown, Massachusetts, gathered together to present a series of plays. They returned the following summer, joined by other artists including Eugene O'Neill, whose plays would help establish the company's credentials. Most of the group lived in New York City, and in the fall of 1916 the Provincetown Players turned the front parlor of a first-floor apartment in a brownstone at 139 MacDougal into a theater. About 140 people could be seated on uncomfortable wooden benches in front of the ten-and-a-half-by-fourteen-foot stage.

By the end of the company's second New York season, with more than six hundred subscribers, the Players knew they had to find a larger space. Fortunately, three doors down at 133 was an unoccupied former-stable-turned-bottling plant owned by the same landlord. The Provincetown Playhouse was born. Among the plays that would be premiered during its early years were O'Neill's *The Emperor Jones* (launching the career of actor Paul Robeson) and *The Hairy Ape*. The Players grew in esteem and were soon producing plays at other, larger venues as well. By 1929 there were hopes of moving to a new theater, but the stock-market crash put an end to that dream—and, eventually, an end to the company itself.

The playhouse managed to live on. In the 1930s it was the base for the Community Theatre division of the Federal Theatre Project. Then, for several years, it was occupied by a troupe dedicated to Gilbert and Sullivan operettas. In 1960 the theater was once again thrust into the limelight when it hosted the now-legendary double bill of Samuel Beckett's *Krapp's Last Tape* and Edward Albee's *The Zoo Story* in their American premieres. The longest-running play in the history of the Provincetown Playhouse—for five years beginning in 1985—was Charles Busch's outrageous campfest, *Vampire Lesbians of Sodom.*

New York University bought the playhouse in the 1980s, and for a decade beginning in 1998, its theater program used the facilities. Between 2008 and fall 2010, the university completely refurbished the building and incorporated it into a new, much larger structure with additional performance spaces. The exterior façade of the Provincetown Playhouse was retained and restored to its 1940s appearance. The theater is currently part of NYU's Steinhardt School of Culture, Education, and Human Development.

For decades up until the time it closed, the theater was home to a ghost who has never been identified. The very visible but dark form would glide by staffers on the staircases, and the air temperature would drop precipitously whenever the shade passed. Front-end employees and members of the stage crew also reported unusual noises throughout the theater. There have been no recent reports of spectral activity. Now that the playhouse is closed to the public, has the phantom left the building? Time will tell.

Before we take leave of the Cherry Lane Theatre and the Provincetown Playhouse, we should take one more look at the poet/playwright/actress they shared. Edna St. Vincent Millay's first successful collection of poetry, *Renascence and Other Poems,* was published in 1917, just before she moved to New York. In that volume was one of the most charming poems ever written about an apparition, entitled "The Little Ghost." It goes, in part,

I knew her for a little ghost
That in my garden walked;
The wall is high—higher than most—
And the green gate was locked.

. . .

And where the wall is built in new
And is of ivy bare
She paused—then opened and passed through
A gate that once was there.

Millay supposedly wrote the poem after encountering the spirit of a girl in her sister Norma's garden on Waverly Place. There's no proof, however, that the poet actually saw "the little ghost" there, or in any other garden for that matter.

In 1923 Millay married Eugen Jan Boissevain, a coffee and sugar importer she had known for some time. It was a very open marriage: Both had other lovers during the twenty-six years they were together. They moved into a three-story, 1873 brownstone at 75½ North Bedford Street that was said to be the narrowest house in Greenwich Village, no more than nine and a half feet wide and forty-two feet deep. Its other occupants have included Margaret Mead and John Barrymore. In 1925 Boissevain and Millay moved to a former blueberry farm they bought in Austerlitz, New York. Millay named it Steepletop. Boissevain died in 1949; Millay followed a year later.

If Millay really did see a ghost on Waverly Place, she wouldn't be the only one.

In the 1980s, screenwriter, novelist, and playwright Paul Rudnick lived in the top-floor apartment of a brownstone at 132 Waverly Place, catercorner across the street from Norma Millay Ellis's house. Best known for his screenplays for *Addams Family Values, In & Out,* and the 2004 remake of *The Stepford Wives,* Rudnick first drew attention for his gay-themed Off Broadway plays *Jeffrey* and *The Most Fabulous Story Ever Told.* He claimed that while he was living on Waverly Place, his flat was haunted by the phantom of actor John Barrymore, who had lived there at some point.

The visitations must have been inspiring. In April 1991 Rudnick's play *I Hate Hamlet* opened on Broadway at the Walter Kerr Theatre. The story involved a young playwright whose apartment was actively haunted by—wait for it—the ghost of John Barrymore.

So within a few years and blocks of each other, five theater-related phantoms popped up: one in a hidden garden, another in a playwright's apartment, and three more in a couple of theaters. But these spectres weren't alone treading the boards Off Broadway. No fewer than three other tiny playhouses in the Village have also had ghosts-in-residence.

From 1915 to 1916 a one-hundred-seat playhouse known as the Little Thimble Theatre operated out of a converted basement floor of the townhouse at 10 Fifth Avenue. On the surface, its directors, Guido Bruno and Charles Edison, were unlikely partners.

Bruno, sometimes affectionately referred to as "the Barnum of Bohemia," was a true Village "character." He led a salon in his garret apartment, to which he charged admission for tourists who wanted to watch real artists at work. For several years he published a series of modest magazines, with titles like *Greenwich Village, Bruno's Weekly,* and *Bruno Chap Books,* filled with witty essays and criticism.

Edison, writing under the pen name Tom Sleeper, was one of the contributors to *Bruno's Weekly.* He was also the son of inventor Thomas Edison. Charles would go on to become the assistant secretary and then secretary of the Navy and, in 1941, forty-second governor of the state of New Jersey. When he was twenty-five, though, he opened the aptly named Little Thimble Theatre with Bruno, who was six years his senior. Together they produced works by serious dramatists such as Shaw and Strindberg. In 1915, in somewhat of a coup for such a minor theater, Edison wrangled an invitation to take the company to Ellis Island, where they put on a special performance for Chief Clerk Augustus Sherman and the four hundred immigrants who were detained there awaiting clearance.

The Little Thimble Theatre was short-lived. Edison left the arts and went into business with his father, and Bruno moved onto new projects. The house fell into other hands after Bruno died in 1942, and the basement was turned into an apartment. At least one subsequent resident reported that a spirit from the time of the Thimble Theatre returned to take a few more curtain calls. How else to explain items on the tables that moved by themselves or the sound of music that wafted through the air with no obvious source?

Then there's the Bouwerie Lane Theatre. The six-story cast-iron edifice at 330 Bowery has gone through several incarnations. The structure was designed in an Italianate style by Henry Englebert for the Atlantic Savings Bank, which had been established in 1860. By the time the building was completed in 1874, the institution had changed its name to the Bond Street Savings Bank. When the bank failed in 1879, the property was purchased by the German Exchange Bank, which primarily serviced the German-speaking community. By the mid-twentieth century the facility had become a fabric warehouse.

In 1963 Honey Waldman acquired the building and converted it into the Bouwerie Lane Theatre. The box-office fixtures and lobby chandelier were holdovers from its days as a bank, and auditorium seats came from a cinema that was being leveled. The theater's first production was *The Immoralist* with Frank Langella, and in 1967 the building received New York City Landmark status.

From 1974 to 2006 the Bouwerie Lane Theatre was home to the Jean Cocteau Repertory Theatre. During the company's tenure, in 1980, the building was added to the National Register of Historic Places. Finally, in 2007, Adam Gordon bought the property and completely renovated it into mixed-used housing with street-level storefronts.

During the building's years as a theater, its rooms were haunted by an invisible spectre. According to staff and ushers who sensed its presence, the phantom was believed to be the spirit of a deceased member of the Jean Cocteau company. There's no report whether the apparition has stuck around.

For some unexplained reason, playhouses worldwide seem to have more than their fair share of hauntings and paranormal phenomena. So why not give yourself a night at the theater? Anything could happen once the house lights dim.

# Chapter 9

# The Ghost on Gay

## The former Frank Paris residence
## 12 Gay Street

*During the twentieth century at least four celebrities lived at the cozy residence at 12 Gay Street—Mayor Jimmy Walker, actress Betty Compton, writer Walter Gibson, and master puppeteer Frank Paris. But none of them seem to be among the phalanx of phantoms that roam its rooms or show up unannounced on the doorstep.*

"Hey, kids, do you know what time it is?"

The puppeteer winced. He knew that his partner, Ted E. Lewis, had probably had one glass of wine too many and was just kidding around. Still, the reference hurt, even though it had been more than a decade since Frank unceremoniously walked off the television show that used the familiar come-on as its opening line.

His guests also knew exactly what Ted was referring to, and you could almost sense a collective gasp as everyone nervously looked at Frank to see his reaction. But Frank was used to Ted's ribbing. (What was the old saying about friends knowing the best place to stick the knife?) Frank smiled, then forced a small laugh. Almost instantly the moment of danger passed, and a sense of genial camaraderie came back to the party.

But it did raise a question in everyone's mind: Where *was* Howdy Doody?

Frank Paris, the evening's host, was one of the most celebrated puppetmeisters in the country. Born in 1914, within thirty years he had become one of the leading commercial puppeteers in twentieth-century America. Along the way, he also helped changed the face of puppetry by being the first major marionette artist to work on stage in full view of the audience, manipulating the short-strung figures in front of himself.

His technique originated at a 1937 performance at the Los Angeles Public Library. With no stage available, Paris stood on top of several tables. He focused borrowed spotlights on the marionettes, figuring the audience would concentrate on what was dangling at his feet instead of the guy pulling the strings.

Paris went on to appear in every possible type of venue, from nightclubs worldwide to cruise ships and theaters. In New York City alone, he was seen at the Strand, the Roxy, the Palace, Loew's State, the Paramount, and Radio City Music Hall, where he made twelve appearances. In addition to his own TV shows, he guest starred on almost every television variety show on the dial.

For three years in the 1950s, Paris taught a class in puppetry at New York University, with each end-of-semester marked by a puppet revue given by the students. Following his tenure at NYU, Paris was also an instructor at Columbia University Teachers College.

Along the way, he created many marionettes to caricature famous celebrities of the day, such as Carmen Miranda and Sonja Henie. And, of course, he designed and brought to life the original Howdy Doody.

Paris was ambivalent about how it all worked out. Back in 1947 NBC tapped Buffalo Bob Smith, the host of a popular radio show for children, to put together a program for its fledgling television network: *The Puppet Playhouse,* also known as *Puppet Television Theater.* At first it was scheduled to run just a few weeks, from December 27, 1947, through February 1948.

Frank Paris, already a noted puppeteer in the entertainment industry, was asked to create an original marionette figure to act as Smith's comic partner and cohost. Paris would also be the show's lead puppeteer.

The figure's "look," along with the puppet's name, was supplied by Buffalo Bob. Back on his radio show *Triple B Ranch,* Smith had provided the voice for Elmer, a silly, country-bumpkin character similar to ventriloquist Edgar Bergen's Mortimer Snerd. Instead of saying "hello" when meeting others, Elmer would drawl, "Well, uh, Howdy Doody."

Unlike Bergen's dummy, no actual Elmer puppet had ever existed for the radio program. So when it came time for Paris to visually transform Elmer into a marionette for *The Puppet Playhouse,* he used the boy's farm-boy "sound" as inspiration. Before long, "Elmer" became "Howdy Doody," a big-eared, blond mop-haired rube. As he had with Elmer, Smith supplied the voice for Howdy Doody. Smith wasn't a ventriloquist, so Howdy's lines were prerecorded for use during the show.

Howdy missed the new program's premiere because Paris was still working on the marionette. For the first three weeks, Buffalo Bob pretended that Howdy was hiding in his desk drawer, too bashful to come out. After three weeks—that is to say, after Paris finished the puppet—Howdy suddenly got over his shyness and emerged.

The immediate success of *The Puppet Playhouse* prompted the network to increase the show's schedule, along with giving the show a new name: *Howdy Doody Time.* Paris continued to work on the program, but he only had a verbal contract with NBC. In the end, the parties weren't able to come to terms, so Paris walked off the show, taking the marionette with him. Buffalo Bob owned Howdy's name, but Paris held the rights to his image. The Howdy we know today was carved to replace Paris's original.

Paris understood why people were curious about his Howdy. The puppet had been out of sight for so long, it became almost mythic.

Well, Paris thought, he did have the "wooden boy" (actually made out of a special lightweight composite material) carefully preserved there in his home. So who knew? If the evening went well and the mood was right, maybe he'd bring Howdy out before the night was over.

He figured his guests also might like to take the grand tour of the house. He had set up a small but complete marionette theater in the basement, and part of his puppet collection was on display. Also, he and Ted lived on the second floor, but several other rooms had been converted into meeting and workshop space.

The visitors would also probably be fascinated to learn that before Paris bought the place, it had been a speakeasy—personally run by the mayor!

It was true. In fact, all of Gay Street had a fascinating history. The short lane, located in the West Village, is just a block long, stretching between Christopher Street and Waverly Place. For most of the distance it parallels nearby Sixth Avenue.

The pathway cut through the site of an early brewery that was owned by Wouter van Twiller, the director-general of New Amsterdam after Peter Minuit. It then became an alley running between stables. The first people who lived alongside it were African-American servants of the prosperous white families residing near Washington Square.

The first upscale houses on Gay Street were built on the west side of the road between 1826 and 1833. The street was not officially christened until it was widened in 1833. The source for its name is uncertain, but the first extant reference to it as Gay Street is in the minutes of an 1827 meeting of the Common Council.

The Panic of 1837 temporarily delayed further construction along Gay Street. Most of the homes on the east side of the street were put up between 1844 and 1860, but what was considered fashionable in architecture changed during the decade-long hiatus. The houses on the west side were built in a Federal style, but the newer ones on the east side of the street contain elements of Greek Revival.

Frank Paris's four-story redbrick townhouse was one of the earliest homes on the tucked-away side street, having been built in 1827. Just under a hundred years later, in 1924, an addition was made to the back of the house, which covered over the old garden.

In the 1920s the row house was owned by one of the most colorful and infamous characters in New York history: Mayor Jimmy Walker. Born James John Walker in 1881, he was the son of an Irish immigrant who had worked himself up to become a Greenwich Village alderman and a state assemblyman. After attending New York Law School, Jimmy followed his father into politics.

He was a natural. Handsome and charismatic, Jimmy was a Dapper Dan and quite the ladies' man. Backed by the Democratic machine in Tammany Hall, he was elected to the New York State Assembly in 1910, then served as a state senator from 1914 to 1925. For the last two of those years, he was also president pro tempore of the Senate.

Sensing the man's promise, Governor Alfred E. Smith threw his weight behind the rising young star. Jimmy Walker became mayor of New York City in 1926, smack dab in the middle of the Roaring Twenties.

Walker roared right along with them. And Beau James, as friends called him, knew how to play the game. Prohibition was in full swing. Walker had his police force conduct the necessary raids for public show, but for the most part he turned a blind eye to the dozens of underground clubs and speakeasies throughout the city. He even ran one himself, the Pirate's Den, which operated out of the cellar of the townhouse he owned at 12 Gay Street.

Walker left his wife and had a number of highly publicized affairs with chorines. He bought the brownstone to set up his mistress, Betty Compton, who was an actress and member of the Ziegfeld Follies. (Technically, Walker leased the house to Compton.) The public didn't seem to care. It was the Jazz Age, and the economy was doing great. Walker was reelected in a landslide in 1929.

All that popularity came to a screeching halt on Black Tuesday 1929 with the crash of the stock market. In subsequent investigations it was alleged that Walker and his cronies had engaged in extortion. Rather than face charges, Walker resigned and fled overseas in September 1932. Compton followed him, and they were married in Europe. Although Walker did eventually return to the United States, he never again held political office, and he died in 1946.

In the meantime, a sculptor had moved into 12 Gay Street, and then, for a while, prolific author and magician Walter B. Gibson took an apartment in the building. Among his many other works, Gibson wrote more than a hundred books on magic and the paranormal, including those he penned as a ghostwriter for Harry Houdini, illusionist Harry Blackstone Sr., and mentalist Joseph Dunninger.

Gibson was most famous, however, for his association with *The Shadow*. The adventures of the mysterious crime-fighter with psychic powers were already being heard on the radio when the program's sponsor, Street & Smith, asked Gibson to write a book-length story for a Shadow periodical they were planning. That first assignment in 1931 went on to last eighteen years. Writing under the name Maxwell Grant, Gibson churned out almost three hundred Shadow novels and innumerable magazine stories. The last issues of *The Shadow* magazine were written in his Gay Street home, as was his final Shadow novel, 1949's *The Whispering Eyes*.

After Gibson moved out, real-estate broker Mary Ellen Strunsky bought the house. Its next owners were Paris and Lewis.

The evening was getting late, and Frank realized it was now or never. He stood up, took a long drag on his Tiparillo, adjusted the turquoise bracelet on his wrist, and playfully asked no one and everyone in particular, "So, would you like to see the place? I thought you might be interested in what we've done with the basement. And I think that little guy—what's his name? Elmer? Howdy?—I think he's down there, too."

His guests didn't have to be asked twice, and in a flash they were on their feet. Frank was leading them toward the stairs when, all of a sudden, a quiet but distinct thump was heard overhead. The room hushed as Frank and Ted exchanged nervous glances. As the company stood there in complete silence, a faint pitter-patter, then a scurry of footsteps—definitely human and not the couple's dog—echoed their way through the ceiling. The sound increased, more definite, to the point it could no longer be ignored. Someone was up there! Then, as quickly as the pounding had started, it was gone.

There was a long, tense pause in which nobody said a word. Finally, one of the guests felt he *had* to break the ice and asked, a bit too anxiously, "Does anyone live up there?"

Ted shot a worried look at Frank. Paris thought the question over, carefully choosing his words, and replied with a knowing smile, "No. Not a living soul."

People have been hearing and seeing spooks in and around the house at 12 Gay Street since the 1920s. Almost everyone who ever lived there saw shadows move up the stairwell wall at one time or another. Disembodied footsteps—that old haunted house staple—have been a regular phenomenon in the place as well. The most common area for the sounds to occur was on or around the staircase.

Famed ghost hunter Hans Holzer heard about the hauntings from *New York World Telegraph* reporter Cindy Hughes, and he got permission from Paris to investigate. On April 30, 1963, Holzer and Hughes took psychic Betty Ritter to the residence without telling her where they were headed. Among her impressions, she "felt" an argument going on between two spirits: a woman and an Oriental man named Ming.

Holzer interviewed the owners about any paranormal activity they had experienced. Both had seen the shades on the staircase and had been unable to find any explanation. Paris said he and their dog had whiffed the distinct scent of violets—well, the canine indicated it smelled *something*—but Lewis had not. Paris had also frequently detected the odor of frying onions throughout the house.

At the time of Holzer's visit, Paris and Lewis were entertaining two guests. One of them, Alice Mary Hall, confided that earlier that year she had been sitting in the couple's living room when she happened to look up at the doorway leading to the hall and the stairs. She saw a man with dark hair dressed in full evening clothes wearing an Inverness cape. She turned to get Paris's attention, but when she looked back at the stranger, the apparition was "gone like a puff of smoke."

Paris saw the spectre the following week. The phantom was wearing the same clothes, but this time he also had on a top hat. Even though the ghost was standing in semidarkness by the stairs, the puppeteer got a good, long look at him. He later recalled that the man was youngish with sparkling eyes. Paris's dog also saw the apparition and bounded over to greet it, but the spirit disappeared before the animal got there.

The canine could not only sense Beings from the Other World, it became one, too. The men told Holzer that after their pet died, both of the men had repeatedly felt the dog nudging their legs, just as it had done when it was alive.

Holzer returned to 12 Gay Street two more times. During his second visit he brought a medium named Mrs. Ethel Johnson-Meyers. Holzer worked with Meyers often throughout his career, and in 1977 they would investigate the Long Island house that inspired the so-called "Amityville Horror."

In the Gay Street home, Meyers made contact with the spirit of a French diplomat, who claimed he was tortured there but said he never gave up his secrets. Shawn Robbins was Holzer's medium for a televised tour in 1991. She claimed she was able to hear a person who had died violently in the house many years before.

Besides seeing the man in white tie and tails, owners and visitors to the house have spotted another male apparition as well. Rather than wearing a tuxedo, that one sported a simple black suit. He never showed up in the building. Instead he stood outside the main entrance or paced the sidewalk out front. Sometimes he'd walk up to the doorstep, smiling pleasantly, just before he vanished.

So who or what is causing all of the commotion at 12 Gay Street? Some say that the lost souls who haunt the residence may have wandered over from a morgue that used to be located next door. And it's tempting to think that the man in formal wear dates to the time of Jimmy Walker.

But Walter Gibson gave one of the strangest yet most intriguing explanations of all. He suggested that the tuxedoed man people were seeing was not a ghost at all but what in Tibetan lore is known as a *tulpa,* which he defined as an "unintentional by-product of a powerfully conceived mind." Gibson theorized that the spectre might be a physical manifestation—made real by some sort of "psychic projection"—of the imaginary character Lewis Cranston, the wealthy, sophisticated playboy alter ego of the Shadow.

Is something like that possible? Maybe the Shadow knows, but it's probably easier to believe in ghosts.

Chapter 10

# The Times That
# Try Men's Souls

## Marie's Crisis
## 59 Grove Street

*Thomas Paine, the Founding Father and author of* Common
Sense, *lived at 59 Grove Street during his final days. Perhaps it's his
otherworldly voice that's heard entering into heated discussions at
the building now on the site. In their own way, the current occupants of the place are revolutionaries, too.*

Well, he wasn't in Kansas anymore!

Ricky couldn't believe his eyes—or his ears. He had been
to piano bars before, which almost by definition were gay
bars. And sure, that was pretty much the main demographic
at this one, too. But at Marie's Crisis, there was a mix of every-
body—ages, genders, types. And everything was so festive!

Of course he *was* in New York, and "if you can make it
there . . . " Ricky mentally cut himself off. He had been
warned about the club's rule. It wasn't ironclad, but generally: show tunes only! No movie melodies, no Top 40. "New
York, New York," the Kander and Ebb hit made popular
by Frank Sinatra—well, with the Marie Crisis crowd, by
Liza Minnelli—had come from a film, not musical theater.
If Ricky asked for it, the guy at the piano bench might
start pounding out the Leonard Bernstein song from *On
the Town* instead.

Wait a second, Ricky corrected himself. He *could* ask for the city's unofficial anthem! He got out his phone and quickly checked ibdb.com, the Internet Broadway Database, to be sure. Yes! Minnelli performed "Theme from New York, New York" in her concert show *Liza's at the Palace* on Broadway from December 3, 2008, to January 4, 2009. So there! It was a Broadway show tune as well!

How sad, Ricky thought, that he actually knew about this stuff. Of course, if he didn't, he probably didn't belong in Marie's Crisis.

You pretty much know what you're in for as soon as you walk in the door. When Ricky first entered, there was a beefy, bald guy, six-foot-two if he was an inch, with tattoos running down his arms and a feather boa around his neck standing at the mic belting out Audrey's solo "Somewhere That's Green" from *Little Shop of Horrors*—and doing a fairly good vocal impression of Ellen Greene, the original star to sing it, to boot.

Within seconds a short Asian guy had joined the man by the piano, and they segued into the reprise of "Suddenly Seymour." Before long, with the help of everyone in the club, they had run through the entire *Little Shop* songbook, including the lesser-known numbers, like "Sominex" and "Mushnik and Son"! (It helped that the overhead monitors weren't showing football; they were flashing lyrics.)

To Ricky, the place felt like home. *If* a little crowded. He was pressed so close to the guy beside him at the bar that they were already on their third date. To paraphrase the old joke, they were packed in so tight he could tell the man's religion.

But before he was tempted to turn to the stranger and deliver what would surely have been the sorriest pickup line ever, Ricky heard someone calling out to him. Well, not to him specifically, but the voice was coming from directly behind Ricky's ear—so close, it was impossible to ignore.

Ricky couldn't make out exactly what the man was talking about, but it had nothing to do with show tunes or divas. Instead it sounded like the guy was arguing with someone—debating might be a better word—about the rights of man, freedom, universal dignity, that sort of thing. It was hard to tell: The room was so noisy that Ricky was only catching every tenth word and now and then a phrase or two.

Whatever the guy was jabbering about, it was getting annoying. The ramblings were muted but clear enough that the sound really carried. Then, without warning, a large man standing directly in front of Ricky spun around with a withering look of total disdain and condescendingly hissed "Shh!" right into his face.

Ricky was stunned. Shushed by a theater queen? Why was the guy upset with *him*? *He* wasn't the one doing the talking. It was some wacko behind him. Ricky gestured over his shoulder as if to indicate the true culprit, but it didn't matter. By then the man who confronted him had whirled around with an exaggerated huff and was back to cheering on a man in black leather singing the score from *Grease*.

Both irritated by the stranger's mumblings and peeved that he had been blamed for them, Ricky turned to face the offender. But the stool directly behind him was empty. Then who was talking? With the room that crammed, there wouldn't have been time for anyone to move away without being seen. Ricky quickly scanned the length of the bar and checked reflections in the WPA-era mirror, etched with scenes from the American and French Revolutions. No one in the immediate vicinity was chattering away. Everyone was engrossed in the performance or silently mouthing along.

Whose voice had it been?

As if he could read Ricky's mind, one of the bartenders wandered over. He waited politely for the applause to start at the end of the number, then motioned to Ricky.

"I heard it, too."

The bartender went on to quickly explain that the disembodied voice is heard all the time at the club, but nobody knows for sure where it comes from or who it belongs to because no apparition has ever shown up. Their best guess, given the site's history and the words that are spoken? The place is haunted by the ghost of Thomas Paine.

The next tune started up, and the entire room full of people burst into song. Ricky smiled in thanks as the server set off to refill a drink at the other end of the bar. The rest of the story would have to wait.

*How appropriate,* Ricky realized as he turned his attention back to the music. *They're doing the songs from* 1776.

Thomas (or more simply Tom) Paine was born in England in 1737. Though intellectually sharp, he was unsuccessful in a variety of early trades. He had just avoided debtor's prison in London in 1774 when he happened to be introduced to Benjamin Franklin, who was on a mission from the colonies. The American statesman, author, and inventor suggested that Paine move to the New World and gave him a letter of recommendation.

Paine arrived in November 1774, having barely survived the crossing. The ship had been poorly supplied, plus five people had died of typhoid. Paine took the better part of two months to mend, but by 1775 he had not simply recovered, he was thriving as the editor of the *Pennsylvania Magazine.*

It was a perilous time, and revolution was in the air. The fight for independence erupted in Lexington and Concord on April 19, 1775, and the Battle of Bunker Hill followed not long thereafter on June 17.

On January 19, 1776, Paine published the pamphlet *Common Sense,* which he had written anonymously but ascribed to "an Englishman." In it he argued that the sole solution for the ongoing troubles in America was complete independence from England. Not only that, the essay was a call to action, virtually challenging the reader to take arms.

The monograph was literate yet easy for the average person to comprehend. And it was highly persuasive. Within three months the booklet sold one hundred thousand copies. Other printers circulated as many as five times that number. Perhaps no other writing did more to inflame everyday citizens and unite them in the cause for freedom.

Later in 1776, Paine penned a series of booklets under the title *The Crisis.* Their purpose was to remind the people of his adopted country what they were fighting for and how important it was to continue in the struggle. The opening words of the first volume ring down through the ages:

> These are the times that try men's souls: The summer soldier and the sunshine patriot will, in this crisis, shrink from the service of their country; but he that stands it now, deserves the love and thanks of man and woman.

In 1787 Paine returned to live in London. His first few years there were uneventful, but he then became an avid supporter of the French Revolution. Inspired by the uprising, he wrote *Rights of Man* in 1791, criticizing the excesses and tyrannies of the monarchy. The problem was, England was a monarchy, too. Paine narrowly escaped to France before he was charged with sedition. (He was tried and found guilty in absentia, but the sentence was never enforced.)

Unfortunately Paine got caught between the bickering sides vying for power during the Reign of Terror, and he was thrown into prison. He narrowly escaped execution and wasn't released until the new American minister to France, James Monroe, successfully interceded on his behalf, pointing out that Paine was a US citizen. Paine returned to the United States in 1802 at the personal invitation of President Thomas Jefferson.

But he was in for a surprise. Since leaving the States, Paine had published *The Age of Reason,* in which he denounced all organized religions, including Christianity. The tract pointed out inconsistencies in the Bible and called both it and established churches man-made inventions. For Paine, the true faith was Deism, which in its simplest form was belief in a single God, no more, no less. According to Paine, there wasn't a need for rituals or congregations; rather, people should practice what he called "moral virtues" to emulate God as closely as possible.

All this didn't bring Paine many fans when he returned to America. In fact, he was a social outcast. He died on June 8, 1809, at the age of seventy-two in the house located at 59 Grove Street in Greenwich Village. His remains were taken to New Rochelle, where he owned a three-hundred-acre farm. Only six people attended the funeral. No church would bury him, so Paine was interred under a walnut tree on his property.

Paine's story has a macabre coda. In 1819 a British journalist named William Cobbett decided that Paine should be buried in honor in his native land. He had Paine's remains removed from their grave and shipped to him in England. Cobbett had not yet reburied Paine when he died more than two decades later, and the skeleton was subsequently lost. Although rumors have cropped up regarding the location of Paine's skull and right hand, all of the bones are still missing.

That apparently hadn't stopped Paine's spirit from returning to the place he died. The original house in which he passed is long gone. The building that replaced it was operating as a house of prostitution by the 1850s. In the 1890s the basement club was literally an underground bar for gay men. Then, during Prohibition, the tavern became a speakeasy known as Marie's.

Since the 1970s the club has operated as a gay-friendly piano bar. At some point it was rechristened Marie's Crisis, the latter word being added to its name as a nod to Thomas Paine's famous treatise. The new nomenclature was certainly appropriate. Gay rights were coming into their own in the '70s, with those who were brave enough to "come out" having to battle prejudice and injustice at every turn. The legendary Stonewall Inn, for instance—where gay riots after a police raid on June 28, 1969, sparked the beginning of the gay rights movement—was less than three blocks away.

For the regulars at Marie's Crisis, the fight for gay equality *was* the new American Revolution. After all, Thomas Paine had written in the very first paragraph of *The Crisis:*

> Tyranny, like hell, is not easily conquered; yet we have this consolation with us, that the harder the conflict, the more glorious the triumph.

No one knows when the spooky voice with nobody (and no body) attached to it started to be heard around the bar. The spirit doesn't stop in every night, but when he's there and starts debating, he sure draws attention to himself.

If you want to try to hear him for yourself, you can't miss the bar from the street. Look for the red window frames, red-and-white-striped awnings, and, impossible to miss, the huge red sign with white, colonial-style letters spelling out MARIE'S CRISIS CAFE hanging above the—what else?—red door. Inside and down a few steps, the club itself is small, usually elbow to elbow, and on weekends busier than that.

The room isn't fancy, and neither are the drinks: a limited selection of beers and simple mixed drinks. But there are other places to go for people who want to get loaded. Marie's Crisis is for people who want to "Sing out, Louise!"

Cozy up to the bar. If over the show tunes you catch the unmistakable sound of a firebrand voice that seems distinctly out of place, say hello to the resident revolutionary from centuries past, Thomas Paine.

# Chapter 11
# Belly Up to the Bar

## Chumley's Bar
## 86 Bedford Street

*By the time a collapsed wall caused Chumley's Bar, a legendary Green-wich Village speakeasy and writers' gathering place, to close in 2007, the ghosts of its original owners, Leland and Henrietta Chumley, had already been haunting the place for years. The bar is undergoing a complete renovation. When it's complete, will the apparitions return?*

Ben stood there, staring up at the scaffolding and green boards covering the front of the building. He knew that things could change overnight in New York—and frequently did—but somehow he assumed that *this* place would be around forever. Now what would happen to the ghosts?

Chumley's, a low-key neighborhood bar that had changed little since its days as a Prohibition-era speakeasy, was, in a word, gone. It had stood there on Bedford Street since the 1800s, wedged between two other houses. The redbrick three-story home to its left seemed fine, and the building to the right, at the intersection with Barrow, was also holding up well. But Chumley's . . .

Ben remembered his first visit. Barely twenty-one, he had just started graduate studies in creative writing at Columbia University. He parents hadn't exactly approved.

"If he's going to Columbia, shouldn't he at least come out a doctor?" his mother would ask, as if Ben wasn't standing right there in the room.

"And what can you do with a degree in fine arts? I don't even know what a fine art is," his dad would answer.

Never mind that Ben was paying his own tuition and that his parents had always known, in their heart of hearts, that all he ever wanted to do was be a writer. Hell, he had notebooks and journals full of stories, plays, bad poetry, you name it, scattered all over the house. And he had a BA in English. You'd think they'd have gotten a clue.

Ben loved his folks, but honestly. Columbia University was one of the most prestigious schools in the country. How many kids got accepted? Still, it was with a long face that Ben flew into Kennedy. Oh, well. Maybe his parents would be happy after he got his first book published.

Ben had heard from everyone that the first year in graduate school was always the hardest, regardless of a person's field of study. After four years as an undergrad, students had to adjust to a whole new mindset. Courses were more intense, expectations from the professors higher, and competition from fellow students fierce.

All that turned out to be true, but Ben reveled in the challenge. Plus, he quickly made a half dozen good friends among his classmates—really talented people, passionate about their work.

"Hey, have you ever heard of a place down in the village called Chumley's?" one of his pals asked out of the blue one day. "Seems it was some sort of hangout for famous writers. Maybe we should go down there sometime and let some of the genius rub off on us."

"Sometime" turned out to be that night. With five others in tow, Ben made his first of what would become dozens of trips to the storied saloon.

He found everything about the place amazing. Even getting into the bar was an adventure. There were two doors, but neither of them was marked. Well, the one on Bedford had a street number, 86, but there was nothing to identify it as the entrance to a bar. The other, the more colorful way in, required people to walk around the corner onto Barrow and pass through a nondescript archway into a courtyard.

From there they had to cross to the far side of the patio and walk up to an old wooden door straight out of "Hernando's Hideaway." As they approached, Ben half expected someone on the other side to open a small barred window and ask for a secret password.

Once inside, Ben could immediately tell that the bar had been a meeting place for many of America's top authors. The tavern's original owners had filled the walls with the writers' photographs and framed copies of their book jackets. Steinbeck. Trumbo. Hemingway!

The interior of the bar was well lit, yet it somehow seemed full of shadows. Perhaps it was the lack of windows or the dark wood. Or maybe it was the closeness of the thick oaken tables, many of them lopsided or mismatched in heights. Sawdust covered the floors, and—were they seeing correctly?—a large St. Bernard casually strolled about the room, weaving between the tables and rubbing up against guests.

Ben and his friends squeezed into a booth. It didn't take them long to figure out that table service was sort of iffy. Half of them held down the fort while the others worked their way up to the bar to order. Soon it was thick, greasy, wonderful burgers (on English muffins: the house specialty) all around, washed down by too many pricey microbrews. Conversation got loud; the laughs were long; and, to quote one of the most clichéd of expressions, it was a night that none of them would ever forget.

After graduation, on one of his last nights in New York, Ben made one last pilgrimage down to what had by then become familiar stomping grounds. He was alone—and felt it—his comrades having all gone their separate ways in the preceding days. It was near closing time, early in the week, and the pub was unusually quiet. He moved to the back, slipped into a shallow booth, and surveyed the room.

He was staring toward the rear wall, focusing on nothing in particular, when he became aware of a woman, sitting by herself in the booth nearest the fireplace, watching him through the semidarkness. She was of an indeterminate age but probably in her forties or fifties, and not unhandsome. She also seemed oddly at home.

Ben had never seen her before on any of his many, many visits, but she seemed to know him. Was she one of the staff? As Ben watched, transfixed, the woman raised her glass in a toast, moved her gaze from Ben's face up to the walls filled with iconic photographs, and then peered back into the young man's eyes. Was she merely saluting the giants, or was she suggesting that one day Ben, too, might be worthy of joining that very exclusive club? Ben unconsciously smiled at the prospect.

Suddenly a warm flood of nostalgia poured over him. As one after another "remembrance of things past" flooded his mind, Ben—who up until then hadn't considered himself to be particularly sentimental—had to force tears from welling in his eyes.

He stood to leave. *Good-bye, old friends,* he thought as he took one last look at the portraits. *I'll try to get back before too long.* Ben slipped on his jacket and started toward the door. Then, as an afterthought, he turned to give a nod of farewell to the mysterious woman in the back booth. But she was gone.

At the time Ben didn't register it as odd. She could have slipped by him easily. The room was dim. And the place was filled with concealed passageways. But in the years since, Ben had heard the rumors: how the ghost of Lee Chumley, who had started the former speakeasy as well as that of his wife Henrietta, had returned to wander the premises.

Now, standing outside the closed tavern, shivering as the chill autumn wind whipped down Bedford, Ben wondered: Had it been the widow's apparition he had seen on his last night in the bar all those years ago? With the old building in ruins, perhaps he'd never know. He'd come back when, if, the place ever reopened. And hopefully she'd be back as well. After all, he now had a book jacket to give her.

In January 1919 the Eighteenth Amendment to the Constitution outlawed the "manufacture, sale, or transportation of intoxicating liquors" in the United States, and in October that same year, Congress passed the Volstead Act to enforce it. Because the demand for alcohol remained unabated, bars were forced to go underground, and a criminal element arose to supply the clandestine taverns known as speakeasies with hooch.

One of the first of these nightspots to open in the Village, on MacDougal Street, was the Black Knight, owned by Sam Schwartz and managed by Leland Stanford Chumley. Known to everyone as Lee, Chumley was quite a character. He had emigrated from England and been everything from a day laborer, stagecoach driver, solider of fortune, and waiter to a newspaper cartoonist and editorialist. He was also an organizer for the International Workers of the World, a wide-reaching union also known as the Wobblies. The IWW was considered to be radical, sharing principles as it did with many socialists and anarchists of the era. As a result, many businessmen and politicians considered the IWW a much greater threat than they did other union groups such as the American Federation of Labor.

In the early 1920s Chumley bought a brick, two-and-a-half-story, Federal-style house located at 86 Bedford Street, near the corner of Barrow Street in the West Village. (Various sources list the date of purchase as 1922, 1926, and 1928.) The building was constructed as a working-class home sometime between 1820 and 1831. At different times, the ground level had been used as a blacksmith shop, stable, dairy, and garage. According to undocumented stories, the building also was a stop on the Underground Railroad during the Civil War.

At first a narrow walkway ran along the north side of the house, allowing access to the back of the building. The home was later extended, and a rear entrance was added, opening onto a horseshoe-shaped courtyard (now known as Pamela Court) shared with 82 Bedford Street and 56–58 Barrow Street. The gated, almost-hidden patio, in turn, emptied onto Barrow.

Chumley used the second-story space in his house to hold union meetings and to publish *The Rebel Worker,* a militant-leaning magazine for the IWW. On the bottom floor he opened an eponymous speakeasy. The date most often cited for its founding is 1926.

People had to know where to find Chumley's, because it was never advertised and neither of its entrances was signposted. Originally patrons entered Chumley's through the rear entrance, the so-called "Garden Door" in the back courtyard. Just like in the movies, there was a peephole in the door that could be used to check out potential customers before the door was opened. The entryway was popular with certain clientele because they could come and go in complete anonymity, much more discreetly than they could by using the Bedford door opening directly onto the street.

Though common in New York during Prohibition, such "teahouses" were against the law, and police raids were a regular part of doing business. Usually an insider on the take would tip off Chumley's when a bust was going to occur so that patrons who were friends of the establishment could escape before patrolmen arrived. The folks left behind in the tavern—those not in the know—would be nominally rounded up and released after a few hours.

How did people get away without being caught if time was tight? One way was through a doorway behind the bar that was decorated to look like part of the wall. When opened, it led to an alley. Another exit was through a false bookcase on the wall about the width of a single person. It could swing open to also allow a quick escape through a private passageway. (In later years waiters would use it as a shortcut between the bar and the kitchen when the room was packed.) A trapdoor in the floor, usually covered by sawdust and a table or barrel, led down to the basement, from which there was another way out onto the street. In the ladies' room there was also a dumbwaiter large enough to hold two people that traveled between the second floor (where, it was rumored, gambling occurred) and the ground level.

People say the often-hasty egress onto 86 Bedford became so well known that the address entered the vernacular.

According to legend, whenever police arrived at the courtyard door, the bartender would call out, "86 it." Customers knew that meant to scram through the Bedford Street
exit. In time, the expression "to be 86ed" came to mean
anything that was removed or gotten rid of (from "86 the
bum" to "86 all the noise") or someone who leaves a place
on his or her own accord (as in, "We 86ed the joint").

From its earliest days, Chumley's became a popular
watering hole for writers of all stripes. Novelists would come
to compare notes, poets would do impromptu readings, and
journalists would exchange tall tales.

The tradition continued up until the bar's closing. Among
the seemingly endless list of greats who frequented the pub
through the years were—almost unbelievably—James Agee,
William Burroughs, Willa Cather, e. e. cummings, Theodore
Dreiser, John Dos Passos, William Faulkner, Edna Ferber, F.
Scott Fitzgerald, Allen Ginsberg, Lillian Hellman, Ernest
Hemingway, A. E. Hotchner, Erica Jong, Ring Lardner, Norman Mailer, Somerset Maugham, Edna St. Vincent Millay,
Eugene O'Neill, Upton Sinclair, John Steinbeck, William Sty-
ron, Gay Talese, and James Thurber. Even J. D. Salinger once
dropped by.

At some point Chumley began to ask authors for copies of
their book jackets whenever they had a new work published.
Many writers complied, and he neatly mounted the covers
and displayed them on the walls behind glass. In addition,
he plastered the bar with hundreds of photos of writers, folk
singers, and other artists of the Beat Generation.

The book covers became such an integral part of the
decor that no less than Simone de Beauvoir mentioned them
in her 1948 book *America Day by Day:*

In Bedford Street is the only place in New York where you can read and work through the day, and talk through the night, without arousing curiosity or criticism: Chumley's! There is no music so that conversation is possible. The room is square, absolutely simple, with little tables set against the walls which are decorated with old book jackets. It has that thing rare in America: "An atmosphere!"

Lee Chumley died of a heart attack in 1935. Everyone assumed he was a bachelor. No one had ever heard tell of a wife or children. With no heirs apparent, it was feared the beloved haunt would be closing. So imagine people's surprise when Chumley's widow, Henrietta, appeared to take up the reins.

Fortunately Henrietta shared her late husband's passion for the saloon. She kept on any of the staff that wished to remain, and she continued to welcome both the working-man and the literati. Henrietta had a favorite booth in the back, close to a fireplace that had been the forge during the building's old blacksmith days. Henrietta would sit there, looking out over the club, chain-smoking, enjoying a drink or two, and playing solitaire. In later years she nodded off so often that, rather than disturb her, waiters would often leave her there when they quietly closed up for the night.

Henrietta held an almost nightly vigil at the pub up until her death in October 1960. She died peacefully in her sleep, there at her favorite table over a half-played game of cards.

It wasn't long before her ghost began showing up. Not very often, but enough to unnerve those who knew her best. Indeed, the spirit was soon accepted as part of the pub's bohemian atmosphere. And it wasn't always

Henrietta who materialized. On occasion, Lee himself would make an appearance.

There were other spirit manifestations, too. Glasses would sometimes break without being touched, and occasionally faint but unexplainable jazz music could be heard. Also, at some point the bar had installed a jukebox. When, more recently, video games were brought in to appeal to a younger crowd, the old jukebox went crazy—cutting out or starting up on its own. It wasn't until the video games were removed that the jukebox went back to normal.

After Henrietta's death Chumley's passed on to her nephew, followed by a number of other owners over the next forty years. Although some writers continued to stop by, the clientele changed considerably to include tourists, college students, and firefighters, especially those from the nearby Engine Company 24/Ladder Company 5/Battalion 2. In 2004 Steve Shlopak, the longtime manager of the bar, partnered with some of the local firefighters to take out a ninety-nine-year lease on the pub. Later that same year Chumley's and some adjacent properties were bought by a holding company called Speakeasy 86, LLC.

In May 2006, while 84 Bedford Street was undergoing repairs, its chimney collapsed and crashed through the roof. Nine people had to vacate their apartments. During more construction, debris fell through to the ground floor, forcing out another eight or nine tenants. The following January, both 84 and 86 Bedford Street were put up for sale. Despite this, the owners continued work to shore up and restore Chumley's façade, with plans to return it to its 1920s appearance.

Just before 2 p.m. on April 5, 2007, while workers were doing unauthorized construction inside the restaurant, a brick chimney fell loose from an interior wall and cascaded into the bar area, punching a six-foot-by-ten-foot hole into the wall. It forced Chumley's to close after more than eighty years of operation.

All four of the buildings that share the common courtyard on Barrow Street were evacuated, including the residents of ten apartments. Some have had to move out permanently.

City engineers quickly ruled that 86 Bedford was not in danger of imminent collapse and could be repaired, but the owners seem to be in no hurry to do so. Work on the property has proceeded in dribs and drabs. In 2008 more structural problems were discovered at Chumley's, and both the second floor and the roof had to be removed, effectively razing the entire interior.

The onetime speakeasy has never reopened. Reports surface from time to time that work will be finished by such and such a date, but so far every deadline has been missed. Shlopak, who retains a lease should the bar ever be rebuilt, has openly questioned the owners' intention for the building. Meanwhile, locals, acting on a rumor that the tavern would be transformed into a rowdy sports bar, circulated a petition to prevent it from reopening as anything other than the quiet, neighborhood hole-in-the-wall it has always been.

If owners are to be taken at their word, 85 to 95 percent of the furnishings have been saved, and Chumley's will be restored to look the same as it once did. And it's possible. But is a total re-creation the same as a restoration? When it's finished, will the new bar also be laced with disguised doors and clandestine exits? And more importantly, will Lee and Henrietta's ghosts still come to visit?

We'll have to wait and see.

# Chapter 12

# 'Twas the Night before Haunting

## The Church of St. Luke in the Fields
## 487 Hudson Street

*The first minister of the Church of St. Luke in the Fields, an off-shoot parish from Trinity Church, was early West Village property owner Clement C. Moore. For a time he was buried at St. Luke's. His remains are now elsewhere, but his spirit seems loath to leave the parish house.*

Justine loved Christmas. And it wasn't because she got presents. Well, not *just* because she got presents.

As a child she couldn't wait to help decorate the tree, hang the stockings, watch her dad put up the lights, and lick the spoon full of leftover dough as mom baked cookies to set out for Santa. Christmas itself comes but once a year, but the holiday glow would last for Justine from early December well into the new year.

The seasonal fever was starting to take hold once again. Thanksgiving was a week in the rearview mirror, so Justine was now seeing yuletide reminders everywhere. She'd already put a wreath on her apartment door, and one morning she'd made her annual pilgrimage to Macy's to sit on Santa's lap—despite the scowls of impatient children and derisive smirks from their parents. Justine's radio was turned to WLTW-106.7 FM for round-the-clock carols, and she'd changed her ring tone to "Jingle Bells." Why, she'd even addressed, stamped, and mailed her cards already! (She had finally given in to sending e-cards for birthdays and anniversaries, but she drew the line at Christmas.)

Okay, maybe she was a bit obsessive. But she found that—except for the last few days before the holiday when everyone went nuts with last-minute shopping—people in New York seemed to be nicer that time of year. Why couldn't it always be like that?

Justine lived just a few blocks away, around the corner on Christopher near Sheridan Square, but she had discovered the place where she was heading completely by accident. During her first week living in the Village, before she had gotten used to the weird layout of its streets, she had cut down Grove only to dead-end at Hudson. And there, standing directly in front of her, was one of the—dare she say it?—quaintest chapels she had ever seen.

There was nothing unique about it. It was a standard rectangular sanctuary, fronted by a tall, maybe four-story, square bell tower. But somehow it spoke to her. Justine immediately forgot whatever errand she was running and walked up to read the plaque attached to the redbrick wall on the front of the church.

No wonder it had attracted her attention. Landmarked by the City of New York, the Church of St. Luke in the Fields is the third-oldest chapel in Manhattan. It was surrounded by newer structures on the property, but the sanctuary itself dated back to 1821. When she read on the plate that Clement C. Moore was a founder and the church's first senior warden, well, she knew what she had to do: She wasn't much of a churchgoer, let alone an Episcopalian, but she was going to become a member of the congregation.

Moore, you see, had written (or is attributed to have written) perhaps the most famous and one of the most often recited pieces of American poetry—and Justine's personal favorite: "A Visit from Saint Nicholas."

It all seemed like ancient history now, but every Christmas Eve when she was growing up—until she was ten or eleven and stopped believing in Santa—there was a family ritual at her house: Just before she and her two little brothers were sent off to bed for the night, her mom and dad would gather them all in the living room, right next to the tree. Dad would make a grand production out of sitting down in his La-Z-Boy—*Do they still make those chairs?* Justine wondered—and, opening a big book he kept for the occasion, he would then start to read:

> 'Twas the night before Christmas,
> When all through the house
> Not a creature was stirring,
> Not even a mouse . . .

Tears swelled involuntarily in Justine's eyes as she stood there in the crisp morning breeze. *God, how hokey*, she thought. It was so "Hallmark television special." Yet how she missed those days. It was another lifetime ago.

Justine had found out a lot about the parish since she joined it. In 1820 a group of West Village residents got together to organize a local Episcopal church. They decided to dedicate it to St. Luke because he was a physician, and the neighborhood had played a large role in New York's expansion as people fled north to escape the yellow fever outbreaks in "the city" in 1798 and 1805. The words "in the Fields" were added to the church's name to acknowledge that, up until the early 1800s, Greenwich Village was mostly open farmland.

The cornerstone for the church was laid in 1821 on Hudson Street property donated by Trinity Church. About sixty years later the congregation moved north to a new church on West 141st Street, and the original sanctuary became an outlying chapel of Trinity Church. Then, in 1976, the Church of St. Luke in the Fields once again became independent. A devastating fire gutted the inside of the chapel in 1981, but fortunately none of the other buildings on the property were damaged. Within four years, the sanctuary was completely restored.

Justine was impressed by the church's outreach to the poor and its commitment to the gay community—especially during the early days of the AIDS crisis in the 1980s. But she had to be honest. What drew her in and kept her there was the church's connection, however ephemeral, to Clement C. Moore.

Born in 1779, Clement Clarke Moore was the son of Benjamin Moore, the second Episcopal bishop of New York, and Charity Clarke, the daughter of Major Thomas Clarke, a British veteran of the French and Indian Wars. After retirement Clarke purchased a massive farm along the Hudson River that, along with further acquisitions, extended from what is now Nineteenth to Twenty-fourth Streets and Eighth Avenue to the river. He named his manor Chelsea, after a London estate owned by Sir Thomas More. The district of Manhattan that encompassed most of Clarke's property bears the name Chelsea to this day.

After the death of his mother and father, Clement C. Moore inherited the property. He had grown up on the family estate in Queens and graduated from Columbia College (now Columbia University) in 1798. He went on to become a professor at the college in Oriental and Greek literature. Most of his land was eventually subdivided and sold, but Moore donated sixty-six tracts in Chelsea—basically, his apple orchard—to the Episcopal Church so it could build the General Theological Seminary, its oldest seminary in the United States. For many years, Moore was a professor of biblical criticism there. He also donated the Chelsea property on which St. Peter's Episcopal Church stands.

When the Episcopal parish of St. Luke's was proposed south of his holdings in Chelsea, Moore was quick to respond to the call. Moore was named its first rector, and the new church was consecrated on May 16, 1822. According to some sources, the land on which the chapel was built was part of a sizable grant Moore had given to the Episcopal Church.

Moore died in Newport, Rhode Island, in 1863. He was buried at St. Luke in the Fields, but in 1899 he was reinterred in the Trinity Church Cemetery in uptown Manhattan. (The graveyard had been established in 1842 when the Trinity Churchyard near Wall Street ran out of space.)

Justine had an hour to spare before meeting a friend for lunch, so she decided to duck into the St. Luke church grounds to take a stroll around its small gardens. Open to the public most days from nine to four, the contemplation park is located behind the vestry buildings, so it's not all that visible from the street. As a result, the place was seldom busy, and this day Justine had the plot of green—well, not all that green in December—to herself.

She sat on a bench placed along one of the pathways and let her mind drift back once again to those Christmas Eve recitations by her father. The poem was first printed in the *Troy Sentinel* on December 23, 1823—anonymously! The work took the country by storm, and it was reprinted for decades without attribution until 1844 when, at the insistence of his children, Moore admitted he was the author and included the verse in a book of his poetry. By then, more than twenty alterations in syntax and spelling had been made in published versions of the poem, and even more changes have been made since.

Moore said the inspiration for the poem came to him while riding home from market in his sleigh. A well-read man, he was no doubt aware of Washington Irving's 1809 description of St. Nicholas in his book *A History of New York*, and the clergyman included details from the Knickerbocker's tome in his poem, such as Santa's riding through the air in a sleigh, his smoking a pipe, and his laying a finger beside his nose. Moore also borrowed the names of the reindeer from old Dutch stories.

Whether consciously or not, Moore made a major contribution to the Santa Claus narrative: At the time, some ministers were voicing their concern about the secularization of one of the holiest days of the Christian calendar. People were gathering with their families on Christmas rather than attending church. Moore's poem helped move the focus of the St. Nicholas legend from Christmas Day to Christmas Eve.

Justine knew that some people thought the poem was actually written by Major Henry Livingston Jr., a Revolutionary War veteran who had died in 1828. Livingston's children claimed their father read it to them as early as 1807. But the Livingston clan had no proof. Even their father's handwritten manuscript supposedly burned in a house fire.

When Moore was questioned why he had published the poem anonymously, he explained that he had written it for just his own family. He considered it too frivolous to be known as having come from the pen of a scholar and college professor. An extended family member had sent a copy of the poem to the newspaper without his consent. When asked, the editor acknowledged it had come from someone connected with the Moore household.

Justine didn't care about the controversy. For her, Christmas was all about tradition, and as far as she was concerned, Clement C. Moore had composed "A Visit from St. Nicholas."

She hated to leave the small, tended gardens. Though it was without much color in December, it still offered a respite from the busy, concrete streets outside the sanctuary. Besides, she'd be back later in the week. St. Luke's was renowned for its choir and organ recitals, and special concerts had been added for the season.

As she headed toward the gate, Justine was surprised to see that there wasn't much activity going on around the parish house. Usually during the holidays, volunteers were always racing in and out of the building to schedule events and coordinate activities. She raised her hand to shield the sun from her face as she peeked through one of the ground-floor windows. Odd. No one was inside. Except, wait, back in the corner, one elderly man, maybe in his eighties, shuffling around. She didn't recognize him, and he seemed to be wearing clothing that would only have been fashionable back in the 1800s. Maybe he was there for a rehearsal of some holiday pageant—"A Christmas Carol," perhaps?

As if on cue, the stranger stopped his meandering, turned, and looked straight at Justine. For some reason,

Moore's poem popped into Justine's mind as the two stared at each other through the glass.

A wink of his eye and a twist of his head,
Soon gave me to know I had nothing to dread

Then the most extraordinary thing happened. The man nodded . . . and smiled . . . and raised his forefinger to his nose. He was signaling he knew that Justine could see him! But then, unlike Kris Kringle in the poem, the curious man didn't rise up some nearby chimney. Instead, as Justine watched, he simply vanished.

Surely Justine hadn't been visited by St. Nick. But had she spied the ghost of Clement C. Moore? Some would say yes. His phantom reportedly haunts the grounds, and his apparition has been spotted in the parish house in particular. Why Moore has chosen to return is up for debate. It's commonly believed that spirits come back to places where they were comfortable when they were alive, and the Church of St. Luke in the Fields certainly played a major role in Moore's life. Perhaps the rector, professor, and sometime poet simply feels at home.

# Chapter 13
# Gentle into That Good Night

## The White Horse Tavern
## 567 Hudson Street

*All sorts of spirits can be found in the White Horse Tavern—some of them alcoholic! Welsh poet Dylan Thomas spent one of his last nights on earth drinking in the pub, boasting of how much he was able to consume. Perhaps he's returned for more. But he doesn't have the place to himself: At least three other shades frequent the bar as well.*

Bohemia is dead!

Or so Derek wanted to yell—howl!—from his table in the back room of the bar. The pub was too well kept, too tidy, to act as a hangout for any true nonconformist. No wonder there were none in sight. All the people in the tavern seemed so . . . hmm, "nice" would be a good word to describe them, Derek decided. He couldn't imagine any of the well-groomed, upwardly mobile folks patronizing the bar that night abandoning his or her microbrew or chicken pita wrap long enough to raise any kind of fuss, much less lift up a head and cry out in a primal scream. Those days, alas, were long gone.

The White Horse Tavern at the southeast corner of West Eleventh and Hudson Streets is one of the West Village's—in fact, the entire city's—oldest saloons. It was opened in

1880 and has operated continuously ever since. Located just three long blocks from the Hudson River waterfront, it was originally a simple workingman's pub popular with seamen, fishermen, and dockworkers, but it also catered to travelers and well-heeled locals as well.

Early in the twentieth century, Greenwich Village became a magnet for artists, writers, actors, political activists—in fact, avant-garde thinkers and nonconformists of all stripes. By the 1950s it had firmly established itself as Grand Central for the counterculture.

Derek, with his three-day-old stubble, considered himself a rebel, as have so many privileged but disaffected youth before him. This was his first foray to New York, so Derek felt it his duty to visit the White Horse. The bar had been a meeting place for his idol, Jack Kerouac, as well as other up-and-coming writers of the Beat Generation, most notably, Allen Ginsberg and William S. Burroughs.

If he had been honest with himself, Derek would have admitted that his knowledge of their literary movement was superficial at best. He knew that Kerouac had originated the term "Beat Generation" in 1948, and it referred to the underground group of discontented, post–World War II youth (especially those in New York City) who used drugs, experimented with their sexuality, and explored other forms of self-expression.

Kerouac is said to have first used the phrase when talking about himself and his circle of like-minded writers, whose lifestyles and written works reflected those values. Nowhere was the Beat Generation better expressed than in Ginsberg's long-form poem *Howl* (1956); Burroughs's third novel, *Naked Lunch* (1959); and Kerouac's masterpiece, *On the Road* (1957).

Derek admired *Howl* and *Naked Lunch,* but it was Kerouac's free-form epic that really spoke to him. Kerouac had mapped out large sections of the book in advance, but he typed the manuscript itself in a three-week period on a single 120-foot scroll of paper that he fed through his typewriter. The rambling tale was based on a series of road trips he had taken with his friend Neal Cassady—hence the novel's title.

Sitting by himself in a room at the back of the bar, Derek imagined the Beats holding court with their pals, high on whatever: art, life, existence. Through the years, other artists, all revolutionaries in their own way, also found the White Horse Tavern. Among them were Bob Dylan and Hunter S. Thompson, both of whom conceded the influence *On the Road* had on them. The Clancy Brothers became regular patrons and would often get up and perform. Jim Morrison, James Baldwin, Norman Mailer, Mary Travers (of Peter, Paul, and Mary) also passed through the tavern's doors.

*Where were such giants today?* Derek thought to himself. All Derek saw out front were tourists, college kids, and young, trend-following professionals. When did the bar stop being hip? Or was it that artists no longer sought out places like the White Horse? Had Tweeting, texting, and all the other social media completely replaced their need to congregate face to face?

Derek threw a couple of dollars on the table. How sad that this first visit would probably be his last. The place was perfectly fine, and everyone inside (and presumably out on the sidewalk patio) seemed to be having a great time. The selection of songs on the jukebox was up to date if not cutting edge, and they were the right tunes for the crowd. Derek was inclined to agree with the bar's menu boasting that it served the "best burger in the West Village." But the gonzo groove—the maverick magic he was looking for—just wasn't there.

He reached to grab his coat and was shocked to discover that he was not alone in the room. When he was seated an hour earlier, the place had been empty. Other than his server, Derek didn't remember anyone else coming or going the whole time he was there.

Normally he wouldn't have paid any attention to the solitary figure huddled at the corner table, but this guy— there was something about him. Was it the fact he didn't seem to be moving? Derek had never seen anyone sit so . . . still. The man appeared to be in his late forties, not exactly overweight, but with a round, almost cherubic face, and he had a full head of thick curly hair. The stranger wore a checkered wool jacket over a black mock turtleneck, and a large silk scarf was knotted around his neck. An empty beer pitcher and glass, both holding remnants of foam, sat on the table in front of the guy, as did a bottle. Its label was turned away, but Derek surmised it was whiskey. The man's hands, which trembled slightly, were cradling a small shot glass filled to the brim with a light, tea-colored liquid.

"I'm sorry, sir," Derek muttered, almost surprised to hear his own voice. "I . . . I thought I was alone. I didn't see you there."

The man looked up from his glass but curiously didn't acknowledge Derek at all. Rather, he slowly lifted the jigger, tilted back his head, threw the drink against the back of his throat, and then slammed the glass back down onto the table.

Silence. Derek stared in wonder. There had been no sound as the shot glass hit the top of the wooden table. How was that possible?

But before Derek had a chance to try to figure it out, the person turned to him and smiled, as if welcoming him to the club. And then he vanished.

Derek stood there, dumbfounded. That howl he had considered earlier must have actually escaped his lips because, suddenly, there was a barman standing next to him, asking him if everything was all right.

"Yes. I think so. I mean, there was this guy sitting there, and then he . . . wasn't."

"Oh," said the server with an understanding grin. "You've seen Dylan. Well, you should feel honored. He doesn't appear for just anybody."

The waiter left him alone with his thoughts. As far as Derek was concerned, the "spirit" of his heroes—the writers of the Beat Generation—was imbedded into the very walls of the tavern. But who would have guessed the place had an *actual* spirit as well?

If Derek had encountered the ghost of Kerouac or even Ginsberg or Burroughs, he wouldn't have been a bit surprised. But he was so focused on the Beats that he'd never heard another writer, one not associated with their radical, provocative literature, also once called the White Horse Tavern home. His name was Dylan Thomas.

Thomas was born on October 27, 1914, in Swansea, Wales. He probably got his love for verse from his father, a grammar-school teacher of English literature, who used to recite Shakespeare to the boy before he could read. Despite being fascinated by language, Thomas was not a good student, and he dropped out of school at sixteen. He was also a sickly child, plagued by bouts of asthma and recurrent bronchitis throughout his life.

He began to write poetry, and more than half of his poems that would ever appear in print were completed when he was a teenager. Although individual works appeared earlier, his first collection of poetry, *18 Poems,* was published to great acclaim in 1934. It won an important competition, and overnight Thomas found himself a major poet. The mellifluous lyricism in his work set him apart from his contemporaries. He would live and write into the era of the Beat Generation, but his style would always hark back to the Romantics.

Thomas made his first visit to the United States in 1950, and his poetry readings are the stuff of legends. Mercurial, flirtatious (though married), theatrical to a fault, a heavy smoker and a heavier drinker, he was every woman's image of a "bad boy" poet. And then there was that Welsh voice.

Dylan Thomas toured the States four times in all, and New York City was always the main stop on his travels. The poet quickly discovered the West Village, and at some point, Scottish poet Ruthven Todd introduced Thomas to the White Horse Tavern. It was a perfect match. From then on, whenever Thomas was in Manhattan, he made a point of visiting the White Horse as often as possible.

Thomas's last visits to America were in 1953. On May 3 he performed what has become his best-known piece, *Under Milk Wood,* as a "work in progress," solo, at Harvard. Eleven days later he read it with other actors at the Poetry Centre in New York, even as he continued to tinker with it. Afterward he returned to Great Britain, and the completed play received its official premiere in Wales on October 8.

Just twelve days later he was back in New York for another series of readings. He stayed in Room 206 at the

Chelsea Hotel, a popular favorite among artists, writers, and musicians, located north of the Village on West Twenty-third Street. On November 3, after all of his scheduled personal appearances were over, the poet took a late-night respite at the White Horse Tavern. He drank himself into oblivion. He roared to anyone who would listen that he had just downed eighteen straight whiskies in a row. "I think that is a record!" he bragged. (The bartender later reported that Thomas had exaggerated: He had probably drunk half that many.)

Regardless, Thomas was smashed. He managed to get back to his hotel, but he canceled all his appointments for the next two days. It wasn't the alcohol: His respiratory problems were back, and the city was blanketed in smog. Nevertheless, on November 4 Thomas dragged himself down to the White Horse Tavern, where he shared a round of drinks with Liz Reitell, his tour manager's assistant. It was his last visit to the bar.

On November 5 Thomas's health dramatically declined, and by midnight he could no longer breathe. He was rushed from the hotel to St. Vincent's Hospital around two in the morning. He never left. Thomas was diagnosed with acute bronchitis and pneumonia. After struggling for four more days, he died on November 9. The immediate cause of death was swelling of the brain due to lack of oxygen brought on by the pneumonia. Thomas was buried back in Wales.

Did Derek see the apparition of Dylan Thomas in the White Horse Tavern? Well, stories have circulated for years that the poet's phantom has returned to his favorite New York watering hole. His semisolid spectre has been spotted wandering throughout the pub, but usually he's seen sitting alone at a corner table in the back room, nursing a drink. A large oil portrait of Thomas hanging in the middle room of the bar makes him instantly recognizable.

People know when the Man of the Hour is present even if he doesn't materialize. His invisible hand sometimes rocks or revolves his favorite table, he'll rattle the glassware, or he'll make an empty beer or whiskey glass appear out of nowhere. Employees have also heard unexplained noises down in the basement that they credit to the Welsh bard.

We have no way of knowing whether Dylan Thomas believed in ghosts. But he was the author of two of the most moving poems about death ever written. The first, "Death Shall Have No Dominion," was published in his collection *Twenty-Five Poems* in 1936. Thomas was a mere twenty-two years of age when the poem was released, but it was one he had written in his teens.

More celebrated was one of the last poems he ever completed, a villanelle (as its poetic form is known) that he wrote for his dying father. Originally published in a literary journal in 1951, "Do not go gentle into that good night" was reprinted in his 1952 collection *In Country Sleep*. (In actuality, the piece has no name. Instead, the first line of the poem, which is repeated throughout, is generally used as its title. The poem has another recurring refrain: It implores those on death's bed to "Rage, rage against the dying of the light.")

If the tales are true, Dylan Thomas isn't the only person associated with the White Horse Tavern who does not want to "go gentle into that good night." Three or perhaps four other ghosts walk the halls as well.

One, a dark figure in a velvet cloak, is thought by many to also be Thomas, but doubters point out that even though the writer could be flamboyant at times, a cape wasn't part of his regular attire.

Perhaps this draped ghost is the same spectre that shows up wearing the sort of coat, hat, and buckled shoes that were popular in the nineteenth century. This wraith meanders through the entire pub, apparently without purpose.

Another male apparition dates back to the tavern's earliest days, when travelers could pay to stay there overnight. Two men whose names are lost to history settled down in makeshift bedding next to the fireplace. Come morning, one of them was gone and the other lay dead. After a quick examination, it was determined that the one left behind had died of natural causes, but the *specific* cause spread more panic than if he had been murdered: He had died of smallpox! To prevent contagion, his body was quickly buried in a makeshift grave.

The location of the man's unmarked burial site remains unknown to this day, as does his identity, but where his ghost frequents is no mystery. The spirit continues to return to the White Horse Tavern, usually appearing in a chair next to the old fireplace. If the spectre waits long enough, maybe his long-gone companion will come back to join him—or to lead him on to the Next World.

The final phantasm is a Native American girl. It's thought that she was the servant who prepared the body of the smallpox victim for burial. She, too, came down with the dreaded disease and, after being forced into quarantine, soon succumbed. Her apparition now roams through the bar, too. She seems to know she's among the living, but she never responds to those who try to talk to her.

The White Horse Tavern is open seven days a week starting at eleven o'clock in the morning. Come early; stay late. Perhaps you'll spy one of the bar's many ghosts for whom death has no dominion.

Chapter 14

# A Night to Remember

## The Jane Hotel
## 113 Jane Street

*Tiny quarters can lead to tiny terrors, especially if you're trapped with a ghost. The spirits of those who lost their lives in the world's most famous shipwreck along with the traumatized souls of some who managed to survive have returned to the hotel where they found safe harbor.*

Lindsay couldn't help laughing. She knew that the room was gonna be small—but come on! Lying on the bed, if she stretched her legs, she could almost touch her toes on the far wall!

To be fair, there was a shelf and perhaps space for a little bag between the end of her bed and the window, but that was about it. The room had been openly advertised as a "remarkably cozy" fifty square feet, but Lindsay never translated that figure into working numbers: The room was about seven feet long and seven feet wide.

As she stood in the doorway looking in from the hall, the thigh-high twin bed stood flush against the left wall, stretching almost the full length of the room. The opposite wall was covered with a giant mirror: Its reflection gave the illusion of greater space in the room than there really was. Next to the bed was a very narrow walk space, barely the width of an average person. It was possible to shove luggage underneath the bed, if Lindsay could figure out how to angle and pivot the suitcase, and there was also a high overhead rack for belongings.

All in all, the room looked more like the berth on a small, private yacht than a hotel room, but perhaps that made sense. The Hotel Jane, where Lindsay was staying, had originally been the Sailors' Home, a way station for mariners and commercial seamen on leave. The boardinghouse had been started by a Christian-leaning group, the American Seamen's Friend Society, and their intention was to provide clean, inexpensive housing for seafarers, hoping to keep them off the streets where they would fall prey to sin and vice.

The current owners had completely refurbished the place top to bottom. They had wisely decided to give the public rooms a luxurious decor best described as early twentieth century, including a lobby with plush hardwood furniture, a period cafe with a checkerboard-pattern tile floor, and a comfortable drawing room with an open fireplace that could have come straight out of the game Clue. A room off the lobby that had been an Off Broadway theater up until the renovation was now a hip bar, the Jane Ballroom. But of all the accoutrements, Lindsay was most drawn to the old-fashioned front desk backed by pigeonhole letter boxes, manned by a clerk in a brass-buttoned, wine-red uniform complete with pillbox hat.

As for Lindsay's room, it had all the amenities most travelers look for these days: a flat-screen TV, a DVD player, free Wi-Fi, an iPod dock (a nice, unexpected touch!), a telephone with personal voice mail setup, an in-room safe, air-conditioning, and three-hundred-thread-count cotton sheets on the bed. True, bathrooms were down the hall—Lindsay hadn't shared a shower with strangers since college—but the price was right for New York City: ninety-nine dollars a night. Well, okay, there was New York State sales tax, New York City sales tax, and city hotel room occupancy tax on top of that, but it was still a pretty good rate for Manhattan.

Yes, the only downside to her room was its size. No wonder it was decorated to resemble a shipboard cabin: "Cabin" was probably short for "cabinet."

Lindsay had taken what was called a "Standard Cabin." If she had been traveling with a friend, she could have rented a double room, or more precisely a "Bunk Bed Cabin." Those were almost identical to the one she was in except for the stacked beds. And if she had wanted to splurge, she could have gone for a "Captain's Cabin." At 250 square feet, those rooms were semispacious. They had all the up-to-date features of the smaller rooms, but they also contained either a full, queen, or king bed—with room to walk around it!—a vanity, a separate table and chairs, and a ceiling fan. The prime rooms also had a river view through tall windows. Some Captain's Cabins also had a terrace. But most importantly, each and every one had a private bathroom with marble sink and countertops, a rainfall showerhead, and a complimentary assortment of C. O. Bigelow toiletries.

Not exactly complimentary, Lindsay corrected herself. Most of the Captain's rooms were pricey—upward of three hundred dollars a night. Maybe that was considered somewhat reasonable by New York standards, but this trip she was on a budget. She would have to make do where she was.

Lindsay had just gotten comfortable and was closing her eyes when she heard an unexpected sound on the other side of her door. The noise was hard to explain exactly. It was definitely human and coming from a male—a man, not a boy. She couldn't make out any words, but the unintelligible voice was gloomy, heavier than a sigh yet not quite a moan, filled with heavy sadness and duress.

Lindsay knew it was none of her business, and normally she wouldn't be the first person to rush up to try to console someone she didn't know, yet she felt herself being compelled to find out who was making the sorrowful cry. She had to see if there was anything she could do to help.

She paused briefly before opening the door, hoping the wail would die down or go away, but when it didn't she peeked outside. No one was there. Not only that, the moment she cracked the doorway, the sound instantly stopped.

Lindsay walked out into the hallway. Her room was located halfway down the corridor, and she looked all the way from one end of the passage to the other. It was completely empty. She hadn't heard a door slam; besides, it would have been impossible for someone to duck into a room that quickly without being seen. Nonetheless, no one was there.

Within minutes Lindsay was back in her room, her door safely locked, and she had fallen fast asleep. The next day she met up for a lunch with an old classmate in midtown. The unusual occurrence of the night before hadn't entered her mind until the friend casually asked, "So did you run into any ghosts? I hear the Jane is haunted. Or used to be. I haven't heard anything about it recently . . ."

But Lindsay had stopped listening as soon as she heard the word "ghosts." She didn't necessarily believe in such things, but what if the hotel really *was* haunted? The place could hold a century's worth of phantoms. She knew the building had been constructed at the turn of the twentieth century and must have welcomed all sorts of people through its doors during its many different incarnations. Newly determined to figure out the identity of the spectre she may have encountered, Lindsay decided to research the hotel, all the way back to its original life as the American Seamen' s Friend Society Sailors' Home and Institute.

As might be expected, in the late 1600s the initial settlement of Greenwich Village—what is now the Far West Village—took place along the Hudson River rather than in the fields and marshland to the immediate east. It was much easier to transport building materials and other supplies to the young hamlet by water than by carting everything the few miles overland from the "city" of New Amsterdam to the south.

Thus, businesses soon grew up to cater to those involved in commercial river trade and seafaring. By the early nineteenth century, these unfortunately included saloons, seedy flophouses, dance-hall dives, brothels, and other lowlife establishments associated with the shady side of seaports.

Beginning in the mid-1800s, several organizations were formed in England and the United States that sought to improve the education, social conditions, and moral behavior of individuals whose activities were thought to be, well, less than ideal. Most of the groups had their start in the evangelical movement of the Christian church.

One of them, the YMCA, even had "Christian" in its full name: the Young Men's Christian Association. It was founded in London by Sir George Williams in 1844 to help men (and later through its sister society, the YWCA, women) develop a "healthy spirit, mind, and body" through good thoughts and actions. The Salvation Army had its start in London as well, in 1852, in the tent meetings of William Booth held in the city's East End.

In New York City, the American Seaman's Friend Society (or ASFS) grew out of prayer meetings that were started in 1816 in the Brick Presbyterian Church on Water Street, where many members of the congregation were sailors. Along with the Marine Bible Society and the Society for Promoting the Gospel Among Seamen in the Port of New York, the ASFS decided that a nonsectarian church was needed if they were to attract large numbers of seafarers to worship. The result was the Mariners Church, which began services on Roosevelt Street near the East River in 1820.

Its pastor, the Rev. John Truair, wanted to expand his ministry, and in 1825, along with several prominent members of society, he proposed a national nondenominational seamen's welfare organization. Its purpose would be to cater to the men's physical well-being as well as their minds and spirits. According to its charter, the ASFS would "improve the social and moral condition of seamen . . . by promoting in every port . . . savings banks, register offices, libraries, museums, reading rooms and schools; and also the ministrations of the gospel, and other religious blessings."

The ASFS adopted a constitution in 1826, but it wasn't formally established with a board of trustees until May 1828. It was five more years before the association was legally incorporated. As part of its stated mission, the ASFS planned to establish "boarding houses of good character" where sailors could stay when they weren't at sea. Besides providing the men with shelter, they would give them access to books, lectures, entertainment, and Bible studies.

The first of these boardinghouses, the Sailor's Home, was opened at 190 Cherry Street off the East River in 1842. It had rooms for three hundred seamen, and it was in use until 1903, when it was demolished so the Manhattan Bridge could be built.

To replace the Sailors' Home, the ASFS planned a new mariners' home-away-from-home in the West Village. In

January 1905 they purchased property on the northeast corner of Jane and West Streets, south of Chelsea and the Meatpacking District, for $70,000. The next year, the society announced its intentions to have the boardinghouse designed by William A. Boring, whose other work (with the architectural firm Boring and Tilton) included the US Immigration Station on Ellis Island. For a time, the project seemed prohibitively expensive, but a donation came in from philanthropist Olivia Sage that would cover half of its $300,000 cost (which also included all of the interior furnishings). The bequest didn't come completely out of the blue. Olivia, the widow of financier and railroad executive Russell Sage, was related to the president of the ASFS, the Rev. Charles A. Stoddard.

The Home's cornerstone was laid on November 26, 1907. Built by Richard Deeves & Son, the Neoclassical five-story building with a basement and partial sixth story was faced in red brick in English bond and cast-stone trim. A decorative cornice lined the top of the building, and a balustrade circled the roof of the tower. Nautical-themed motifs appeared in decorations throughout the building. Finally, a one-story octagonal tower topped by a steel-and-copper-framed beacon and flagpole was positioned on the roof at the corner where Jane and West Streets meet.

Although the riverfront side of the building takes up 505–507 West Street, its main entrance, with a high arched doorway accessed by a short flight of stairs, was placed at 113 Jane Street. (The Jane Street façade was approximately twice as long as the West Street frontage.)

The American Seaman's Friend Society Sailors' Home and Institute first welcomed guests on October 7, 1908. The word "Institute" was added to its name to signal that the

ASFS flagship would be more than a clean, reasonably priced boardinghouse. It would also have educational and recreational facilities including a four-hundred-seat auditorium and concert hall, a billiards table, swimming pool, bowling alley, library, and reading rooms—even a small observatory in the tower. There was also a restaurant, bank, laundry, post office, and baggage storage room. And, true to the organization's Christian calling, there was an interfaith chapel, dubbed the Chapel of the Sea, where nightly services were held.

The sleeping quarters were tiny, even then furnished to resemble shipboard cabins, lining both sides of a corridor that itself wasn't very wide. Most of the rooms were rented out, but there were always some available free of charge for seamen who were too poor to pay, were sick, or had been shipwrecked.

There were separate quarters for the different ranks of seamen. Reports vary as to the number of single rooms available for regular sailors and firemen, but it was somewhere between 107 and 156. There were thirty-two additional rooms for officers and engineers, and a dormitory could house twenty-four stewards or cooks. The officers' quarters had their own bathrooms; other tenants shared communal showers and toilets at the end of each floor. When the "hotel" first opened, a single room cost most seamen twenty-five cents per night. Depending upon the accommodations, it was fifty or seventy-five cents for officers. Dinner was twenty-five cents extra.

As the nineteenth century drew to a close, the ASFS decided to concentrate on providing for commercial merchant mariners. (Up to that time, members of the US Navy were also encouraged to use their facilities.) Even so, by the early 1920s it became obvious that the Sailors' Home on Jane Street was too small and would have to be replaced.

By then there were three main seamen's welfare groups in New York City: the ASFA, the YMCA Merchant Seamen's Branch, and the Seamen's Christian Association. Rather than duplicate their efforts, they decided to work together to fund a larger, more modern seamen's retreat. Ground was broken for an eight-story structure in Chelsea at 550 West Twentieth Street (near Eleventh Avenue), and the completed building was dedicated on November 2, 1931.

Instead of being sold, the ASFS Sailors' Home and Institute was turned into the Seamen's Relief Center Annex. It provided free beds and meals to destitute mariners during the Depression and into World War II. The building was transferred to the YMCA in 1944, and two years later the light beacon and flagpole were removed from the roof, signaling the end of the Home's service as a seamen's haven. The American Seamen's Friend Society closed its office in New York in 1976, and the association completely disbanded ten years later.

In 1946 the former Sailors' Home and Institute was bought by Jane-West Corporation and, after refurbishment, was reopened as the Jane-West Hotel. Five years later it was acquired by Benbar Associates, then, in 1967, by Hotel Associates. For the next several decades the former Sailors' Home was known as the Riverview Hotel.

Classified as an SRO (Single Resident Occupancy or Single Room Occupancy) hotel, the Riverview Hotel operated as a low-budget dive, and it gained a notorious reputation as one of the worst transient hotels in New York. Rooms were very cheap, however—some less than fifty dollars a night all the way up to the 1990s—so the hotel catered to the hostel crowd, the poor, and the disadvantaged. For several years the city leased rooms in the winter months for use as a homeless shelter.

In addition to its hotel rooms, the building also housed various commercial tenants dating back to the 1930s, including a dance club, office space, and, at one point, the trendy bar and restaurant Socialista in the basement. In the 1970s the old ballroom was made into an Off Broadway theater, the Jane Street Theatre, with a small thrust stage and seating for around 280 people. Among the noteworthy productions that appeared there were *Hedwig and the Angry Inch* and *tick, tick . . . BOOM!*

Then, in 2008—in the building's centennial year—the old Sailors' Home got another new lease on life. It was purchased by developers Sean MacPherson, Eric Goode, and two other partners who completely revamped the property. MacPherson and Goode knew what they were doing: They had already renovated the Maritime Hotel, another former seamen's hostel that had been built in the 1960s. Plus, they were the boys behind the upscale Bowery Hotel in the East Village. Now they had another feather in their cap: the Jane Hotel. Its single rooms were indeed minuscule, yet the boutique hotel became fashionable to a certain clientele, not the least because of its unique heritage.

Part of that legacy was its connection to one of the worst disasters in maritime history. Around 2:20 a.m. on April 15, 1912, the White Star Line's luxury ship, the RMS *Titanic,* sank while on its maiden voyage after hitting an iceberg in the North Atlantic. The tragic story is well known. Approximately two hours before the *Titanic* slipped beneath the waves, a Cunard vessel, the RMS *Carpathia,* picked up its distress signal. The *Carpathia's* captain, Arthur Henry Rostron, changed course and raced to the scene.

It took about three-and-a-half hours to travel the fifty-eight-mile distance. When the *Carpathia* reached the *Titanic's* last known position, everyone onboard was stunned. There was no sign of a damaged ship in the ice field. Eventually eighteen small lifeboats from the *Titanic* were spotted, and over the next four hours just over seven hundred survivors were pulled to safety.

Because of incomplete records, no one will ever know for sure how many passengers and crew members were on the *Titanic* when she left her last port in Ireland, but sources place the number between 2,223 and 2,240. There is even a slight discrepancy in how many survived, but an official inquiry, Lord Mersey's Report to the British Parliament, stated that 712 survivors were rescued. One of those died en route to New York and was later counted as a casualty.

Thousands of people met the *Carpathia* on the evening of April 18 when she tied up at Pier 54 off West Twelfth Street in New York City—five berths from where the *Titanic* should have docked at Pier 59. Several charitable groups, including the Travelers Aid Society, the Women's Relief Committee, and the Council of Jewish Women rushed survivors to shelters.

Many of the *Titanic* crew members that were saved were taken in by the ASFS Sailors' Home, where they received food, shelter, and clothing. Traumatized and mourning the loss of their friends and coworkers, most of them had no money: They had not yet received their wages and, besides, the White Star Line would only pay them for the work they had done up to the time the ship sank. On the night of April 19, about a hundred people, including the *Titanic* crew members, held a memorial service in the Home for those who had lost their lives in the tragedy.

To this day, there are unexplained "cold spots" through-out the building. (Paranormal experts theorize that such unnatural, small columns of cold air might be portals between the mortal world and the Beyond.) The elevator sometimes acts as if it has a mind of its own. Then there are the disembodied, grief-stricken sighs that reverberate up and down the hallways. It's been hypothesized that the hauntings, especially the woeful grunts and groans, come from the spirits of the *Titanic* survivors who were brought to the old Sailor's Home. Some people believe that a few of those who died in the catastrophe have made their way to the Jane as well. And why shouldn't they?

It's also possible that the Jane Hotel isn't haunted at all, at least not by active apparitions. The phenomena in the for-mer boardinghouse might be what paranormal experts refer to as a "residual haunting." In such cases, a person in an extreme emotional state, such as elation, panic, or despair, somehow impresses his or her feelings and activities—for lack of a better word, "essence"—onto the surroundings. This aura remains seared onto the environment as a kind of psychic scar and replays itself like a film loop, over and over again throughout eternity. Then, today, "sensitives" who can perceive such things happen upon that impression and see or experience it anew, even though the actual events happened long ago.

Are there apparitions haunting the Hotel Jane, or are overnight guests tapping into a time gone by? Regardless, the Jane—which has certainly seen its good days and bad in more than a century of continuous operation—remains a timeless testament to the past.

# Chapter 15

# The Face on
# the Ten-Dollar Bill

## The former Francis House
## 27 Jane Street

*For years, residents of a Jane Street house once owned by physician John Francis believed the place was haunted by the ghost of Alexander Hamilton. The politician was brought there, mortally wounded, after his duel with Aaron Burr. The Rembrandt apartment building now stands on the site. Has Hamilton's spirit stuck around?*

What was it with that ghost and the toilet?

Jean Karsavina had lived in the old brownstone since 1939. At first the disturbances in her home were minor—a few disembodied footsteps, doors that opened and shut by themselves, creaking on the staircase, appliances going crazy, a hazy form floating around the rooms. You know, the usual stuff.

But then the damn toilet started flushing on its own. One time she even walked in to find the pull chain—the toilet was one of those with an old British-style flush cord—swinging back and forth. Her conclusion was that whatever spook was fooling around in the bathroom had no idea what to make of indoor plumbing.

This revelation was reinforced when she found out another person in the building had gotten a good look at the spirit: a man dressed in clothing from the 1700s. In addition, he either had his hair pulled back in a small ponytail or was wearing a wig, which was common with men at the end of the eighteenth century. The apparition leisurely sauntered into her neighbor's room, making no notice of her, and then just as casually strolled back out.

It made sense. A lot of work had been done to the building over the years, but the house at 27 Jane Street dated back to Revolutionary times. The spectre could easily be someone hanging on from its early years.

Karsavina had already done a little checking on the place, and it turned out that the residence was a fascinating footnote in American history. Alexander Hamilton was brought there, mortally wounded, after his infamous duel with Aaron Burr in 1804.

Hamilton was one of the most influential—and in some ways one of the unlikeliest—of the nation's Founding Fathers. He was born to unwed parents in 1755 or 1757 in Nevis in the British West Indies. His mother, Rachel Faucett Lavian, had left a husband and child in St. Croix and gone to St. Kitts, where she met James A. Hamilton. The pair moved to Nevis, where Rachel had inherited property, and they had two children, James Jr. and Alexander. The father abandoned the family, supposedly to avoid being arrested for bigamy, though he and Rachel had never married. When Rachel died in 1768, her actual husband seized her estate. At first the boys were adopted by a cousin, Peter Lytton, but when Lytton later committed suicide, James and Alexander were sent to different homes.

Amazingly, despite this calamitous childhood straight out of Charles Dickens, Alexander was able to forge a remarkable career. An essay he wrote in 1772 so impressed the island's civic leaders that they sent Alexander abroad—to America—where he could be properly educated.

He was enrolled at King's College (now Columbia University) in New York. At the beginning of the American Revolution, Hamilton put together an artillery company that drew the attention of George Washington. The general made him his aide-de-camp, or chief of staff.

Hamilton had political ambitions, and he was soon elected to the Continental Congress and later the New York Legislature. While practicing law in New York City, he founded the Bank of New York. Hamilton was one of three New Yorkers in the delegation that helped draft the US Constitution, and he wrote more than half of the *Federalist Papers* to help persuade states to ratify the document. Once the new government was in place, President Washington named Hamilton the first US secretary of the treasury. During his time in the cabinet, Hamilton helped establish the first national bank and the United States Mint.

Hamilton believed in a powerful central government, but with the country having just come out of a war against a monarchy, there were many people who didn't share his point of view. Much of the conflict was over Hamilton's demand that the federal government have the authority to regulate currency and tax. Hamilton's supporters became known as the Federalist Party; the opposition party, whose members included Thomas Jefferson and James Madison, went by a number of different names. Today they're usually referred to as Democratic-Republicans.

Hamilton was a man of strong opinions, and he didn't mince words. Among the political enemies he made along the way was the man who would be his eventual undoing: Aaron Burr.

In the run-up to the presidential election of 1800, Hamilton naturally fought against the candidates of the Democratic-Republican Party, but he also circulated a pamphlet he had written to his fellow Federalists that was highly critical of their own man, President John Adams. Unfortunately Hamilton's essay fell into the wrong hands and was made public. Its contents tarnished Adams enough that he lost his bid for reelection. When Jefferson and Burr then tied for votes in the Electoral College, Hamilton campaigned behind the scenes for Jefferson to win, considering him the lesser of two evils. Burr blamed Hamilton when he had to settle for the vice presidency.

When it became obvious to Burr that Jefferson was not going to ask him to be his running mate in 1804, Burr decided to run for governor of New York. Once again, Hamilton actively worked against Burr. For Hamilton, this type of backroom electioneering often occurred at private parties where, after dinner, he would try to convince anyone who would listen not to support Burr.

Dr. Charles D. Cooper was an attendee at one of these soirees in February 1804. Afterward, he wrote a letter to Philip Schuyler, a politician and Alexander Hamilton's father-in-law, in which he noted that the former treasury secretary had a "despicable opinion" of Burr and "looked upon Mr. Burr to be a dangerous man and one who ought not to be trusted with the reins of government."

On April 24, 1804, the *Albany Register* newspaper published Cooper's letter. For Burr, who had lost the gubernatorial election, that was the last straw. Burr insisted Hamilton apologize for his remarks. Hamilton responded through an intermediary that he couldn't be held responsible for Cooper's interpretation of what he may or may not have said that night—most of which he didn't remember in any case. He claimed his comments focused on political principles and in no way should be construed as suggesting dishonorable conduct or anything relating to Burr's private character.

That was not enough to mollify Burr, and he challenged Hamilton to an interview on the field of honor, that being what duels where euphemistically being called. The fact was, such confrontations were illegal in New York and several adjoining states. Hamilton accepted the challenge.

As dawn rose over the Hudson River on July 11, 1804, Hamilton and his party rowed across to the Heights of Weehawken in New Jersey where they were to meet the sitting vice president of the United States. Dueling was also forbidden in New Jersey, but the site was chosen because dueling was being less severely prosecuted there than in New York. Pistols were fired shortly after 7 a.m.

Exactly what took place that morning is still in dispute, partially because no one saw the actual exchange. Several people accompanied Hamilton and Burr, but to avoid being a witness to a crime, the duelists' seconds and supporters had either turned their backs or remained in the rowboats down on the river. Two shots were fired, but the length of time between them is unclear. Who fired first is also uncertain, although it was probably Hamilton who had the honor. Usually in such contests, if the intent is to show courage and defend one's name but not to kill the adversary, both men fired into the ground. Hamilton discharged his bullet into the air, however, and it passed into the trees by Burr's head. Perhaps assuming Hamilton was not playing by the unwritten rules of conduct, Burr returned fire. Whatever the reason, he struck Hamilton in the lower gut above the right hip. The lethal ball bounced off a rib, pierced vital organs, and lodged in Hamilton's spine.

According to a letter he had written the night before, Hamilton had planned to "throw away" his shot. But why, then, had he aimed the gun anywhere in Burr's direction? Wouldn't he have known his actions could be misinterpreted? Historians suggest that it may have been a premature misfire, because the guns (which Hamilton had provided) had a secret hair trigger that, if set, would have allowed Hamilton's gun to fire slightly quicker than Burr's. Had Hamilton's gun accidentally gone off while it was still pointing toward Burr? Or had he really hoped to kill Burr, despite what he had said in his note, but the unexpected discharge of his weapon caused the plan to backfire? Of course, there's always the possibility that Burr had fired first, and Hamilton's gun went off after he was hit.

Despite the horrendous injury, Hamilton was not killed instantly. His dueling party rowed him back to Manhattan, where they docked at the foot of Horatio Street, one block away from Jane. The mortally wounded Hamilton was rushed to the home of his physician, Dr. John Francis, who lived at 27 Jane—where Karsavina would be residing 150 years later!

Francis could tell immediately that there was no hope for Hamilton. He dressed the wound and no doubt comforted the patient as much as possible with whatever anesthetics were available in that day and age. Hamilton's own mansion was far away, up at the northern end of Manhattan near what is today West 141st Street, so Hamilton was moved to the home of a friend, William Bayard, at nearby 80 Jane Street. (The house has since been torn down.)

After a grueling night and in constant, intense pain, Hamilton died about two o'clock the next afternoon. He was buried in a rectangular, above-ground tomb at the south end of the old Trinity Churchyard in the Wall Street area of Lower Manhattan. Large urns at the four corners and a pyramid with a flat peak decorate the top of the sarcophagus.

It's unknown when Hamilton started to return to 27 Jane Street, nor is the reason clear. Ghosts often come back to places where their lives were cut short, such as battlefields or murder sites, but perhaps Hamilton's last conscious thoughts were in his doctor's house on Jane Street instead. No one will ever know.

Karsavina was curious enough to contact Hans Holzer, the noted phantom chaser, and he and a medium, Mrs. Ethel Meyers, investigated the house in March 1960. Meyers, who had not been informed of the house's past, sensed the presence of various spirits, one of whom could have been Hamilton. The descriptions matched, but she did not positively identify him. She also felt the spectres of several other people who were connected with the building in one way or another. Holzer documented the meeting, but he didn't try to help any of the spirits "move on."

Hamilton's ghost certainly stuck around. He continued to be seen by tenants, both inside the house and on the pavement out front, for years. The Francis home was later demolished along with all of the structures up to the corner of Eighth Avenue. In 1963 a seventeen-story, 127-unit redbrick apartment building was put up in its place. The Rembrandt, a co-op, has its main entrance at 31 Jane Street. Word is mixed as to whether Hamilton has shown up in the new abode.

Regardless, some say his apparition has begun to appear near his crypt in the Trinity Churchyard. If it does, he wouldn't be the only spirit in the graveyard. Anglicans founded the original Trinity Church in 1698. The building burned down during the American Revolution, and weather so damaged the replacement church that it had to be razed in 1839. The current Neo-Gothic church, an Episcopal chapel with a distinctive 280-foot steeple, dates to 1846. Its burial ground lies in two sections, one on either side of the sanctuary. At least two other ghosts besides Hamilton are making the rounds within the wrought-iron fence enclosing the cemetery: Adam Allyn, whose tombstone is marked "Comedian," and Lt. Augustus C. Ludlow, who was second-in-command of the frigate *Chesapeake* during the War of 1812.

Shortly after Hamilton was struck by that fatal blow on the bluffs in New Jersey, he whispered to Dr. David Hosack, a physician who attended the duel, "This is a mortal wound, doctor." Perhaps that was true for his corporeal self, but Hamilton's spirit proved to be immortal, as many who have lived at 27 Jane Street or visited Trinity Churchyard can attest.

# Chapter 16

# The House on Bank Street

## The Bank Street House
## 11 Bank Street

*When disembodied footsteps started ascending the stairs of the onetime boardinghouse, the new owners didn't know what to make of them—that is, until repairs in a bedroom revealed a box of cremated ashes! The urn dated to 1931, so how did it get hidden behind a ceiling from the 1880s?*

There the footsteps were again! The ghost was back!

By that time, everyone in the house had gotten used to the sound of the delicate footfalls on the narrow staircase as well as the pitter-patter of feet lightly crossing overhead on the second floor. It was assumed that the spirit making the ethereal noises was a woman, as the tread was so soft.

The owner, Harvey Slatin, had taken it upon himself to figure out when and how often the sounds appeared. Neither he, his wife, their maid Sadie, nor the workman who was renovating the house ever heard the faint yet distinct noises before eleven in the morning. And the steps had always stopped by night-fall. Interesting, Slatin thought, since almost all hauntings—not that he believed in ghosts—took place after dark.

The footsteps weren't the only paranormal sounds reverberating through the house. There were also occasional rap, tap, tappings, as Edgar Allan Poe might have put it.

It suddenly occurred to Slatin that neither he nor his wife had ever seen an apparition, so they'd assumed all the footsteps and bangings were coming from one lone spirit. But what if there were more?

The house dated back to the nineteenth century. In 1798 the Bank of New York was quarantined when one of its clerks came down with yellow fever. To prevent similar business interruptions in the future, the bank decided they needed a branch office far out of the city, say, up north in that little hamlet Greenwich Village. The company bought property lining a small lane about five blocks long that stretched from Greenwich Street (the main route from the city to the village) and the Hudson River. The road, logically enough, became known as Bank Street.

Another epidemic in 1822 found more and more people wanting to escape the congested—and contagious—confines of the city, which resulted in a flood of new settlers in the Village. To help house them, a series of two- and three-story brownstones went up along Bank Street. One of those homes, at 11 Bank Street, was built in or around 1832.

The brick townhouse was originally intended for a single family, but at some point it was converted into a nineteen-room boardinghouse. It was owned by a Mrs. Maccario and had been multi-occupant housing for at least twenty years when the Slatins bought the property in 1948. Dr. Slatin, a nuclear physicist, had worked on the Manhattan Project. His wife, Yeffe Kimball, an Osage Indian born in Oklahoma, was a painter.

Together they planned a complete remodel of the three-story row house. Most significantly, the first floor would be transformed into one long room running all the way from front to back, then open into a garden. To make the renovations, the Slatins hired a local carpenter, an English-man named Arthur Brodie. The couple decided to stay in their new home while the restorations were taking place.

The ghostly footsteps and knockings started within weeks after the Slatins moved in. At first they thought they were imagining them, but both of their employees assured them that they were hearing the noises as well. Slatin could also sometimes smell an inexpensive perfume in the room and sense an invisible presence when the unexplainable sounds occurred. But whoever the phantom was, she never showed herself.

No one felt frightened or threatened by the ghost, nor did it ever do any damage. If he had to pick a single word to describe the spirit, Slatin would almost be tempted to call her friendly.

Brodie knew from experience that old buildings produce all sorts of strange sounds. As a result, he didn't believe for a second that the noises, whatever they were, came from a ghost. That may have changed a bit in February 1957 when he was doing work in a bedroom on the second level. As he was repairing the ceiling that dated back to around 1880, a large patch of plaster broke loose without warning and fell. Along with it, a small metal container crashed to the floor.

The box was about the size and shape of a coffee can, and it had been japanned with a heavy black varnish. Brodie picked up the curious object, dusted off a faded label, and read:

UNITED STATES CREMATORY CO., QUEENS, NY

THE LAST REMAINS OF ELIZABETH BULLOCK, DECEASED, CREMATED JANUARY 21, 1931

Well if that didn't beat all! Brodie, his tongue firmly in cheek, strolled over to Mrs. Slatin's bedroom and knocked on the door. "It's me, ma'am," he called. "I'm leaving the job! I found the body!"

The story was too good not to be shared, and it made its way into a *New York Times* column, Meyer Berger's "About New York," on June 26, 1957.

Enter the ghost hunter! Hans Holzer read the notice and contacted the Slatins. Could he come to investigate the house? Perhaps with the assistance of one his favorite mediums, Mrs. Ethel Meyers, he might be able to provide some answers about Elizabeth Bullock and why she was, presumably, haunting the house.

The Slatins agreed, and a séance of sorts took place on the evening of Wednesday, July 17. As usual with his cases, Holzer did not inform Meyers in advance where she would be taken or any other details about the alleged haunting. Once the social preliminaries were out of the way, Meyers went into a trance. She soon made contact with a spirit who identified herself as "Betty." The wraith, in essence, took over the medium's body and spoke through her—in an Irish brogue, no less.

Betty wasn't exactly easy to understand. Her words were jumbled, confusing, sometimes contradictory, and in broken phrases rather than full sentences. At times Holzer would question her and ask for clarifications. Betty claimed to be paralyzed on one side, had a heart condition, and needed to walk slowly. She was born in Pleasantville, New York, and her mother's maiden name was Elizabeth McCuller. She had lived nearby and had two children: a son, Eddie, who was alive and in California, and a daughter, Gracie, who had died as a baby.

Betty spoke of a Charlie, who seemed to be her husband, as well as an Eddie, who may have been a brother. She said her Catholic family had disapproved when she married a Protestant. In fact, they didn't consider it to be a real marriage! But she knew in her heart that she was married in the eyes of God. After her death, Betty's parents wanted to bury her in the family plot. Charlie, a Presbyterian, refused to grant permission. Betty seemed to agree. She yearned for "a Christian burial in the shades of the Cross . . . any place where the Cross is—but not with them." Charlie ordered the mortuary to cremate the body, and he took the ashes before Betty's family could put their hands on them. Although Holzer specifically asked how the urn had made it ways to the rafters above the Slatin's ceiling, Betty never gave a coherent answer.

After Meyers awoke from her trance, Holzer told the Slatins that Elizabeth Bullock—Betty—was a restless and unhappy spirit, first, because her family had never forgiven her and, second, because she had never received a proper burial. Indeed, the spectre still seemed to be a bit conflicted as to where she should be interred. Holzer's advice? The Slatins should bury the urn as respectfully as possible in their garden out back.

The Slatins thanked Holzer and Meyers for their troubles, but when all was said and done they decided to keep the box in an honored spot on their living room piano. Besides, who knew? Someday someone might show up looking for the ashes!

And you know what? Once the memorial urn was set in place, the hauntings stopped!

It's remarkable the messages that mediums, sensitives, and other spirit readers are able to receive. It's even more remarkable if any of the details in those messages turn out to be true. It's not very often that ghosts share exact dates, full names, and complete addresses. One has to sort through the ramblings, half sentences, and seemingly meaningless statements produced during a séance to make sense of the communication. Then there's the problem of verification. Fortunately, that has become easier in the days of the Internet.

Stacy Horn, who studied the early twentieth-century ESP tests conducted by paranormal researcher J. B. Rhine, fact-checked Holzer's account of the Bank Street ghost as well as what the spectre, speaking through Mrs. Meyers, had to say.

Here's what we now know is true: Elizabeth Bullock died at the age of fifty-one. Her husband's name was Edward, not Charlie. According to legend, eyewitnesses saw Elizabeth being struck by a speeding car while crossing Hudson Street, and the dying woman was carried into a pharmacy. She died in the drugstore before an ambulance could arrive, but Elizabeth's death certificate says she expired from chronic myocarditis, an inflammation of the heart. No mention was made of trauma from any kind of impact.

Elizabeth Bullock was born in New York and did not speak in an Irish brogue. It would have been unlikely if she had: Her father was from Germany, and her mother, Mary Schwieker—not Elizabeth McCuller—was American. Bullock was living at 113 Perry Street at the time of her death. Her body was taken to a funeral home on West Eleventh Street, and soon thereafter it was cremated. She had no children.

According to an old wives' tale, one or two members of Elizabeth's family caught her husband stealing the ashes from the funeral home and gave chase. To elude them, Edward Bullock ducked into a vacant house on Bank Street that was undergoing repairs. He snuck up to the second floor and stashed the urn on a beam behind a partially restored ceiling, figuring that eventually he could finagle his way into the building to recover the remains. For whatever reason, he never made it back.

What actually happened is this: Edward *did* receive the ashes from the mortuary, but if there were any objections from his wife's side of the family, they were never noted by the funeral director. Bullock definitely moved out of the Perry Street home he had shared with Elizabeth and went to stay in the Bank Street apartment house. It's presumed he took the box containing his wife's ashes with him. There's no record as to which room he stayed in, how the urn got into its hiding place above a century-old ceiling, or why he didn't take it along when he left. And unfortunately, the trail of both Elizabeth and Edward Bullock pretty much goes dead at 11 Bank Street.

As for the rest of the account, including the religious conflict between the two families and Elizabeth's comments about where she'd liked to be buried, well, for those we'll have to take the medium—or Betty's spirit—at her word.

The tale of Elizabeth Bullock soon entered ghost folklore. In 1981 the *Washington Post* tracked down the Slatins and did a follow-up article about the mysterious haunting. It turned out they had contacted a Catholic church about giving them the remains for a consecrated burial but were rebuffed because Elizabeth had married outside the faith.

After the story appeared in the *Post,* the Slatins got a letter from Father Devereaux, a priest in the small community of Loleta in Humboldt County, California. He offered to provide the Christian burial Elizabeth sought, and the Slatins sent him the ashes. About fifty people celebrated the funeral mass, followed by the urn's burial in Patrick's Cemetery on Table Bluff outside town. As she wished, Elizabeth's grave lies in sight of a cross.

There's a final, chilling twist to the story. After the séance with Holzer and Meyers was finished, Yeffe Slatin recalled that not too long before the box dropped from the ceiling, a well-groomed youngish man had shown up at the door. He obviously didn't know that the place was no longer a boardinghouse, because he asked whether there were any rooms for rent. Yeffe assured him there weren't, but the stranger left his calling card just in case the situation changed. It was engraved "E. C. Bullock."

Had Elizabeth's husband, Edward, come back to claim her ashes after all?

# Chapter 17

# The Accidental Arsonist

## The Waverly Inn
## 16 Bank Street

*Built in 1844, the Waverly Inn has been occupied by a ghost as far back as anyone can recall. He likes to play around the fireplaces, especially the one in what used to be the smoking lounge. Oddly, it was the only room undamaged by a fire in the restaurant back in 1997.*

The fire marshal was not amused. There was no immediate indication of exactly where the flames had started, nor was there an obvious cause. The fire had begun somewhere in a part of the restaurant without electrical outlets, and no easily flammable items or incendiary materials had been stored in the area. Puzzling.

But any staff member who had ever had trouble starting up any of the fireplaces in the restaurant had a simple explanation: The Waverly Inn phantom did it. The claim was made with such sincerity that, to be diplomatic, the inspector didn't want to ridicule it outright. Instead, he dismissed the theory by tersely responding, "Ghosts don't start fires—we don't think."

Whether an otherworldly spirit set the fire or not, even accidentally, at least one ghost has been in the building almost from the day it opened. The restaurant was founded as a tavern in 1844. For a time the facilities were turned into a brothel. One transformation had the building become a carriage house for prosperous residents in the Village. The Waverly Inn finally returned to its roots as a bar, but there was a problem with the timing: Prohibition was right around the corner.

From 1920 to 1933, when the sale of alcohol was illegal in the United States, the Waverly Inn operated as a "teahouse." If a customer requested English tea, for example, he was really ordering gin served in a teacup. "Tennessee tea" was code for Jack Daniel's. "Canadian tea" was actually a call for either Seagram's Seven or Canadian Club whiskey. Sometimes the liquor was the real deal. If so, it had been smuggled into the country. Otherwise, the liquor was "bathtub gin," brewed in illegal stills.

The speakeasy years hardly put a dent in the Waverly Inn's popularity, if it did at all. Citizens of all characters and classes easily commingled for the chance to wet their whistles. Two of its regulars, for instance, were poets Robert Frost and Edna St. Vincent Millay. What could be more respectable than that? Once the Twenty-first Amendment repealed the ban on booze, the tavern's doors were flung wide open, and business never looked back.

For thirty years, Murray and Daisy Sellack owned Ye Waverly Inn & Garden, but in 1993 another husband-and-wife team, Israeli restaurateurs Hanna and Sarid Drory, bought it. While modernizing the operation behind the scenes, out front they were careful to maintain its ambience and the country inn charm that patrons loved.

The Waverly Inn was renowned for its quaint atmosphere, warm decor, original hardwood floors, moody lighting, and intimate dining spaces, including seating on a veranda out back. On chilly evenings guests liked to curl up in front of crackling logs burning in one of the tavern's four cozy fireplaces. One of the most popular areas to settle in was by the hearth in the smoking room, which the house had designated Room 16.

It was part of the staff's duties to tend the fireplaces, so it was probably one of them who first noticed when weird stuff started happening. Oftentimes employees would come in to work only to discover that the andirons, pokers, and other fireplace paraphernalia were not where they had left them the evening before.

Some nights, no matter how long anyone worked on the kindling in one fireplace or another, he or she just couldn't get the wood to ignite. But all the person had to do was give up and start to walk away, and the tinder would burst into flames.

At the end of the night, it was essential that all of the fires be doused and the cinders raked to make sure that there were no live embers. Nevertheless, on more than one occasion, after everything had been checked and double-checked, a tiny, playful lick of fire would flare up in one of the fireplaces—even though the wood was completely spent.

One of the restaurant's chefs, Patrick Haynes, also noticed that candles had a tendency to blow out on their own and then somehow spontaneously relight.

At first glance, people familiar with the Other Side might have suspected there was a poltergeist at work, because they like to set fires. The word "poltergeist" comes from two German words, *poltern* (meaning "to make noise") and *geist* (or "ghost"). Hence, a poltergeist is a "noisy ghost," and, as the name suggests, its presence is usually indicated by the sound of loud knocks and pounding. Often, objects move or fly across the room, and people get punched, pinched, shoved, or bitten by unseen forces.

Paranormalists believe that poltergeists are not ghosts, not in the vernacular sense. Rather than being the soul or remnant of someone who was once alive, a poltergeist is an entirely different type of spirit entity, not demonic but certainly malicious and overly playful to the point of being dangerous.

Fortunately, except for the spirit's fascination with fire, none of the other activity associated with poltergeists occurred at the Waverly Inn. The restaurant was dealing with a regular run-of-the-mill ghost. If there were any doubt, poltergeists almost never show themselves, and their activity tends to center on the presence of a particular individual. Lots of people—guests, employees, managers, and owners alike—had seen the apparition in the Waverly Inn!

The phantom, it seems, was a man dressed in nineteenth-century formal wear, including a waistcoat and a top hat. According to Therese Lanigan-Schmidt's well-researched *Ghosts of New York City*, a former manager named Maria Ennes caught a fleeting glimpse of the spectre in a mirror. Haynes also spied the apparition of a man in his forties—which may or may not have been the same spirit as the one in the looking glass—drifting through the restaurant.

(Chef Haynes once saw another spectre—the vision of a cheerful woman in her twenties dressed in clothing from the late 1800s. It was a onetime haunting, however. She never showed up at the Waverly again, or at least the wraith has never been reported.)

People used to sense the spirit's presence when it was in the room. Patrons sitting in the smoking parlor would sometimes feel a mysterious whish on the sides of their faces as an invisible "something" passed by. Other times, the hairs on the back of their necks stood on end. Many such encounters took place in Room 16, which at some point was renamed the Edgar Allan Poe room. (But don't jump to conclusions: Although Poe's ghost is thought to haunt several places in Greenwich Village, the Waverly Inn is not one of them.)

Other freaky phenomena in the bar? Well, lights would turn themselves on and off. Doors would open and shut by themselves. Now and then the sound of something heavy being dragged up a staircase echoed from the rear of the building. All that's pretty standard for places that are haunted, but the Waverly spectres also liked to mess around with the house computers. They'd change items that servers had tapped into the keypad, so the kitchen prepared the wrong dishes. Lots of fun, right?

But maybe the ghost's high-spirited hijinks went too far. The fire that was being investigated broke out in the wee hours one night during the winter of 1997 and quickly swept through much of the building. Was it the Waverly Inn spectre fooling with matches? There wasn't a shred of evidence that anything supernatural caused the blaze, so it was never mentioned in the final report. But one thing's curious: Despite damage throughout the rest of the restaurant, Room 16—the ghost's favorite hangout—was completely untouched by flames.

The inn was reopened within two months of the blaze, and talk of the spectre subsided. Then in 2006 new owners bought the Waverly Inn. The partnership was spearheaded by Graydon Carter, the longtime editor of *Vanity Fair,* but it also included Sean MacPherson and Eric Goode, who are responsible for two other very haunted sites in the Village: the Jane and the Bowery Hotels.

Under its new management the Waverly Inn has become very elite. For the first few months it was open, patrons who called the bar received prerecorded information but couldn't make reservations. You had to know somebody—or know somebody who knew somebody—to get in. Exclusive, chic, celebrity-filled: not bad for a place that spent time as a bordello.

It's pricey, but with the exception of prime seating times on a weekend night, it's no longer impossible to score a table, either by telephone, by dropping into the restaurant during the afternoon to make a reservation, or through an online service such as OpenTable.com.

The Waverly Inn still has the buzz, but does it still have a ghost? It's hard to say. The phantom, who never acquired even a nickname, hasn't been seen for a while. Maybe the place just doesn't feel like the same old haunt anymore.

Part Three

# THE NEW KID ON THE BLOCK— THE EAST VILLAGE

As the rest of Greenwich Village gentrified and rents soared in the 1950s, many "artist types"—beatniks, hippies, artists, and musicians—moved eastward, and soon the quarter they adopted developed a new, artier (though still gritty) character all its own. Up until the 1960s the area was known as the Bowery or simply the Lower East Side.

Before long, however, people had a new name for the area bordered by Fourteenth Street, Houston Street, Broadway, and, originally, First Avenue: the East Village. Today the blocks east of First Avenue all the way to the East River (a neighborhood known as Alphabet City) are also generally included.

Beginning around 1980 the East Village started going upscale as well, once again changing the face of the district. What has remained constant is its many ghosts: from those haunting the Public Theater and the Astor Place subway station to the city's last Dutch governor, Peter Stuyvesant himself, who roams St. Mark's Church in-the-Bowery.

Chapter 18

# The Astor Apparitions

## The Public Theater
## (the former Astor Library)
## 425 Lafayette Street

*The massive building that houses the Public Theater was originally the Astor Library, and two of its phantoms come from that period. A few others date to the early twentieth century. The most recent addition to its gallery of ghosts is the building's current namesake, theater visionary Joseph Papp.*

Cogswell sat almost dozing at his desk. The library had long since closed for the night, and he was savoring the solitude. Not that there had been that many visitors during the day. The collection was open to the public—it had been since the library's inception—and its use was free, unlike many private libraries scattered about the city. But not many people took advantage of the opportunity.

Cogswell was well aware of the library's limited appeal. It housed only reference materials, and none of the items could be removed from the premises. Also, it was open weekdays, when men not of the privileged class were at work. Then, too, the library had been built with money bequeathed by the richest man in the country, so, like it or not, the place had an unmistakable elitist aura to it. The people who seemed to make use of the facilities were scholars and researchers, the wealthy, those who had attended the right universities, and people who had been friends or business associates of the late John Jacob Astor.

Cogswell was Joseph Green Cogswell, a former professor and librarian at Harvard, the cofounder of Round Hill School (a private boys' preparatory school in Massachusetts), and from 1839 to 1842 the editor of *New York Review,* an important critical journal of the time.

Astor, America's first multimillionaire was born in Germany. He moved to the United States in 1784, just after the end of the Revolutionary War, and began a career in fur trading. Before long he was a major importer and exporter to and from Europe. In 1808 he established the American Fur Company, and by the 1820s he controlled the fur trade in both the Great Lakes region and the Pacific Northwest. In the 1830s Astor moved into real estate, buying up huge tracts of land in Manhattan. After having amassed a fortune of about $20 million—more than one billion in today's dollars—Astor retired and became a patron of the arts.

He enlisted his friend, confidant, and counselor, Joseph Cogswell, along with famed author Washington Irving and poet Fitz-Greene Halleck, to help plan a monumental library to serve the citizens of New York.

Astor knew Irving from his standing in the literary world and the writer's public fame. Born in 1783, Irving was one of the first truly great American authors. In an 1807 story in *Salmagundi,* a satirical magazine he cocreated, Irving became the first person to use the word "Gotham," an Anglo-Saxon word meaning "goat's town," to refer to New York City. In 1809 he completed his first major work under a pseudonym, *A History of New-York, from the Beginning of the World to the End of the Dutch Dynasty,* by Diedrich Knickerbocker.

In 1829 Irving became a sensation with the publication of *The Sketch Book of Geoffrey Crayon, Gent,* a collection of short stories that included "Rip Van Winkle" and "The

Legend of Sleepy Hollow." "Winkle" was set in the Catskill Mountains, which Irving had visited as a teenager. "Sleepy Hollow," which many consider to be America's first original ghost story, grew out of Irving's time in Tarrytown, which lies along the Hudson about twenty miles north of Manhattan. Irving fell in love with the hamlet and purchased a cottage and property there in 1835, later naming his estate Sunnyside.

Irving was internationally known by 1834 when Astor asked him to write a history of the trading settlement the fur tycoon had established in the Oregon Territory. Irving jumped at the opportunity—though famous, he was always short of cash due to bad investments—and he delivered the flattering account, *Astoria,* in just two years.

Little remembered today, Halleck was very popular in his day. Born in 1790, he was often referred to as "the American Byron" (after the British Romantic poet Lord Byron). Halleck was one of the Knickerbocker group of writers whose work reflected early Americana and was headed unofficially by Irving, James Fenimore Cooper, and William Cullen Bryant. In 1932 Halleck became John Jacob Astor's personal secretary, and he also advised the magnate on his purchase of artwork and other cultural matters.

In 1842 President John Tyler appointed Irving a minister to Spain on the recommendation of Secretary of State Daniel Webster. Irving had spent many years there in the 1820s, was well known and liked by the Spaniards, and had written books on Granada, the Alhambra, and Christopher Columbus. (In one of his two books on the navigator, Irving started the erroneous myth repeated throughout the centuries that Europeans of the 1400s believed the world was flat.)

Irving requested that his friend Cogswell be made his secretary of legation, and the commission came through. But Astor had other ideas. Concerned that the preparations for his library would be put on hold indefinitely, Astor named Cogswell its superintendent as well one of its trustees. Cogswell chose to stay with Astor. For their own part, Irving and Halleck were made trustees of the library as well.

Astor died in 1848, and he left $400,000 in his will to build the facility, amass the collection, and endow its operation. Irving, who had returned from Spain in 1846, was retained as one of the executors of the will, which had also designated him chairman of the library. Meanwhile, Cogswell traveled to Europe to purchase much of the library's holdings. In 1849 Halleck retired. He moved to Guilford, Connecticut, where he stayed with his sister until his death in 1867.

While the Astor collection was temporarily housed at 32 Bond Street, the task of designing the library fell to architect Alexander Saeltzer. The style would be Rundbogenstil, a German form of Romanesque Revival, and construction took place between 1849 and 1853. Cogswell became chief librarian, while Irving opted to return to Tarrytown. Irving continued to work out of Sunnyside until his death on November 28, 1859.

Cogswell often stayed late at the library, cataloguing the materials. It was during one of those evenings, sometime during the winter of 1859–60 that the first haunting at the library took place. Looking up from his papers in the dim light, Cogswell saw a shadowy form moving among the stacks. It drifted, seemingly without purpose, and finally stopped in front of shelf B30. *The library shut its doors, as usual, at five this afternoon,* Cogswell thought. *Who is this interloper?*

Cogswell's eyes widened in wonder as the mysterious guest turned to him, and the weary librarian recognized the apparition's features. It was Austin L. Sands, a prosperous merchant and a bigwig in the insurance industry. The problem was: Cogswell knew for a fact that Sands was dead these many months and lay buried in his grave. The phantasm had to be a ghost!

Nonplussed, the always-composed and logical Cogswell challenged the spirit. "You have no business here. We've closed for the night. I must insist that you leave."

He continued: "Besides, my dear sir, you never bothered to visit the library while you were alive, so you can't come in now that you're dead."

The spectre, embarrassed at having been found out, said nothing. But as Cogswell continued his accusatory glare, the apparition faded away.

Cogswell ended his tenure as resident librarian in 1861, and he gave up his trusteeship three years later. We know about the ghostly incident because of George Templeton Strong, a distinguished attorney and trustee of Columbia University who, as it turned out, was a tireless diarist. He began a journal in 1835, recording historical events and making observations of human nature, right up until his death in 1875. But for many years his logs were a secret or lost. The 2,250-page chronicle wasn't discovered until the 1930s.

Strong had made two entries about ghosts in the diary. One, dated August 30, 1859, recounts a brief story about a haunted house in Astoria, a neighborhood in Queens. His entry about Cogswell was made on March 12, 1860. He told the tale in the form of a loose poem and then followed it with a few personal notes.

Cogswell claimed to have seen Sands's ghost three separate times that winter, and on one occasion the spirit told the librarian that the reason he visited the stacks was "for variety." Cogswell had shared details about his encounter with dinner companions, and the story made its way to Strong.

The diarist opined that Cogswell was working late at night and was "nervous and shakey [sic], and quite an old man." He concluded that Cogswell was "a likely subject for spectral illusions" and that the haunting was probably no more than "an instance of hallucination."

Maybe it happened, and maybe it didn't. But around the same time, people (including Cogswell, according to other sources) began to see another ghost, the spectre of one of the other original trustees, sitting among the stacks: Washington Irving! Eventually sightings of both Sands and Irving stopped at the Astor Library, but it was said that Irving's apparition moved across the street to the nine Greek Revival residences known as Colonnade Row. The homes, located at 428–434 Lafayette Street, received their name because their second and third stories were fronted by one long line of towering Corinthian pillars.

Irving may have been an uninvited guest in them at one time, but there have been no recent reports of hauntings in the four houses that still stand. One of them, number 434, now contains the Astor Place Theatre, the longtime home of Blue Man Group.

According to Irving's nephew Pierre, the author also used to show up in his old home, Sunnyside, in Tarrytown, New York.

Is it possible to visit the Astor Library to see if Alan Sands and Washington Irving are hanging around? Well, yes and no. The library's books are long gone, but the place is now one of New York's premier theaters.

When former New York governor and Democratic presidential candidate Samuel J. Tilden died in 1886, he left about two-and-a-half million of his estimated seven-million-dollar fortune "to establish and maintain a free public library and reading room in the city of New York," despite Manhattan already having several private lending libraries and two large institutions: the Astor and the Lenox. (The latter library housed philanthropist James Lenox's rare books, including the first Gutenberg Bible brought to America.)

Most of the small libraries charged either an admission or usage fee; the two big libraries were free but weren't particularly welcoming to the common man. Tilden envisioned a library that could be enjoyed by the masses at no cost whatsoever.

John Bigelow, one of the trustees of Tilden's estate, came up with idea of merging the Astor and the Lenox into one great athenaeum: the New York Public Library. His timing was perfect because the endowments of both institutions were dwindling, placing them in financial jeopardy. With additional funding from other benefactors, Bigelow sealed the deal with the Astor and the Lenox libraries on May 23, 1895.

After the Astor Library's collection was moved, it left behind an enormous shell of a building. Between 1856 and 1869 architect Griffith Thomas had added an extension to the north side of the original structure, and designer Thomas Stent added a third section, again to the north side, between 1879 and 1881. So perfectly did the three architects' work blend together that today it's next to impossible to see where one part leaves off and the next one begins.

In 1921 the former book repository was bought by
the Hebrew Immigrant Aid Society. The organization was
established in 1881 to provide assistance and protection to
the large Jewish community that had migrated to America
and settled in New York. (Today the group's mission has
expanded to "rescue, reunion, and resettlement" of Jewish
immigrants and refugees worldwide.) The HIAS, as it became
known, started as a storefront operation in the Lower East
Side, but with the outbreak of World War I and the flood
of new arrivals to Ellis Island, the society knew it needed
a larger headquarters. The old Astor Library fit the bill.
Offices, classrooms, a kosher kitchen, and a synagogue were
set up on the first two floors, and lodgings took up the third
and fourth. The gigantic, faded "HIAS" painted on the north
exterior wall of the building can be seen to this day.

HIAS relocated in 1960, and by mid-decade the place had
fallen into disrepair. Rumors spread that wraiths had taken
up residence inside. The spectres were thought to belong to
some of the immigrants who had passed through the doors
of the Aid Society seeking comfort. Even though the building has now had a new tenant for more than forty years, the
apparitions are still occasionally seen in the upper rooms
where they would have been housed while they were alive.

The structure had been set for demolition in 1965 when
a savior came along. He was Joseph Papp, who had founded
the New York Shakespeare Festival in 1954 with the goal of
making the playwright's canon accessible to the public. His
plan included free productions in Central Park and other
venues throughout the boroughs. Papp managed to convince
the city to landmark the former Astor Library to save it
from the wrecking ball. He, in turn, bought the building and
hired architect–urban preservationist Giorgio Cavaglieri to

convert the interior into what has become an amazing complex of theaters, rehearsal rooms, studio spaces, a cabaret (Joe's Pub), and offices.

The Public hit gold with its first production, the controversial antiwar "hippie" musical, *Hair*. The rock musical, unlike anything that had been seen on Broadway up to that time, moved to the Great White Way, where it played for five years. More Broadway transfers followed, including the groundbreaking musical *A Chorus Line*, but the theater's focus was never coming up with "hits." It's been to create challenging, cutting-edge works, to nurture emerging as well as established artists, and to produce innovative, revelatory stagings of the classics. Until his death on Halloween 1991, impresario Papp oversaw it all. On April 23, 1992, the playhouse was officially renamed in his honor the Joseph Papp Public Theater.

In recent years, staff members have sometimes caught sight of a familiar if unsubstantive figure as they make their rounds. Theatergoers, too, occasionally spot the man, almost always dressed in a signature white suit, his piercing eyes surveying the room. By the time any of them recognizes the phantom as Papp from the old posters and photographs on display, the guardian spirit has gone.

A century and a half ago, illustrious ghosts roamed within the walls of the Astor Library. By the middle of the twentieth century, those apparitions had been replaced by the ragged spectres of the Jewish diaspora. It only makes sense that today it's Joseph Papp who's still around, watching over his baby.

Chapter 19

# The Subway Spectre

## Astor Place subway station
## Lafayette Street and Astor Place

*A phantom subway car rides the rails of the IRT. Could it be the private carriage August Belmont Jr. used to travel out to Long Island to the Belmont Racetrack? And are those who see it today spotting an apparition out of the past, or is it possible they're stepping back in time?*

Five hours. And all he had to show for it was twenty-five bucks? Sure, it was a Tuesday, not exactly date night, so there hadn't been a lot of foot traffic in the subway station.

Many times Jim didn't bother to busk midweek. He knew from sad experience that the "take" would be poor. But rent was due in a few days, and he didn't have anything better to do that night. Besides, who couldn't use a little more spare change—which is all that people ever seemed to drop into his instrument case as they walked by.

Although he was adept at several instruments, Jim chose to play his banjo whenever he went out street performing. There were too many singer-guitarists out there already, and the sound of a banjo was unique. (Of course, so was the twangy drone of a set of bagpipes, Jim mused, but he wanted to draw people in, not have them run off screaming with their hands over their ears.)

Jim was on the approved roster of street artists at South Street Seaport, but he found it more profitable to pass the hat after impromptu concerts in the city parks—even though there was never-ending competition to secure one of the high-traffic areas. But Jim was a master at drawing a crowd and soliciting tips.

In recent months, however, police had begun to enforce a new law intended to limit congestion and noise in the city parks. The rule made it illegal for buskers to set up within fifty feet of a monument or landmark. Authorized spots were set aside and marked with medallions.

Jim decided to move down into the subways. The MTA and New York City Transit allowed artists to work on the mezzanines and platforms but not on the cars themselves. There was a long list of don'ts for performers, but Jim knew all the rules: Entertainers couldn't perform during public service announcements, while construction was going on, or within twenty-five feet of a token booth. They couldn't block a stairwell, escalator, or elevator, and amplification was forbidden. But performers were completely free to accept all the "donations" they could solicit.

Street musicians, singers, and break dancers had already overrun the passageways directly beneath Times Square, so Jim steered clear. Besides, he found it too hectic. People rushing through the tunnels in that area were usually frantic or, if they did pause long enough for him to build a crowd, it soon became too difficult to easily gather tips. The decibel level was also unbearable.

His favorite place to set up shop was Astor Place because it was in the middle of an arts (or arty) district. Folks went out to dinner on their way to the cinema; shoppers sauntered up and down Broadway; and several playhouses, including the Public, the Astor Place Theatre, the Union Square Theatre, the Orpheum, and the Daryl Roth Theatre, were within a stone's throw. Every night hundreds of people out on the town, their wallets full of disposable income, passed through the Astor Place subway station.

Typically, Jim positioned himself on the southbound platform around 7 p.m. to catch the Upper East Side crowd as they arrived in the Village. He then moved over to the northbound side around 10 or 11 to catch them on their way home as the movies and theaters let out. For some reason, tonight he had tried it the other way around, and the experiment had been a bust.

Oh, well. *What was it Scarlett O'Hara said?* Jim thought to himself. *Tomorrow is another day.*

As he stuffed what little money he had collected into his jeans and closed up the banjo in its case, he noticed that the few people standing around him on the platform were soaking wet. It must have just started raining—and raining hard.

Damn. He was supposed to meet friends in the West Village in about half an hour, and normally he would have walked over, cutting through Washington Square on the way. But if it was raining that much . . .

Jim decided to catch the next train south to Bleecker Street—it was only one stop—then transfer to the F train and take it one stop north to West Fourth Street. Any other time, taking the subway would have been silly, more trouble than it was worth, but tonight it would keep him dry a little longer. Once out on the street, he could jog the last couple of blocks to the cafe and not look like a drowned rat when he got there.

Impatient, Jim leaned forward and peered up the tracks. He heard the telltale rumble long before the light appeared in the tunnel, and soon the subway train was screeching to a halt in front of him.

Jim stepped inside without a second thought. As the doors slid silently shut behind him and the train started to move, he slowly became aware that what he was standing in was not a subway car, at least not like any he had ever seen. There were no seats along the walls, no poles. Rather, he was inside what seemed to be—if what he had seen in the movies was correct—a private train car, like the Pullman coaches rich people traveled in at the turn of the twentieth century.

He spun around to face the doors through which he had entered. They were no longer there! In their place was a solid wall, made out of what looked to be mahogany. As for the rest of the car, the coach had tall, sparking, clear-glass panes, framed by mulberry silk curtains. Soft, deep-pile carpeting covered the floor, and the room was furnished with taste-ful salon chairs and a long, low sofa for those who wished to recline. Oval brass striker plates were conveniently spaced on the walls for smokers to light their matches, and a small table was set up for dining, complete with custom-made IRT-pattern china and glassware. Obviously outfitted for comfort, the railway car no doubt doubled as a movable office: A wide swivel chair and a roll-top desk sat at the far end of the room.

What was this . . . place? Jim couldn't think of it in terms of a subway car. Hell, he couldn't even figure out how he'd gotten into it. Maybe it was some sort of touring museum on wheels that was being transported by rail to an exhibition? Or had he somehow passed through time and wandered into a parlor coach on the Orient Express?

Before he had time to consider the possibilities, the train slowed to a stop. Looking through the window, Jim could see the tiles in the subway wall spelling out Bleecker Street.

It was like a magic trick. In the instant he had gazed through the glass, everything inside the mysterious coach had changed. He was back inside a regular subway car, what Jim *thought* he had boarded just minutes before. With a familiar swish, the metal doors slid open in front of him. Jim stepped out onto the platform in stunned silence. He stood, rooted to the spot, as other passengers rushed by him onto the train. He heard the doors close behind him and the subway started off.

Jim turned slightly to his left to catch the tail end of the last car as it barreled down the dark tunnel toward Spring Street, Canal, and then City Hall. Whatever it had been, the ghost train was gone.

The plush subway car Jim stepped into that night has been seen—and, if the claims are true, ridden—by countless other people since the late 1920s. It's believed to be the apparition of the private car once owned by August Belmont Jr., whose company built the IRT subway system. It has been spotted all along the Manhattan portion of the Lexington Avenue line, but most of the passengers who have entered the phantom club car did so at the Astor Place station.

Belmont was born in 1853, the son of a prosperous New York banker. A sprinter while at Harvard, he is credited with having introduced spiked track shoes to the United States. Upon the death of Belmont Sr. in 1890, the younger Belmont assumed control of his father's banking and other business interests, including the breeding of thoroughbred horses. (The greatest horse to come out of the son's stables was Man o' War, born in 1917.) In 1905 Belmont Jr. built the Belmont Park racetrack in Elmont, Queens, Long Island, and it became the new home for the Belmont Stakes, the third leg of the famed Triple Crown. (The race, originally backrolled by Belmont Sr., had started out in 1866 at Jerome Park Racetrack, then was held at Morris Park Racecourse for fifteen years before moving to Belmont Park.)

By the end of the nineteenth century, New York was already densely populated, but, despite massive population growth in the 1800s, the city had done little planning in the way of mass transit. London had alleviated some of its traffic problems in the 1860s with the world's first underground railway system. Boston became the first city in America to open a fully operational subway system in 1897.

In 1894 a New York City commission had been set up to consider possible subway routes. Rather than dig the tunnels and lay the tracks itself, the city decided in 1900 to lease the rights, allowing independent companies to do so. The private contractor that won the first bid was the Rapid Transit Construction Company, organized by John B. McDonald.

In May 1902 August Belmont Jr. incorporated the Interborough Rapid Transit Company to finance construction. Belmont was named president of the company and, starting in 1907, chairman as well. The line opened on October 27, 1904, running from City Hall station to 145th and Broadway.

Today the IRT's Lexington Avenue Local 6 is a single trunk line, partly subterranean and partly aboveground. The Lexington Avenue Local follows a fairly straight line up the east side of Manhattan from City Hall to 125th Street. It then crosses over into the Bronx, where it extends aboveground to Pelham Bay Park.

The original City Hall station is now out of service and lies dormant, inaccessible to the public. The landmarked station was designed by architects Heins and LaFarge to be a showcase, with Roman brick wainscoting along the walls, polychrome tiled arches, leaded-glass vaulted skylights, and twelve chandeliers of wrought iron and brass. Ridership through the station was down to just six hundred people a day when it was closed in 1945. Local passengers now board instead at the nearby Brooklyn Bridge–City Hall station.

(The original City Hall station has been put under the jurisdiction of New York City's Transit Museum, which occasionally provides tours of it. But riders on the southbound 6 can catch a quick glimpse of the dimly lit, defunct station if they stay on the subway to the end of the line before it loops around to return on the northbound tracks.)

While Belmont advocated public transportation for the masses, that didn't necessarily mean he wanted to hobnob with the hoi polloi. Before the subway opened he commissioned a private car for personal use from the Wason Manufacturing Company of Brightwood, Massachusetts. No expense was spared.

Technically, the car was part of the rolling stock of the IRT and was assigned number 3344, but the Mineola, as Belmont named it, never entered general service. The reason for the nomenclature is uncertain, but the name "Mineola" comes from a Native American word for "pleasant place."

And a pleasant place the railcar was! Up until his death in December 1924, Belmont used the carriage to give private tours of the IRT and to entertain guests. It had an opulent sitting area with an Empire-style arched ceiling bordered by Tiffany glass. Food and drink was served from an onboard kitchenette, which had a kerosene stove and a 600-volt coffee urn. The car even had a toilet, which emptied onto the tracks. A bag of sand was always kept at the ready to help "flush" the bowl after use if necessary.

It's said that Belmont sometimes took Mineola when he went out to his racetrack. The IRT had been extended into

Brooklyn, but none of its routes continued as far as the racecourse. Belmont arranged for his car to be transferred from the IRT onto Long Island Railroad (LIRR) tracks at the Atlantic Avenue station. That way, he and his companions could travel in style from a siding under the now-demolished Belmont Hotel on Forty-second Street all the way to Belmont Park.

After Belmont's death the car went into storage in the Bronx and was soon forgotten. It was discovered in the 1940s and was purchased by a salvager for scrap metal. After the coach was stripped, the dealer gave what remained to his father-in-law, who put the boxlike shell in his backyard in Flemington, New Jersey.

The historic subway car was tracked down in the 1960s and purchased by a Pennsylvania train museum. During its time there, the retired coach was further damaged in a flood and was struck by lightning. In 1973 the Shore Line Trolley Museum in East Haven, Connecticut, bought the Mineola. Because of its fragile condition, it has not been put on display. Generally, what's left of the carriage stays stored in a barn on the property, as it continues to undergo restoration.

So what was it that Jim and so many others like him experienced? Ghost lore abounds with tales of people giving hitchhikers a lift, only to have the riders somehow vanish from the vehicles. In the archetypal version of the story, a man driving down a dark stretch of highway at night spies a lone woman along the side of the road. He offers to drop her off at her home, and she climbs into the back seat. As the man pulls up to the driveway he looks into the rearview mirror to discover that the girl is somehow gone.

The story of the ethereal subway car falls into the related genre of phantom vehicles, of which there have been some notable examples throughout history. The most mythic, perhaps, is the *Flying Dutchman,* the ghost ship that appears off the Cape of Good Hope. Then there's the apparition of the funeral train that carried the body of Abraham Lincoln from Washington, D.C., to his burial site in Springfield, Illinois. It's been seen on isolated stretches of the original track on the anniversary of its 1865 passage. In more recent times, the late Telly Savalas claimed that back in the early 1960s, when he was starting his acting career, he was picked up in rainstorm by a man driving a black Cadillac after his own car ran out of gas on a deserted road on Long Island. When Savalas later sought out the Good Samaritan to return the money the stranger had loaned him to buy gas, he discovered the person was dead—and had been for several years.

The story of the Mineola may be unique, however, because the actual coach still exists. How can it be a "ghost" if everyone knows where the railcar is located, albeit in ruins?

The quandary begs the question that has plagued paranormal researchers for years: What exactly *is* a ghost? Experts in spirit phenomena have tried to come up with what physicists would call a unified theory to explain all the different kinds of otherworldly activity that takes place. Why, for example, do some folks see a full apparition, while others merely sense an invisible presence, feel a chill in the air, or hear disembodied sounds?

According to the vernacular, a ghost is the returning soul or spirit of someone who is deceased. If that's the case, researchers ponder, why do animals like George Washington's horse sometimes materialize? Do animals have souls? Specialists in paranormal inquiry also pose questions that seem ridiculous to people outside their field, things like: If ghosts are spirits returning from the Great Beyond, why aren't they naked? Did their clothing pass over to the Other Side as well?

Which brings us back to the Mineola. How can an inanimate object return from the dead if it was never alive in the first place?

Paranormalists have come up with one possible solution, but it hasn't gained many supporters—even among people who believe in ghosts—because it involves a kind of time travel. It relies on an open interpretation of Einstein's General Theory of Relativity that suggests matter warps both space and time.

Applied to the case of the Mineola, what appears to be a haunting might really be a sudden shift in time, an occurrence that's been termed retrocognition, or sometimes postcognition. When it happens, people find themselves temporarily relocated into a three-dimensional past. Such displacements are extraordinarily rare, instantaneous, and usually very brief.

Retrocognition could explain why people have seen full armies fighting on old battlefields when no reenactments were taking place. It could explain how, for a half hour in 1910, two British women found themselves among people (who were not costumed staff members) dressed in Louis XVI–era wardrobe during a visit to Versailles. It could also explain encounters with the Mineola. In all of these cases, the onlookers may not have been seeing ghosts *from* the past. Instead, they may have momentarily been transported *into* the past.

Whatever the ghostly subway car is—whether it's an apparition or a wrinkle in time—it continues to show up on the Lexington Avenue Local line. So if you ever accidentally find yourself onboard, make yourself at home. You've been invited to ride as the special guest of one of New York's most famous entrepreneurs, Mr. August Belmont Jr.

Chapter 20

# Escape from Beyond

### McSorley's Old Ale House
### 15 East Seventh Street

*It's said that when Harry Houdini made his home in New York City
he was particularly fond of a particular pub—McSorley's Old Ale
House. Is it possible a phantom black cat that shows up in its window from time to time signifies the presence of the world-famous
magician's ghost?*

Ty knew better. There was no way Houdini's ghost could be
inside. And even if it were, why would the master escape
artist, perhaps the most famous magician in history, have
returned to *this* place?

Ty stood in front of McSorley's Old Ale House in the East
Village. According to the large green-and-white sign above
the windows and doorway, the bar had been established in
1854, twenty years before Houdini was born Erich Weiss in
Budapest, Hungary. Yes, for much of his life, Houdini called
New York City home, but why, Ty wondered, have rumors
surfaced that the great magician's ghost has returned to
take up residence at this particular bar?

Ty himself was an "escapologist"—the fancy word for
anyone who could free himself from ropes, shackles, straitjackets, you name it. He had started performing simple tricks
as a kid when he received a magic set for Christmas. The
hobby turned into somewhat of an obsession as he devoured
any book he could find on the subject. Normally, playing

with cards and pulling coins out of someone's ear would have marked him as a geek at school, but because Doug Henning and David Copperfield were appearing on television, it was cool to be a magician. Not only did girls start huddling around Ty, but he also began making money by doing shows at Rotary clubs and birthday parties. He was proud that he got all the way through his teenage years without ever having to ask, "Would you like fries with that?"

It was the same year as Copperfield's first TV special that Ty's interest began to switch from bunny rabbits to handcuffs, and it was all because of *Happy Days*. Yes, *Happy Days*, that classic sitcom with Richie, Mr. C, and The Fonz. In an episode called, aptly enough, "The Magic Show," the Leopard Lodge, Mr. Cunningham's fraternal club, sponsors a show to benefit an orphanage.

When the magician who was scheduled gets injured trying to escape from an oversize milk can, a dangerous trick made famous by Houdini, Fonzie tells his friends about another guy who can do the trick: The Amazing Randi. The boys track him down—in the middle of his performing a straitjacket escape suspended from a building—and convince him to take over. When Randi, too, becomes incapacitated, Fonzie saves the day by doing the milk can escape himself.

Ty was mesmerized. And he was stunned when he realized the Amazing Randi wasn't just the fictional character's name in the TV episode; it was also the stage name of the real-life internationally famous escape artist, James Randi, who portrayed him.

Well, Ty was hooked. He *had* to learn how to escape from a sealed milk can! *And* how to get out of a straitjacket. And ropes and chains and, perhaps one day, the infamous Water Torture Cell that Houdini had introduced in 1908 and publicized with posters that read "Failure Means a Drowning Death."

With a few years of dedicated research and rehearsal, Ty transformed himself from a novice picklock to one of the top performers in his very specialized field of daredevilry. Soon he was a headliner at state fairs and sports arenas, where he would allow himself to be bound, confined, or otherwise locked into impossible restraints. His signature piece? He would be handcuffed, wrapped in a hundred feet of chain, and locked into a small pinewood crate. The "coffin" would be nailed shut and set at one end of the home stretch of a racecourse. Then, on the starter's signal, a sports car would barrel down the track toward the box. Either the magician escaped, or the collision would mean certain death.

After one close call too many, Ty decided it was time to take a few months off, to reconsider his calling, and to decide on what direction his career should take in the future. He was no longer a spring chicken. He was nearly fifty, ironically the age Randi had been the year of that *Happy Days* taping so many years before. Ty knew he couldn't be struggling his way out of shackles and holding his breath underwater for too much longer.

Even Houdini must have had some second thoughts. His act took an enormous physical toll on his body. By the time of his death from peritonitis at the age of fifty-two on Halloween 1926, Houdini had cut back on the escapes. A full third of his evening show was dedicated to exposing the work of fake mediums. Ty noted that the Amazing Randi followed Houdini's example and had reinvented himself as an expert on the paranormal. *Will that be the next step for me?* Ty wondered.

Perhaps reacquainting himself with Houdini's life would give him some sort of answer. He was already in New York and was up for an adventure, so he decided to retrace Houdini's footsteps in the city. While that would be impossible literally, of course, Ty set out to visit as many of the spots associated with the "King of Handcuffs" as he could find.

Houdini's father, the Rabbi Mayer Samuel Weiss, had preceded the rest of the family to the New World in an attempt to make a better life. He originally settled in Appleton, Wisconsin, where he led a small Reform congregation. In 1878 the rabbi's family (including four-year-old Erich) joined him. By the age of nine, Erich was showing theatrical talent, performing in a backyard circus he put together with friends. When the rabbi's term of employment was ended in 1887, the Weisses moved to a boardinghouse on East Seventy-ninth Street in Manhattan. Erich was already practicing sleight-of-hand by that time. About the age of seventeen, he took the stage name Harry Houdini. (He named himself after France's greatest magician, Jean Eugène Robert-Houdin. He had heard that adding the suffix "i" to a word made it mean "like" or "as," and since he wanted to be "like Houdin," he dubbed himself Houdini. (Harry was an Anglicized form of his own name, Erich.)

For a time, Harry performed with a friend, Jacob, and then his own brother Theodore (who would later work as Hardeen). But in 1893 Harry met the girl of his dreams, eighteen-year-old Wilhelmina Beatrice "Bess" Rahner, who was performing at Coney Island in a song-and-dance act called The Floral Sisters. Harry and Bess wed after a whirlwind courtship of three weeks.

It would be six years before Martin Beck, a vaudeville impresario, caught the Houdinis' act in St. Paul, Minnesota. Harry and Bess performed an impressive illusion in which the couple changes places in and out of a locked trunk, but it was Houdini's unique handcuff escapes that impressed Beck.

Despite becoming a star on the vaudeville circuit, Houdini wanted more. He and Bess sailed to England in 1900 without any bookings but were determined to create a sensation. He managed to get London authorities to challenge him to escape from Scotland Yard. He got out, and the resultant publicity led to five years of work in Great Britain and on the Continent. By the time Houdini returned to America in 1905, he was world famous.

Houdini's claim to fame was that he could escape from anything: regulation straitjackets from insane asylums; a set of handcuffs that a British blacksmith had taken five years to craft; the Washington, D.C., jail cell that held President Garfield's assassin, Charles Guiteau; locked trunks thrown into rivers; the carcass of a whale. Then there was the milk can escape, introduced in 1908, that had so captivated Ty in his youth. And finally, the Water Torture Cell, in which a generation of filmgoers believed Houdini died.

The 1953 biopic *Houdini* ended with actor Tony Curtis, portraying the title role, trying to get out of the water cabinet. Ty often told his audiences the old magicians' joke: "Houdini didn't die in the Water Torture Cell. Tony Curtis died in the Water Torture Cell." For those who cared to hear the full story, Ty would explain how three male students from McGill University came into the star's dressing room during his engagement at the Princess Theatre in Montreal. The young men asked Houdini if it were true that he could withstand any kind of blow to his stomach. When the magician said yes, they thought it was an immediate invitation. Houdini, surprised, did not have time to properly tense his muscles to take the series of punches that followed, and although Houdini recovered from the assault, his appendix had unknowingly been ruptured. Houdini became ill over the next few days as toxins spread through his bloodstream, but he refused to cancel shows. He collapsed after a performance in Detroit and was rushed to the hospital, but by then, in an age before antibiotics, it was too late to save his life.

Houdini's remains were returned to New York City, where about two thousand people attended his funeral, held in the ballroom of the Elks Club Lodge #1 on November 4, 1926. The illusionist was buried in Machpelah Cemetery in Queens, where a large monument complete with a statue of a weeping woman now marks his grave. (There is a cenotaph for Bess at the gravesite, but she is buried at the Gate of Heaven Cemetery in Westchester, New York. Her Catholic family would not allow her to be interred at Machpelah, a Jewish cemetery.)

Manhattan had changed since Houdini's time. Ty walked past 108 West Forty-third Street where the Elks Club had been located, but the building had, first, become the Diplomat Hotel, and then been torn down years later. Ty was never able to ascertain the exact address of Houdini's boyhood home, but he dutifully walked the incredibly long blocks of Seventy-ninth Street between Fifth Avenue and the East River along which it must have stood. Ty found no trace of the gigantic Hippodrome Theatre at 1120 Sixth Avenue where in 1918 Houdini made a five-ton elephant disappear from the stage. (The theater was demolished in 1939, and an office building was raised in its place in 1952.) Then, at last, Ty found one place associated with his idol that was still standing: the reddish-brown row house at 278 West 113th Street that Houdini bought in 1905 and was his main residence during the last twenty-one years of his life.

The next day, Ty went to pay his respects at Houdini's gravesite, which he thought was going to be the last stop on his pilgrimage. But while he was standing in front of the memorial, a stranger sauntered up and began to engage him in small talk. He was a magician, too, and recognized Ty from his TV appearances. No, he said, Ty would never have heard of him; he was just a local hobbyist. But unlike Ty, he wasn't an escape artist. Instead, he performed what fellow illusionists sometimes call "bizarre magick," routines with supernatural or parapsychological themes and story lines.

"I'm fascinated," the fellow visitor whispered conspiratorially, "that Houdini spent all those years debunking mediums and the Spirit World. Especially now that Houdini's ghost haunts a bar he used to go to in the Village."

The words struck Ty like a thunderbolt. *What? Houdini has returned from the dead?*

Ty knew better, of course. Mediums, magicians, even Bess herself had tried unsuccessfully for years to contact Houdini's spirit.

By the time Houdini began his life's calling, Spiritualism was already in full swing. The religion's most controversial tenet is that spirits of the dead can visit and talk with the living. Every civilization in history has had people such as oracles and shamans who claimed they could talk to the dead. But modern Spiritualism dates to March 31, 1848, when Kate and Margaret Fox, two young girls in Hydesville, New York, said they were receiving messages from a murdered peddler buried underneath their house. The man's ghost never appeared. Instead, it communicated through a series of disembodied knocks and rappings, which, when used as a code, allowed the phantom to answer yes-or-no questions and, eventually, to spell out words.

Before long, mediums (as the "sensitives" were called who could conjure up spirits) were conducting "sittings" or séances throughout the United States. The controversial craze soon traveled to England and Europe. In 1882 the Society for Psychical Research was founded in London to investigate and authenticate or discredit the mediums and the paranormal phenomena they were producing.

Houdini was well aware of the hoopla surrounding the most eminent mediums of the day. How could he not be? Many of them were giving demonstrations in the same theaters where he performed. But he considered the mediums to be charlatans, nothing more than magicians who used their methods to play on the sympathies of the public and defraud people who were in mourning. Houdini decided to undertake a personal crusade to expose fake mediums and their methods.

Houdini's most famous encounter came in July 1924, when he agreed to attend a séance held by the renowned Boston medium Mina Crandon, who worked under the name Margery. She was being tested by *Scientific American,* and the panel was all set to declare her legitimate and award her a large monetary prize until Houdini intervened.

Ty knew there could have been many reasons for Houdini to declare war on Spiritualism. Perhaps he *was* doing it on ethical grounds alone. But as an illusionist, Houdini had spent a lifetime exploring the border between the possible and the impossible. Did he not have a natural curiosity as to what, if anything, was on the Other Side?

Then, too, it may have just been good business. The publicity surrounding Houdini's exposés guaranteed that people would flock to his shows to see him reveal how things went bump in the night.

Ty believed that Houdini had a much more personal investment in his crusade. Harry worshipped his mother, Cecilia Weiss, but he was on tour in Europe in 1913 when she died. Houdini collapsed in grief upon hearing the news. The man who could escape anything had to confront the fact that he had no power over death. Was Harry's anti-Spiritualist campaign actually an attempt to find a real medium so he could say good-bye to his beloved mama?

Though Houdini never publicly acknowledged that spirit messages might be possible, he made a pact with his wife. Whichever one of them died first would try to reach out Across the Veil to contact the one who survived. But to be sure that an actual connection had been made, one particular word known just to them had to be part of any spirit message.

For ten years after Houdini's untimely death, every Halloween night Bess would take part in a séance on the roof of the Knickerbocker Hotel in Hollywood, California. Houdini never appeared. Or did he? As the last candle was blown out at the end of the final séance in 1936, a clap of thunder sounded and a freak, brief shower rained down on the participants. Was it Houdini saying farewell?

It wouldn't be the only time people claimed Houdini had reappeared.

In 1926, Bess agreed to take part in a séance conducted by a well-known medium, the Reverend Arthur Ford. At first Mrs. Houdini thought the secret code word ("believe") had come through, but as time went by she changed her mind and denied that the correct message had been received.

Others believe that Houdini returned to haunt the property where he had lived in Hollywood. Around 1920, while the magician was in town making a series of movies, he and

Bess stayed in the guesthouse of an estate on Laurel Canyon Boulevard.

The Houdinis never owned the place. It belonged to Los Angeles department store magnate Ralf M. Walker, who welcomed the couple to his home. Over the years, however, locals began referring to the place as the Houdini Mansion. For several years after Houdini's death, Bess once again stayed in the guesthouse, up until Walker's death in 1935. The guesthouse itself was eventually torn down. The main house was destroyed when a wildfire laid waste to the canyon in 1959, and the burned-out structure was finally razed in 1968.

The gardens remained, unkempt but otherwise complete with their crumbling terraces, concrete walkways, and stone staircases. By the early 1970s rumors circulated that Houdini's ghost was sometimes spied on the grounds, and phantom light orbs could be seen darting through the trees on the hill behind the old mansion's foundations. There was a simple earthly explanation: The shadowy forms seen in the overgrown, untended gardens were probably vagrants trespassing, and the mysterious lights could have been come from young "hippies" partying up in the brush. But such logic was lost on those who wanted to "believe."

So here Ty was at the end of a long day, in Greenwich Village standing in front of McSorley's Old Ale House. Before his encounter with the stranger at Houdini's grave he had never heard of the bar. But he was determined to visit every place in Manhattan he could find that was associated with the legendary escape artist, haunted or not.

When Houdini passed through New York City as a four-year-old boy, McSorley's had already been in business for two decades. John McSorley, an Irish immigrant, moved to

America in 1851 during the Great Potato Famine and founded his pub three years later. It was an immediate success: a true workingman's bar, with sawdust on the floor, raw onions and cheese served on the house, and its own hearty ale. The saloon's reputation spread, and soon celebrities, politicians, artists, and authors were attracted to its doors. Visitors included an eclectic assortment of luminaries such as Abraham Lincoln, Teddy Roosevelt, Boss Tweed, John Sloan, e. e. cummings, Brendan Behan, Woody Guthrie, and John Lennon. Inside the tavern, everyone was equal, regardless of their social standing elsewhere.

Except for women. McSorley's was a male bastion until 1970 when, after a court order was issued, women were allowed inside for the first time.

Ty entered the front doors. It was as if he had walked back in time, back to 1910, the year McSorley had died. Ty wasn't sure at first whether he was in a friendly neighborhood bar or a museum. Since McSorley's death, no memorabilia had been removed from the premises. The old-time sawdust was there scattered beneath his feet, the walls were covered with yellowing newspaper articles, and wishbones were hung above the bar. (They had been left behind by doughboys heading off to World War I, and they were only to be removed by the men themselves upon their return.)

And there at the end of bar was, for Ty, the Holy Grail: a set of handcuffs dating to the early twentieth century, with its one cuff closed up tight around the gleaming bar rail. According to popular belief—and more specifically to the stranger Ty had met earlier that day in Queens, the manacles had belonged to Houdini. It was in part because of the cuffs that Houdini's phantom supposedly dropped in to visit.

Ty settled into a chair across from the bar. He couldn't take his eyes off the handcuffs. Supposedly Houdini loved the brew house, and in the 1920s he stopped in whenever his touring schedule would allow. As for the cuffs themselves, it's unknown whether Houdini happened to be carrying them with him when he arrived one day, whether they had belonged to an obliging policeman who lent them to Houdini for a demonstration, or whether someone who knew that the magician frequented the place brought them to challenge Houdini on the spot.

An hour went by. Then two. Ty enjoyed first one ale, then another. By the time he had finished a third glass, he could understand why Houdini would want to come back to this place. Ty felt strangely at home. Many ghosts return to places where they were most comfortable while they were alive. Ty could easily envision the celebrated entertainer feeling that way here, holding court by the bar, the center of attention.

But no amount of imagination, or alcohol, could convince Ty that Houdini was going to show up that night. At one point Ty had jumped when he caught the motion of a silhouette moving across the wall at the far side of the room, but it had turned out to be some guy heading toward the john. As midnight neared, Ty made the call: The great illusionist was not going to materialize. It was time to go.

Ty took one more sip out of his glass, dropped a couple of bucks on the table, and stood. He surveyed the room, took a last, longing gaze at the cuffs on the rail, then walked outdoors. Immediately the sounds of the city engulfed him. He quickly cut across Seventh Street and headed toward Astor Place to catch the subway.

If he had glanced over his shoulder Ty might have caught a glimpse of what he had come to find. There in the front window, so much of a shadow that it was hard to tell if it was real, stood a sinewy black cat with piercing green eyes, its head cocked to one side and—was it winking?

Ty had forgotten the most important part of the old wives' tale the stranger told him at the grave. You could always tell when the great escape artist's spirit was going to make an appearance. A phantom black cat would appear in the window, sometimes for no more than a few seconds, to announce the impending visit.

Ty had left too soon. It was now the witching hour. Houdini was in the house.

Chapter 21

# The Bouwerie Bogey

## St. Mark's Church in-the-Bowery
## 131 East Tenth Street

*St. Mark's Church in-the-Bowery has been haunted by no fewer than four phantoms for as long as anyone can remember. By far the most famous ghost is none other than Peter Stuyvesant, the seventeenth-century director governor of New Amsterdam and on whose former farmland the church is located.*

What on earth could be causing all the commotion at the church? The short, wiry man pulled his cloak around him as he rushed through the foggy streets toward the sanctuary.

Our anonymous protagonist—shall we call him Mister Appleby?—was St. Mark's Church in-the-Bowery's sexton, the most recent in a long succession of vergers dating back to 1799, when the Episcopal house of worship first began welcoming parishioners. He was not a clergyman, not even a lay brother, but his round-the-clock dedication to his post helped free the reverend to minister to the flock.

As sexton, it was Appleby's responsibility to care for the sanctuary, its contents, the graveyards, and the rest of the church property. He was an able handyman, so he could do most of the upkeep on his own, but if specialized repairs were necessary, he would supervise the workmen. He kept the grounds tidy, the interior of the sanctuary spotless, and the altarpieces and fixtures polished. He maintained the burial records and, when required, he helped dig the graves.

Among the deceased whose tombs Appleby tended were some of New York City's most important and influential citizens: military men such as Commodore Matthew C. Perry, who "opened" Japan to the West; political figures such as Vice President Daniel D. Tompkins; legal minds such as Josiah Ogden Hoffman; and, perhaps best known of all, Peter Stuyvesant, the last director general of New Amsterdam before it became New York City.

On top of all of his other duties, Appleby was also responsible for the large cast-iron bell hanging in the belfry of the steeple—and for ringing it to announce services or special occasions. And *that* was what had Appleby hurrying back to the church so late that night. Someone was tolling the bell—and it certainly wasn't him!

It had been somewhere between 10:15 and 10:30 p.m.— Appleby wasn't sure—when he first noticed the wild tolling of the bell echoing through the neighborhood. It was Good Friday, but services had ended hours before. No one should have been anywhere near the church anymore. He had personally closed the sanctuary, walked the grounds to make sure everyone had departed, and locked up everything before heading home.

Appleby reached the entrance and pulled at the gate in the fence surrounding the property. It was still shut up tight. He hastily inserted the heavy key, turned the tumbler, and swung the gate wide. Appleby looked up toward the sound of the bell, pealing away, but the mist had thickened that evening to the point that he could barely make out the steeple. He dashed toward the portico, all the while looking for the key that would open the sanctuary's door.

It was then that he heard it. A quiet thump like a walking stick being gently tapped on the hardened ground, followed by a shuffling sound. Was it a piece of wood being drawn along the earth? Rap. Swish. Rap. Swish. Appleby's curiosity turned to terror as he realized the noise was coming from right behind him.

He turned. At first, nothing was visible through the dense haze. Then, slowly, ever so slowly, a form materialized as it stepped out of the murky shroud. The figure was a tall, robust gentleman, carrying a cane and dressed in clothes from the last century: a velvet jacket, puffed shirt, knee breeches, and white-gartered hose. If the unearthly intruder's garb had not been enough to identify him, Appleby would have recognized the man from his many portraits around the city as well as the unmistakable silver-studded wooden leg. The wraith before him could be none other than Peter Stuyvesant himself!

Appleby wasn't aware that he was screaming until he was well outside the gate. Drawn by his loud shrieks and the continuing clanging of the bell, people were beginning to gather on the other side of Tenth Street. After catching his breath, Appleby tried to tell them—was he making any sense?—what he had seen, and finally a few brave souls agreed to accompany him back into the churchyard.

To the secret relief of many, the ghost was nowhere to be found. The men crept cautiously into the meeting hall and tiptoed toward the stairs up to the tower. Appleby insisted that as sexton he lead the charge, but as he touched his foot to the first step, the chiming overhead abruptly stopped. The last bong reverberated through the air, then silence. Newly emboldened, the group quickly made its way upward. Whoever was chiming the bell couldn't escape; he would have to pass them on the way down.

They reached the pull cord, or rather the platform where the bottom of the cord should have been. It was gone! Or so it seemed at first. Appleby asked one of the crew to lift his lantern as high as possible, and as he peered into the darkness above him, his eyes could just make out the end of a short piece of rope hanging from the bell. Either the cord had snapped or someone had deliberately cut it in two. Regardless, with the lower half of the rope missing, who or what could have reached up far enough to ring the bell?

The replacement of the rope had to wait until morning. And by then tragic news had reached New York City. The night before, two hundred miles to the south in the nation's capital, an assassin had entered the Presidential Box at Ford's Theatre and shot Abraham Lincoln at point-blank range. The country's leader had taken his last breath at 7:22 a.m.

Appleby, like the rest of the country, was stunned. But his mourning took a metaphysical twist as he realized the bell in St. Mark's belfry had begun to toll at the exact same time that the fatal bullet was fired. Perhaps the appearance of Peter Stuyvesant's spectre the previous night was not a coincidence.

As the sexton wandered over toward Stuyvesant's gravesite, his mind was racing. Was it possible? Had the old Knickerbocker come back from the Other Side to announce the Great Emancipator's crossing into the Next World? When Appleby reached the Dutchman's vault, he couldn't believe his eyes. If he had had any doubts up to that point, they instantly vanished. There on the ground, directly in front of Stuyvesant's crypt, lay a long piece of rope. Appleby knew it well. It was the lower half of the pull cord that was missing from the steeple high overhead.

The legend of the sexton's encounter with Peter Stuyvesant's spirit has been told time and again by ghost enthusiasts. As with so many old wives' tales, details vary with each retelling. In some versions it's not a sexton but the church rector who sees the ghost on the night of the bell's tolling. The year seems to change from one storyteller to another as well, all the way from the late 1700s to 1960, but most renditions say the haunting took place during the Civil War. More than one narrative specifically gives the date as the night of Lincoln's assassination. Until some primary document surfaces, though, like a newspaper article or even a church bulletin, it's impossible to confirm any single account.

Peter (originally Petrus or Pieter) Stuyvesant was one of the major figures of early New York City history. Just who was this man whose ghost has never come to rest?

Stuyvesant was born around 1592 in the Netherlands. After his studies, he joined the Dutch West India Company sometime between 1632 and 1635 and worked his way up through the ranks. In 1644 he was named director of their colonies on Aruba, Bonaire, and Curaçao, the Dutch Lesser Antilles commonly known as the ABC Islands located off the coast of Venezuela.

Shortly after his stewardship there began, he led an attack against Spanish colonists in the region. In the battle his right leg was wounded by a cannonball. Stuyvesant returned to the Netherlands, where the lower half of his leg was amputated and replaced with a wooden peg decorated with silver studs or nails (although some sources refer to them as bands of silver). He would go on to acquire a variety of nicknames, including Peg-Leg, Father Wooden Leg, and Old Silver Nails. Then in May 1645 Stuyvesant was made the fourth (and what would turn out to be the last) director general of New Amsterdam.

He wouldn't arrive in New Netherland for two more years. When Stuyvesant stepped ashore on May 11, 1647, the settlement consisted of Fort Amsterdam and several blocks of houses clustered around it. Under his watch, New Amsterdam grew from about two thousand to eight thousand inhabitants, and in 1653 it was formally incorporated as a city. Stuyvesant had a defensive wall constructed (along the route of today's Wall Street), laid out Broadway, and had water channeled through the lower city into a canal (which, when filled in years later, became Broad Street). Trade boomed during Stuyvesant's eighteen years at the helm, and he enforced a measure of law and order that was often lacking before his appearance on the scene.

He set up a Council of Nine to represent the colonists, but the settlers' input was very limited. Stuyvesant was a true company man. Though sometimes benevolent, he was a demanding, autocratic ruler—a relationship he described "as a father over his children." He was often cold and blunt, and when he wanted to make a point, he was known to holler, wave his walking stick, or stamp his wooden leg.

The reforms Stuyvesant put in place were sorely needed in the rowdy settlement, but they didn't make him particularly popular. His edicts controlled the consumption and sale of alcohol, including its prohibition to Native Americans, and he attempted to enforce a monopoly on the fur trade. Farm animals were no longer allowed to run free. Stuyvesant enforced the observance of the Sabbath and enacted laws regulating public decency. Bars and brothels were closed.

He was also intolerant of (and sometimes punished) settlers who didn't follow his Dutch Reformed church. Perhaps the best description of Stuyvesant came from author Washington Irving, who portrayed him in his *A History of New York, from the Beginning of the World to the End of the Dutch Dynasty* as "a tough, sturdy, valiant, weather-beaten, mettlesome, obstinate, leathern-sided, lion-hearted, generous-spirited old governor."

On August 27, 1664, four English frigates with 450 men aboard sailed into the harbor demanding New Amsterdam's surrender. When the British offered the settlers "life, estate, and liberty to all who would submit to the king's authority," the colonists refused to follow Stuyvesant's orders to put up a fight. The director general was forced to admit defeat and turned over the island to the British. In June 1665 the settlement was officially rechristened New York City, named for the Duke of York (who would later become King James II).

In 1665 Stuyvesant sailed back to the Netherlands to make an official report on his time as governor of the island. Afterward, he returned to his farm in New York City, where he lived peaceably enough until his death at the age of eighty in 1672.

During Stuyvesant's tenure as director general, the executive mansion where he lived and conducted business was Whitehall, a white-roofed stone house he built at the tip of Manhattan on a small piece of land jutting out into the East River. Beginning in 1651 he resided elsewhere: about two miles north of the city on sixty-two acres he purchased from the Dutch West India Company. He called his property the Great Bouwerie—*bouwerie* or *bouwerij* being the Dutch word for "farm."

The land, situated in what is now the East Village, stretched from modern-day East Third Street up to East Twenty-third Street and from what is now Fourth Avenue to somewhere between First Avenue and Avenue D. The grounds were tended by forty to fifty slaves. Stuyvesant's main house, which was designed in typical Dutch architecture of the time and cost 6,400 guilders to build, was located near what is now the intersection of Tenth or Eleventh Street and Third Avenue. The manor stood until 1777, when it was destroyed by fire. A pear tree that Stuyvesant brought from the Netherlands and planted in 1647 at the corner of today's Thirteenth Street and Third Avenue stood until 1867. The trail that led from town to the farm eventually became, appropriately enough, Stuyvesant Lane.

A deeply religious man, Stuyvesant had built a private family chapel on his property by 1660. When he died in 1672, he was buried in a vault underneath the church.

But he didn't stay there. Within days of Stuyvesant's death, household servants and workers on his *bouwerie* started seeing their recently passed master walking the grounds of the farm. Sometimes the spirit would break pottery or china in the house. Whenever the ghost was around, whether it materialized or not, people could feel its presence. When the Stuyvesant mansion burned to the ground a century later, his phantom was seen wandering through the ashes.

By the end of the eighteenth century, the city was rapidly growing northward. Roads were being built through the old Stuyvesant land, and the Great Bouwerie was subdivided for real estate. In 1793 Stuyvesant's great grandson Petrus Stuyvesant donated the property on which the family chapel stood to the Episcopal Church on two conditions: A new church had to be built on the spot, and the Stuyvesant family vault had to remain on the grounds. On April 25, 1795, the cornerstone was laid for St. Mark's Church in-the-Bowery, and the two-story, Georgian-style fieldstone sanctuary was completed four years later. It was consecrated on May 9, 1799.

The Greek Revival church steeple was a later addition, in 1828. A weathervane was affixed in 1836, and the cast-and wrought-iron fence around the property was put up in 1838. Also around that time, the interior of the church was renovated, with the bulky pillars that originally held up the balcony being replaced by slender Egyptian Revival columns to improve sightlines. Today there are no fixed pews inside the sanctuary, which allows seating to be arranged in any number of ways. In 1858 the current cast-iron portico was added to the front of the building, both for aesthetic purposes and to shield arriving and departing worshippers from the elements. Finally, a clock was added to the steeple sometime near the end of the nineteenth century.

Other structures and monuments on the church grounds include a parish hall, a rectory, two statues of Native Americans, two lion sculptures, busts of Peter Stuyvesant and Daniel D. Tompkins, and a stone fountain. There are cemetery plots on both sides of the church, known as the East Yard and the West Yard. Wealthy members of the congregation were interred in stone vaults under both yards until city law forbade earthen burials in Manhattan. Cremation burials are still allowed, however, and today take place in the West Yard.

Perhaps most notably, when the sanctuary was built, Stuyvesant's remains were removed from beneath the old chapel and were reinterred in a vault along a wall on the outside of the church. A slab mounted above the tomb reads:

IN THIS VAULT LIES BURIED

PETRUS STUYVESANT

LATE CAPTAIN GENERAL AND GOVERNOR IN CHIEF OF AMSTERDAM

IN NEW NETHERLAND NOW CALLED NEW YORK.

AND THE DUTCH WEST INDIA ISLANDS. DIED FEB. A.D. 1671-2

AGED 80 YEARS

Despite his new home in a place of honor, Stuyvesant's spirit is just as restless as always. His familiar form is now seen strolling through the Bowery, especially along Stuyvesant Street. And he's particularly active whenever the church or its grounds are disturbed.

In 1831, for example, when Second Avenue was extended to the north, it cut through the edge of the East Yard. Throughout construction, unnerving bumps and thuds could be heard in and around Stuyvesant's vault. The odd noises continued as houses were built along the avenue. Second Avenue was widened around 1900, and once again Stuyvesant was awakened from his repose. That time he didn't confine his complaints to his crypt. Instead the bell in the steeple began to peal uncontrollably—and not by human hand. Perhaps Stuyvesant decided it was time to repeat the trick he had played on that sexton a century earlier.

Peter Stuyvesant's spectre has been a frequent visitor in or around the church as well. Most often he is merely heard.

Apparently in the 1880s the tap of his cane and the disembodied sound of his peg leg shuffling in the aisle occurred with some regularity.

Once in 1884 an incorporeal voice boomed out during services, singing Dutch Reformed hymns in the original tongue. Was Stuyvesant objecting to the new church on his former property being an Episcopalian chapel? In the 1930s, over the course of several Sundays, a parishioner spied Stuyvesant and a female companion, both in full period Dutch wardrobe, sitting across from him in the pews.

The Reverend Dr. W. Norman Guthrie, who was Rector of St. Mark's from 1910 to 1937, believed the performing arts could help a person connect with one's spirituality. He invited Isadora Duncan to dance for the congregation, beginning a tradition that has led to dance, poetry, and theater being presented within the main sanctuary. Martha Graham danced there; William Carlos Williams, W. H. Auden, and Allen Ginsberg recited their poetry, and many of the early plays of Sam Shepard had their first performances at St. Mark's. Today, three ongoing series—the Poetry Project, the Danspace Project, and the Incubator Arts Project—present their works in the church.

Peter Stuyvesant, who was deeply conservative and highly disapproved of anything that went against his Calvinist teachings, has not been quiet on the subject. Perhaps he considers using the space for anything other than church services offensive, if not downright sacrilegious. In any event, sometimes during rehearsals, especially when women are in the cast, he will shift around small objects, make the electricity go haywire, or even voice his objections aloud.

Incidentally, Peter Stuyvesant isn't the only ghost to haunt St. Mark's in-the-Bowery.

In addition to Stuyvesant's pew sharer, two other female phantoms appear in the sanctuary as well. One is a worshipper who shows up in the center aisle of the nave during services. Another woman dressed in a wide skirt has been spotted by the rear entrance, and on occasion she's also seen in the balcony. In addition, a figure of undetermined gender manifests itself near the organ. One of these ghosts might be the spectre that a 1981 *New York Times* article identified as Matilda Hoffman, the daughter of Judge Josiah Ogden Hoffman.

St. Mark's Church in-the-Bowery is the second-oldest church (after St. Paul's Chapel) in Manhattan, but if the original Stuyvesant chapel is taken into consideration, it is the oldest site of continuous religious worship in the city. It was designated a New York City Landmark on April 19, 1966, and was added to the National Register of Historic Places on June 19, 1972. In 1978 a major fire ravaged the sanctuary, almost destroying it, but the church has been painstakingly restored.

If you choose to attend services or one of the many artistic performances held at St. Mark's Church in-the-Bowery, you will not only have the opportunity to visit one of the city's most significant buildings, you may also get to see one of the city's most important founders: the final governor of old New Amsterdam, Peter Stuyvesant.

Chapter 22

# The Bird Still "Sings"

**Tompkins Square Park**
**Between East Seventh and Tenth Streets and**
**Avenues A and B**

*The scene of a notorious riot in the 1980s, Tompkins Square Park is now a shady refuge from the busy streets of the East Village. It's also been the site of an annual jazz festival honoring saxophonist Charlie Parker, who lived nearby. The ghost of the legendary musician himself may roam the grounds—as well as haunt his former townhouse on Avenue B.*

Alphabet City. What a strange name for a neighborhood!

Bobby knew that many of the districts in Manhattan had colorful nicknames. Some dated from colonial days: The word "bowery," for example, is an Anglicization of a Dutch word for "farm." Harlem was originally Nieuw Haarlem, which in turn was named for the city of Haarlem in the Netherlands.

Other parish names came from their geographical location on the island: SoHo is the area immediately *So*uth of *Ho*uston Street. Some neighborhoods are named for historical individuals, such as Stuyvesant Town or Peter Cooper Village. Other wards, like Chinatown and Little Italy, got their names from the ethnicity of the local inhabitants.

So when a friend suggested that Bobby look for an apartment in Alphabet City, he knew right where to head. Spanning parts of both the East Village and the Lower East Side, the area contains Avenues A, B, C, and D, the only single-letter-named streets in New York City. What little he knew about the neighborhood, however, came from a couple of shows he had seen on the Broadway stage that are set there—*Rent* and *Avenue Q*.

As Bobby wandered through the actual community, he was surprised by what he saw. It bore no resemblance to how it had been portrayed in the theater. Also, he had heard nightmare stories about how dangerous the local streets were at night, how run-down the houses and stores were, and basically how unpleasant it was to be there. That, too, must have been sometime in the past. Now the place seemed almost trendy. A new breath of life must have blown through Alphabet City.

The search was on. Bobby eventually found an apartment. Unfortunately it was no longer one of the inexpensive flats he could have found there a decade earlier, but it was reasonable enough. And one of its main attractions was that the building allowed residents to keep pets. *And* it was a stone's throw from Tompkins Square Park, which had a popular dog run. (When the patch of crushed stone and sand opened in 1990, it was the first dog run in New York City.)

Bobby had a toy terrier that in a moment of inspiration he had named Scotty, and on this particular day it was a good thing the park was so close. Scotty was telling Bobby it was time to go out. Now! Bobby took the hint. He leashed his pal, picked up the pooper-scooper and a plastic bag, and headed for the door.

Evening neared as the pair rode down the elevator and made their way toward the park. Twilight. Bobby's favorite time of the day. The weather was perfect. It was midsummer, but without a trace of the mugginess that often plagues New York in July and August. An unseasonable cool breeze was whipping up Tenth Street from the river as the two reached the northeast corner of Tompkins Square.

It was almost impossible for Bobby to believe that, up until the 1800s, much of that area of Manhattan was wetlands filled with brackish water. Known as the Salt Meadows and the Stuyvesant Meadows, the swampland was unsuitable for farming. As the population expanded north, the water was diverted, opening the property to, first, agriculture and, later, real estate.

As the middle of the nineteenth century approached, German immigrants moved in, and soon they made up the majority of the residents. By the end of the century, they had been replaced by Eastern European Jews, as well as Irish and Italian émigrés. The early tenements in which they lived were anything but plush, often overcrowded with no running water. The district also had a distinctly unsavory undercurrent, and it became known for petty crime and prostitution. The neighborhood oasis—the central place where everyone could relax and take a brief respite—was Tompkins Square Park.

In the early nineteenth century, the Stuyvesant family owned the land that now makes up the park. They had inherited it from their ancestor, the early Dutch governor Peter Stuyvesant, who had been granted the property in the 1600s. The city acquired the tract in 1834, and over the next fifteen years, the land was drained and graded. Sycamore trees were planted and walkways added, and the grounds were enclosed by a shoulder-high metal fence. The ten-and-a-half-acre park was opened to the public in 1850, named for Daniel D. Tompkins, the director-general of Dutch New Netherland from 1807 to 1817 and vice president of the United States under James Monroe from 1817 to 1825.

In 1866 the New York State Legislature ruled that most of the trees in the park had to be removed to create a parade ground for New York's Seventh Regiment. (Today, only three of the original sycamores remain, two along Tenth Street and one on Avenue A near Ninth Street.)

Locals were incensed. How dare the government kick them out of their own park? It took more than a decade, but in 1878 area residents were finally able to convince the legislature to turn the grounds back into a public space, which it has remained ever since. The square was re-landscaped, and almost 450 trees were planted, including American elm, black locust, and Oriental plane. Over the past century, several statues, a playground, recreational facilities, and two large fountains have been installed.

People have literally been up in arms in Tompkins Square Park on a number of occasions. In 1857 it was the site of a demonstration protesting the poor economy, lack of jobs, and food shortages. But that was nothing compared to the seven thousand workers who gathered there on January 13, 1874. The protesters were met with massive police resistance in what has become known as the first Tompkins Square Riot. Then, in 1877, the National Guard descended on twenty thousand people who gathered to listen to Communist organizers speak.

A hundred years later a very different dilemma faced the neighborhood. By the mid-1980s, Tompkins Square had become a hotbed for drug dealers and users alike, the homeless had set up camp, and a certain "skinhead" element had moved in as well. In the summer of 1988, in an attempt to combat the growing problem, the local community board set a 1 a.m. curfew for the park. Protests grew, and on the night of August 6, open conflict broke out with police who were charged with clearing the square. Clashes in this second Tompkins Square Park Riot continued until about six o'clock the next morning.

Like all of the Lower East Side, the neighborhood was undergoing a seismic shift. Developers were buying up cheap row houses and renovating them for upscale living. Fashionable shops were moving in. By the late 1990s the neighborhood was almost completely gentrified.

And nowhere could you see the difference more than in Tompkins Square Park. Bobby smiled in gratitude. On more than one occasion he had found the quad's shady lawn a great place to stretch out and while away a few leisurely hours. As Scotty recognized the corner of the park, he instinctively turned down Avenue B and picked up his pace as they neared the Ninth Street entrance.

The two were nearing the flagpole as Scotty suddenly stopped, his ears peaking up and his hair standing on end. Slowly, Bobby noticed that his dog was making a weird noise he had never made before. Not a bark or growl, exactly. No, it was something between a whine and a whimper. And all the time, the dog stared straight ahead.

Bobby followed Scotty's gaze about fifteen feet down the pathway. There in the shadow of a large tree sat a disheveled man all alone on a park bench. Clearly the guy had fallen on hard times. That, or he had no need to keep up appearances—or was too oblivious to know the difference. From the fit of his suit, Bobby could tell that the man had once been a formidable presence, but he was now gaunt and slumped over.

It was then that Bobby noticed the saxophone pressed to the man's lips. Bobby was so used to the ever-present music permeating the Village that it had almost become background noise in his mind. He was surprised to discover that the soft strains he was hearing were coming from the stranger's saxophone.

Bobby was—what?—entranced? No, *spellbound* seemed more like it. Against his own better judgment, Bobby found himself unconsciously being drawn to the man and the source of the music.

Keeping a discreet distance, Bobby paused in front of the park bench and studied the troubled soul. He had seen that look on street people before: The man was strung out—heroin, Bobby suspected—and his general unsteadiness suggested recent consumption of large amounts of alcohol.

But if the musician was aware of Bobby's presence, he didn't show it. He was in a world of his own, possessed, his eyes shut tight, his head bobbing back and forth. As dissipated as the rest of his frame might have been, the man's fingers flew sure across the saxophone's keys. The music that exploded from the instrument's bell wasn't the smooth, dreamy elevator strains of a modern-day Kenny G or even the cool, sweet jive of a Gerry Mulligan. No, this man's sound was raw, fast, intoxicating, hypnotic.

As Bobby stood there, riveted by the sound, he noticed a hat sitting on the bench next to the man, its brim upward. Was the guy busking? If he was working for tips, it hadn't been a good day: The hat lay there completely empty.

Bobby reached into his wallet and pulled out a bill. He gingerly stepped forward and dropped it into the man's cap. Usually quite frugal by necessity, Bobby was so caught up in the music he hadn't even glanced at the currency to see what denomination it was.

As the bill hit its mark, the enigmatic figure paused in his playing, looked up briefly, gave the smallest of nods in thanks, then dropped his head as he placed his lips back on the mouthpiece.

Leaving the man to his reverie, Bobby began to head down the path toward the Temperance Fountain. But Scotty had other ideas. Despite a small tug on the leash, the terrier wouldn't budge. When a second yank also had no effect, Bobby turned to see what the problem was. Surprisingly, as he spun round, the saxophone music instantly ceased. The mysterious musician was no longer on the bench—even though Bobby had been hearing the indescribable melodies mere moments before.

Scotty looked up at his master, with his head cocked to one side and a puzzled expression on his bearded face. "Where did the guy go?" the canine companion seemed to be asking. Bobby had no explanation for his little friend. He had no clue. There hadn't been time for the person to shuffle off without being seen or heard. It was as if the man making those heavenly sounds had simply disappeared.

By anyone's reckoning Charlie Parker was a brilliant but harrowed man. It's universally accepted that he was—and continues to be—one of the most influential American musicians of the twentieth century. He played jazz, but his new style was so significant and radically different that some separate the musical genre into two periods: "before Bird" and "after Bird."

Parker (actually Charles Parker Jr.) was born in Kansas City, Kansas, on August 29, 1920. His near-absent father was a onetime musician, singer, and dancer working for the Theater Owners Booking Association, a vaudeville circuit featuring African-American artists in the 1920s and 1930s. Young Parker showed no real musical aptitude until the age of thirteen, when he started playing alto sax. He quit school the following year and began gigging with youth bands before graduating to the professional league. He moved to the Big Apple in 1939. At first he had to work a variety of odd jobs—including street performing—to pay the bills.

Before long, Parker had developed a breakthrough, original melodic style, distinguished by a revolutionary use of harmonics and chord intervals. Parker was being noticed and was in demand. Soon he was an integral part of the jazz scene in New York, and he was given a cool new moniker to match: "Bird," affectionately shortened from his childhood nickname, "Yardbird."

Parker played with a number of notable bands, led by such jazz greats as Buster Smith, Jay McShann, Earl Hines, and Bill Eckstine. But it was Parker's friendship with trumpeter Dizzy Gillespie that led to perhaps his greatest creative collaboration. Although their new sound had its antecedents, Parker's expressive improvisation and musical experimentation led to a fast-tempo jazz, filled with eighth notes, heavy rhythm, irregular phrasing, and unusual chromatic scales. The style acquired its own name: bebop, or bop. (Gillespie claimed to have coined the term; Parker never used it.)

Parker continued to tour, both with Gillespie and other bands. In 1946, while playing in Los Angeles, Parker had a breakdown, caused by his heroin addiction and alcoholism. He spent six months in a state mental hospital before being released, but he was never completely clean.

Parker formed a quintet and went back on the road. Musical milestones continued to pile up, including a legendary

1947 concert at Carnegie Hall. He was also composing, often naming pieces after his sobriquet—works like "Ornithology," "Chasin' the Bird," and "Bird's Nest." Some of his most popular, though atypical, recordings were made in 1949 and 1950: a series of popular songs with virtuoso saxophone breaks, all backed by strings. His stature in the jazz world was unquestioned. When a nightclub opened at 1678 Broadway in 1949, it named itself Birdland after the superstar and invited Parker to be its first headliner.

(In 1952 jazz pianist George Shearing and lyricist George David Weiss made the nitery internationally famous when they composed the hit song "Lullaby of Birdland." The location of Birdland Jazz Club has changed over the years, but it still exists. Currently, it's at 315 West Forty-fourth Street in midtown Manhattan.)

By the 1950s Parker's excessive drinking and drug use began to take a toll on his body, resulting in ulcers and cirrhosis of the liver. He began to miss dates and would sometimes be unable to pay his musicians. At one point he was barred from playing in New York City clubs for fifteen months, so he went on the road and recorded.

If his professional life and his health were in turmoil, he entered one of the most tranquil periods in his personal life. In 1950 Parker moved into a ground-floor apartment in a four-story row house located at 151 Avenue B in the East Village. Living with him in the Gothic Revival–style building, built in 1849, were his wife Chan and their three children. Within the confines of the apartment, Bird tried to live a "normal" existence, if such a thing was possible for a jazz musician of his stature. Sunday dinners with the family were sacrosanct; Parker would come to the table in coat and tie. Jam sessions were usually held elsewhere, and fellow musicians knew better than to ask to crash there overnight. Parker could often be seen walking the street out front, alone or with his family, and he frequently ducked into Tompkins Square Park, which was right across the street.

On Wednesday, March 9, 1955, before departing for a gig in Boston, Parker visited a friend and patron, the jazz aficionado Baroness Nica de Koenigswater. A descendant of the Rothschild family, the baroness was living at the Hotel Stanhope at 995 Fifth Avenue. During the stopover Parker became so ill that Nica called a doctor who had offices in the building. The physician urged the musician to enter a hospital, but he refused. The baroness insisted that Bird not leave for Boston until he had recovered, and he agreed to stay. After rallying for a time, Parker died around 8:15 on the night of March 12 while quietly watching television. The immediate cause of death was listed as lobar pneumonia, but the musician's preexisting conditions (including, at one point, a heart attack) and his continued consumption of alcohol and narcotics all contributed to his eventual and not-unexpected early demise. Bird's body was so ravished from a lifetime of abuse that the coroner who examined him estimated Parker to be fifty-three years old. He was thirty-four.

Some theorize that many ghosts return to the mortal world because their time on earth was cut short. They died too soon to fulfill their promise. On the surface, that would not seem to be the case for Charlie Parker. The Bird is still held in awe and is remembered by the many dazzling recordings he left behind. But who knows what other heights the man might have reached?

Others suggest that spirits return to places where they felt most comfortable while alive. Is it any wonder, then, that Charlie Parker's apparition has been reported walking the blocks of Avenue B in front of his former home? The phantom has also been seen in Tompkins Square Park itself, either sauntering down the trails or sitting on a park bench. Whenever he's spotted or recognized, however, he instantly disappears.

There's been talk of his phantom materializing inside his old apartment, but the rumors have been dismissed by the building's current owner and resident, Judy Rhodes. And she should know! A lifelong jazz fan and former concert promoter, she bought the house in 1979 when she was in her late forties. She's had plenty of time to spot Parker if he had ever turned up. In 2010 Rhodes completely refurbished the exterior of the brownstone, returning it to its look when Parker lived there in the '50s.

In 1992 the three blocks of Avenue B between Seventh and Tenth Street were officially renamed Charlie Parker Place in his honor. A year later the first annual Charlie Parker Jazz Festival was held in Tompkins Square Park. In 1994 Bird's former home on Avenue B was placed on the National Register of Historic Places, and in 1999 it was named a New York City Landmark. Finally, in 2011, a small brass plaque was fixed to the outside wall of the house, identifying it as the onetime residence of the jazz great. If you pause to read the sign, don't be surprised if you feel a chill pass behind you. The Bird himself may be walking by.

# Chapter 23
# The Banshees at the Bowery

## The Bowery Hotel
## 335 Bowery

*Even though the Bowery Hotel didn't open its doors until 2007, the deluxe accommodations already have a few otherworldly guests. And who knows what causes the elevator to act up in the dead of night? Is it possible some of the spirits "living" in the cemetery next door have wandered over?*

Michael couldn't get the song out of his head.

> The Bowery! The Bowery!
> They say such things and they do such things,
> On the Bowery! The Bowery!
> I'll never go there anymore!

The Charles H. Hoyt tune came from a long-forgotten Broadway show, *A Trip to Chinatown*, which ran way back in 1891. But for Michael it was almost impossible to go through that part of the city without humming a few bars. And on this visit it was happening much more often than usual because he was staying at the new Bowery Hotel.

As recently as twenty years earlier, Michael wouldn't have wanted to stay overnight in the neighborhood. It might not have been safe. But fortunately that no longer seemed to be the case.

Dutch colonists first settled in the area back in the 1600s. Indeed, Bowery means "farm" in the original Dutch. Bowery, the street, was originally a Lenape footpath long before Europeans came to the New World, and at one time the trail extended the length of the entire island, north to south. Prior to 1807 settlers referred to the track as Bowery Lane.

Beginning around 1654, houses were built on former farmland in the Chatham Square section of the Bowery as the gentry moved north. The trend continued through the 1700s as taverns, shops, and theaters were also established. By the 1800s even the Astors had moved into the area. The four borders of the Bowery generally came to be accepted as East Fourth Street to the north, Canal Street to the South, Allen Street to the east, and, of course Bowery to the west.

By the time of the Civil War, the district had undergone an alarming change. Prosperous families no longer found the East Side fashionable, and they left in droves. What was left behind were mainly tenements, flophouses, brothels, bars, dance halls, and second-rate music halls. Street crime increased, and one of America's earliest gangs took root: the anti-Catholic, anti-Irish Bowery Boys.

Through the first half of the twentieth century, the Bowery got worse. To add insult to injury, from 1878 to 1955 the Third Avenue El ran above Bowery, casting the sidewalks into shadow on even the brightest days. The streets became a haven for prostitutes, bums, and the homeless, and by the 1970s "the Bowery" had become synonymous with "Skid Row" in New York City. As gentrification came to the Lower East Side in the 1990s, the Bowery began to feel its effects. Although the Bowery isn't yet as upscale as some of the rest of the East Village, it has certainly been revitalized.

In 2007 two high-end hoteliers, Eric Goode and Sean MacPherson, decided to take a chance on the rapidly evolving quarter and built an opulent seventeen-story, 135-room boutique hotel smack dab in the middle of the Bowery. Four years earlier the pair had renovated the National Maritime Union building in Chelsea, making it into the glamorous Maritime Hotel, and in 2006 they helped transform a West Village coach house into the now-trendy Waverly Inn. They would later turn the Hotel Riverview into the luxurious Jane Hotel. As opposed to the Maritime and Jane, the Bowery Hotel was built from scratch.

As he headed toward the elevator, Michael could hardly tell the place was brand new. Everything looked as if it had come from an earlier, more sumptuous era. The spacious lobby, broken up by leather screens into discreet seating nooks, was paneled with dark woods and filled with potted palms, Edwardian furniture, Art Deco knickknacks, and Oriental carpets, all set off by a warm fireplace. The hallway to the lift was dimly lit for mood and had floors that seemed to be Moroccan tiles.

Michael had no idea what to expect as he rode up to his room. What could four hundred dollars get you in New York these days? Would the room live up to the expectations created by the lobby? He fingered the old-fashioned, tasseled metal key to his room in anticipation.

His first instinct upon opening the door was that the room was sizable but not overly spacious, but then it *was* New York. Space was at a premium. The room had a generous bed—with a ridiculously high thread count on the sheets, he would discover—Oushak carpets over hardwood floors, a couple of plushy cushioned chairs, a marble-topped table, and all of the high-end amenities one would expect from a four- or five-star hotel. What immediately sold Michael on the room, however, was the bank of incredible floor-to-ceiling windows. During the day sunlight streamed into the room, and at night his unimpeded view of the city, all the way up to the Empire State Building, was breathtakingly spectacular.

The hotel also lived up to its reputation if you were into stargazing. A veritable A-list of movie actors, musicians, fashionistas, and trendsetters regularly walked through its doors. Most nights Michael was sure the people sitting at the tables next to his in the hotel's Gemma restaurant were famous, even if he couldn't put names to their faces.

Sitting in the restaurant veranda for breakfast the last morning of his stay, Michael looked down to a grassy, open plot of land directly adjacent to the hotel. When he looked closer, he realized it was a neatly tended cemetery.

When Michael later asked about it, the concierge immediately became apologetic—that is, until he realized Michael had no problem with a graveyard being next door. It turned out that the New York Marble Cemetery, as it was known, was founded in 1830. The burial ground is almost completely hidden from view these days, taking up the interior of a block bordered by East Second and Third Streets, Second Avenue, and Bowery. Its only entrance is a gate at 41–43 Second Avenue.

(A similarly named graveyard located one block east, the New York City Marble Cemetery, is much more visible to passersby. Both burial grounds were named New York City Landmarks in 1969 and were added to the National Register of Historic Places in 1980.)

Three partners, Perkins Nichols and lawyers Anthony Dey and George W. Strong, created the New York Marble Cemetery as a commercial, nonsectarian venture in 1830. At the time the land was at the northern edge of the city. Yellow fever had recently decimated New York, and earthen burials had been outlawed. New York Marble Cemetery offered interment in belowground vaults. There were 156 barrel vaults in all, none of which were marked with monuments on the lawn. Eventually there were more than 2,100 burials on the site, mostly from merchant and professional class families. Perhaps the cemetery's most famous "resident" is Charles Scribner, who cofounded the publishing company that evolved into Charles Scribner's Sons.

Michael desperately wanted to visit the graveyard before he left town, but there wasn't time. Unfortunately the place was locked up tight, and from what the concierge could tell, from April to October visitors were only allowed onto the grounds on the last Sunday of the month, though occasionally people did seem to be there on other weekends as well.

"I don't know what you're looking for," the concierge cautioned with a sly smile, "but the cemetery isn't haunted." He leaned forward and whispered conspiratorially, "We have their ghosts over here."

Michael was dumbstruck. The Bowery Hotel was haunted? But the place had just opened. It hadn't had time to develop its own coterie of spirits. As for spectres drifting over from the cemetery next door, that sort of thing only happens in the movies. Doesn't it?

There are those who say otherwise.

Rumor has it that the apparition of a woman with brown eyes and wearing a white dress roams the hallway on the second floor. Because there's nothing to link her to any of the guests who have stayed at the hotel during its few years of operation, some have suggested that she had to be a spirit moonlighting from New York Marble Cemetery.

There's another unusual, possibly paranormal, phenomenon that takes place in the hotel: The elevator sometimes goes crazy, either starting without being called or stopping on floors despite no buttons having been pushed. The antics usually take place between the hours of 1 a.m. and 2 a.m. Supposedly there are other unexplainable electrical disturbances throughout the building, most of which also occur in the wee hours of the morning. They, too, have been blamed on wandering spirits.

Despite having been titillated by the possibility of running into a ghost, Michael never did get to see one. At least not on that visit. He knew there'd always be another chance. The Bowery Hotel had won him over, and he'd be coming back when he returned to the city. And next time he'd ask for a room on the second floor.

## Chapter 24

# As Luck Would Have It

### KGB Bar
### 85 East Fourth Street

*The brick building at 85 East Fourth Street, home of the KGB Bar, has played host to a number ghosts, from a Mephisthophelean face in a mirror to a nameless spirit on the staircase. Then there are the unaccountable accidents, grisly murders, and mysterious deaths that have occurred there.*

Ryan was not a Communist. Nor was he a Socialist. But there was no way he could tag along with his cousin Jack to try out a saloon they had heard about in the East Village. Ryan, a liberal Democrat, was running for office, and he knew what the right-wingers—not to mention the rabid tabloid press—would say if he were seen in a place called the KGB Bar. According to an old maxim, a politician can survive anything except being caught in bed with a teenage boy or a dead hooker. Ryan figured being photographed in a bar with KGB in its name might run a close third.

Fortunately Jack had no such constraints. All he knew was the bar sponsored readings by writers who hung out at the club, so as an author himself he thought he should check it out. The place had quite a history. At one time, a wooden tenement stood on the site. The house collapsed in 1882, killing thirty-one Italian immigrants. The lot was cleared, but it stood empty for twenty years.

Frank Conroy built the current four-story structure. For years afterward, the place seemed jinxed. In 1908 Conroy's wife hanged herself in the building while grieving for the couple's only son, a young boy who had died after falling down the stairs. Two years later, on July 31, 1910, a scab textile worker named Herman Liebowitz attended a union meeting in the building to apologize for crossing a picket line. He was thanked by being beaten to death and dumped on the sidewalk out front.

On July 11, 1912, a rent boy named Toby was found on the stoop, dazed and confused and covered in blood. He was also holding a man's severed hand. Seven years later Rebecca Mittlebaum, a mentally challenged immigrant, was raped in her upstairs apartment. She managed to kill her assailant, nearly decapitating him in the process. Then in 1928 Frances Green, a female prostitute, was murdered in a gangland speakeasy on the second floor.

The saloon was run by Charlie "Lucky" Luciano, who became the father of organized crime in America in the 1930s by bringing warring mob families together under his leadership to work in their common interest. People say he got his nickname as a teenager because he was so good at avoiding arrest. More likely it dates to a 1929 attack in which he was forced into a limo, beaten, stabbed, and left for dead along the waterfront. But he was "lucky." Somehow he survived.

Luciano's early rise came during the Prohibition years. By 1921 he was running a bootlegging operation throughout the Northeast. One of his New York speakeasies was the one located on the second floor of 85 East Third, a bar and gambling joint called the Palm Casino. During the club's heyday, bribes and kickbacks to police and politicians helped keep the place open. When Prohibition ended in 1933, business waned. By then Lucky had bigger fish to fry, and at some point the bar closed.

In 1948 the building became the Ukrainian Labor Home, a sort of fraternal club for Ukrainian Socialists, but the place kept its political interests on the Q.T. It was the McCarthy era, after all. The first floor was made into a giant hall, about one hundred feet long by twenty feet wide. The space was used for meetings, dances, and dinners. The shuttered Palm Casino upstairs was transformed into a bar with a small kitchen.

In the 1980s lawyer Denis Woychuk, who had visited the place with his father as a boy, rented the first floor to open an art gallery. By the early 1990s the Kraine Gallery, as he had named it, was out of business, but then the barroom upstairs became available. In 1993 Woychuk opened a new saloon on the second story. With a nod to the building's notorious past as a den for radicals, he wanted to call it KGB. When state officials objected, he told them the appellation was short for Kraine Gallery Bar, so his application was finally approved. Up went the decorations, from red walls lined with Marxist propaganda posters and lithographs of Lenin to a Communist flag hanging over the bar.

In 1994 KGB began an authors' reading series, and it's been going on ever since. Sunday was set aside for fiction, Monday for poetry, and Tuesday through Thursday became a hodgepodge, catch as catch can. It was the promise of a fun evening among kindred spirits that drew Jack to the bar. He wrote true crime, both histories and biographies, and he thought that it might be apropos to read a couple of passages from one of his books about the early days of the Mafia.

Jack had settled at a table comfortably far enough away from, but with a full view of, the "stage." The atmosphere was exactly what he had hoped it would be, and waiting for the first author to take the mic, he had already decided he wanted to come back to read.

As he mulled over the possibilities, he noticed a man, all alone, leaning against the wall on the opposite side of the room. The guy had on a broad pinstriped suit, spats, and a black fedora tilted low over his brow. Jack laughed silently to himself. Talk about dressing the part! But it wasn't just the dated wardrobe that drew Jack's attention. There was something else.

When the recognition came, it almost knocked Jack out of his chair. The guy was a dead ringer for Lucky Luciano! Dead ringer indeed: The mobster died all the way back in 1962.

The author's mind began to race. He knew the bar he was sitting in was Luciano's speakeasy in the 1920s. Also, while researching one of his books, Jack had run across a stray tidbit: Lucky Luciano's ghost supposedly showed up in the East Village Music Store when it was located on the ground floor of the building. Jack remembered being amused at the time. Why would the gangster's ghost come back to peruse the dozens of new and used musical instruments on display? Was he shopping for a violin case to hold his Tommy gun?

Regardless, with the music store now located down on East Third Street, Luciano's spirit apparently was coming back to his old nightclub when he visited the building. He must have been surprised the first time he showed up, Jack mused. The red banners and Marxist portraitures certainly weren't part of the decorative motif when Lucky was there in the '20s. But the place was packed, and the liquor flowed freely, just as it did in the old days.

And, Jack figured, Luciano's ghost could get away with haunting the place without anyone knowing. All these years later, his face wouldn't be familiar to the general public.

"Can I get you anything?"

Jack was startled by the server's voice. He'd been so busy covertly scrutinizing the stranger that he hadn't seen the waiter walk up to him.

"Uh, yeah. I'll take another beer. Say, do you see that guy over there?" Jack motioned over to the man he'd been studying, who somehow had sunk further into the shadows. "He looks familiar. Do you know him?"

"Which guy? Where?"

Jack panicked. Was it possible the server couldn't see him? Was he the only one able to make out the ghost?

But his fear ended when the waiter replied offhandedly, "Oh, yeah, him. Johnny. He's one of the writers, or tries to be. He gets up every so often with some of his stuff. It's not bad. But I doubt if you would know him. I mean, he's not famous or anything."

Relieved, Jack watched the server as he headed back to the bar to fill his order. How could he have thought, even for an instant, that some random person was a ghost—no matter how much he resembled one?

Jack's story is a cautionary tale. Many times people convince themselves that a place is haunted when no ghosts exist. In Jack's case there *were* rumors Luciano's spectre had appeared in East Village Music when it was located downstairs. But the apparition has never turned up in EastVille Comedy Club, which took over the ground level after the shop's departure.

That being said, ghosts have been known to return after a long dry spell.

So far there haven't been any reports that the phantom floated up to KGB on the second floor. But, again, never say never. The crime boss *might* drop in someday, but for now the place seems to be free of spirits—if you don't count the alcoholic kind sitting behind the bar.

Of course, that doesn't mean the rest of the building isn't haunted.

Over the years there have been more than forty sightings of Frank Conroy on the pavement outside the building. Inside, a headless phantom—Rebecca Mittlebaum's attacker?—has been spotted skulking around in dimly lit corners.

A spectre that's been seen floating up and down the interior stairwell for about twenty years was finally captured in a 1949 photograph. The translucent white form is indistinct, so it's impossible to identify the phantom. Could be it one of the Conroys or possibly Frances Green? Or maybe someone else entirely?

A few phantoms have been invited into the building voluntarily. In the 1920s a vaudeville magician and mind reader named the Great Alexander lived on the top floor. Billed as "The Man Who Knows," Alexander held weekly séances in his darkened chambers. Apparently on at least one occasion an actual spirit came through—much to the surprise of the startled prestidigitator.

Perhaps the creepiest haunting at 85 West Third concerns a large mirror located on the stairwell landing outside the KGB Bar. Patrons who stop to check themselves are sometimes in for a shock. Every so often a shadowy figure with burning red eyes stares back at them from the other

side of the glass. One woman ran out of the building screaming that the leering face was that of Satan himself!

Scrying, a form of fortunetelling in which seers concentrate on shiny surfaces such as crystals, polished wood, or
water to receive their messages, has been practiced since
ancient times. Today it's much more common for clairvoy-
ants adept in scrying to use a crystal ball.

Some soothsayers say they see images on the reflec-
tive surfaces; others use them as focal points to clear their
minds so that the spirit communications can seep into
their consciousness.

Likewise, ghost lore is filled with examples of faces or
other ethereal figures appearing in a mirror. One of the oldest
is the story of Snow White, in which the Evil Queen possesses
a Magic Mirror. Who can't recite the rhyme chanted to the
looking glass in the classic Grimm fairy tale?

Mirror, mirror, on the wall,
Who in this land is fairest of all?

The most typical haunting associated with a mirror has
people catching an unexpected reflection out of the corner
of their eyes as they walk by. If the person stops and faces
the mirror, the image is gone. The phantom in the glass is
almost always someone the person knows, and invariably
the spectral individual is deceased.

In another common scenario, while a person is looking into a mirror someone walks up from behind and peers
over his or her shoulder. Or the individual may spot the
reflection of somebody standing elsewhere in the room. In
either case, when the person spins to see who's there, he
or she is alone.

Perhaps the most famous haunted mirror in existence is owned by the Roosevelt Hotel in Hollywood, California. According to legend, a maid was cleaning a tall vertical mirror in one of the suites when she saw a beautiful blonde woman with a distinctive beauty mark come up behind her. The cleaner instantly recognized the newcomer: It was Marilyn Monroe. But the domestic couldn't believe her eyes, because she knew the sex symbol was long dead. When she turned to confront the ghostly intruder, the spectre was gone. News of the encounter soon leaked out. Rather than deny the rumors, for about two decades the hotel kept the "haunted mirror" on public display, first by the downstairs elevators, then on the mezzanine overlooking the lobby. It was never labeled, but fans of the paranormal could always find it. The mirror was taken down a few years ago when the hotel underwent renovations, and it's been in storage ever since.

Maybe you'll have more luck catching an apparition in the KGB mirror if it's still there when you visit. It stands about seven feet tall, so it's hard to miss. No one remembers where the mirror came from. The accepted theory is that immigrants escaping Czarist Russia brought it with them when they moved to New York. But is it actually Lucifer inside the looking glass? Or some nameless person who has passed through the building? Who can tell?

Even if the looking glass ghost doesn't materialize, never fear. There are ghosts everywhere in the building!

# Chapter 25

# The Spinster Spirit

## Merchant's House Museum
## 29 East Fourth Street

*Gertrude, the resident ghost at the Merchant's House Museum in the East Village, isn't too thrilled about people touching the original Federal-era furnishings. While she lived there—for ninety-three years—she liked things in their place. That hasn't changed now that she's returned to take up her spectral residency.*

This time Jamie had to get it right. His last show, a new musical comedy based on the movie *Psycho,* had been an unmitigated disaster. It had seemed a good idea at the time. Well, if truth be told, he knew it was a *terrible* idea, but when he was asked he didn't have anything else on the horizon. And work *was* work.

But really. *Psycho?* The whole time he had been working on the show he couldn't get those shrieking chords from the Bernard Hermann film score out of his brain, even though they were never used in the Broadway score. (Maybe, Jamie figured, it was too hard to come up with lyrics for them.)

Perhaps they could have worked out the kinks in the show if they had opened out of town. But the novice producers hoped to get a buzz going on the Main Stem by starting previews cold. Well, the plan worked, but it wasn't the buzz they were hoping for. In fact, bad word of mouth was being tweeted by the intermission of the first preview.

When the show finally opened, the critics panned everything about it, including Jamie's minimalist set designs—
which the director had insisted be made up primarily of
plastic shower curtains. Hundreds of them!

The sad thing was, Jamie knew the concept wasn't going
to work from the start. He could have fought the director;
he could have quit. But, no, he acquiesced.

Fortunately Jamie wasn't being blamed for the show's
failure. (Songs such as "Knife to Know You," "Mother Lover,"
and "Rocking Chair Blues" took care of that.) In the end, to
paraphrase the old Gay Nineties ballad, Jamie was more to
be pitied than censured.

So Jamie was thrilled when another tentative offer
quickly came his way. And like manna from Heaven, it was a
drama that required a realistic set: a major regional revival
of *The Heiress*. The play, written by Ruth and Augustus
Goetz and based on the 1880 Henry James novel *Washington
Square,* had first been produced in 1947.

The single room in which all of the onstage action
occurs is described in the script as "the front parlor of Doctor Sloper's house in Washington Square. 1850." There were
no specifics as to how it should be decorated, so Jamie had
lots of possibilities. All he had to do was come up with an
accurate design for the drawing room of an upper-class New
York family in the mid-nineteenth century.

Fortunately it was pretty simple to get an idea of what
the average parlor of the era looked like. Illustrated books
and photographs abound.

But the devil is always in the details. And he knew that,
even with such a conventional setting, there were many
ways it could go horribly wrong. One of the things Jamie
feared most was an anachronism—putting some item in the

room, such as a type of lampshade or divan, that didn't exist in the 1850s. And Jamie also wanted to make sure that he didn't accidentally duplicate the design of some previous production of the show.

An old theater joke goes: "How do you get to Carnegie Hall? Practice." Well, Jamie knew that instead of practice, his discipline required research. And lots of it.

The first obvious point of reference would be the 1949 William Wyler film. Shot two years after the opening of the Broadway show, the movie's screenplay was by the same writers, so there were bound to be many similarities between the two scripts. Also, Harry Horner, production designer, and Emile Kuri, set decorator, both won Academy Awards for their work on *The Heiress*.

But film and stage are two different mediums. Things that look great on screen might not read well from the seats in a darkened theater.

At first Jamie didn't think he had a ghost of a chance of finding out what the sets looked like in the various Broadway incarnations. But then he remembered the New York Public Library for the Performing Arts housed at Lincoln Center. A vital repository of books, playbills, posters, artist sketches, manuscripts, scripts, pictures—well, you name it—Lincoln Center holds more than five million pieces of theater ephemera in its collection. With financial assistance from major donors, the library is also able to shoot archival videos of several Broadway shows each season.

With a quick phone call, Jamie discovered that the library had a box full of black-and-white press photographs from all four of the New York productions in its Billy Rose Theatre collection. It also had a videotape of the 1995 revival! Surely some of them showed the sets.

Excited about the prospect of getting to leaf through the material, Jamie checked the visiting hours. He had forgotten: The stuff he wanted to see wasn't sitting out on the stacks. Access—especially permission to screen the videotapes—was restricted to theater professionals with a valid reason to view it. Not only that, it was only available by reservation.

His bona fides would allow to him to see the press pix and the archival footage without any problem. A quick call to the library secured him a slot for the next afternoon.

Swearing the staffer to secrecy, Jamie described his new project. The *Heiress* revival he'd be working on was long rumored—nothing spreads faster than theater gossip—but the production hadn't been formally announced. Also, nothing was signed, so the whole thing might never materialize.

"In the meantime, have you checked out the Old Merchant's House?" the librarian asked. "It's open as a museum, and it dates to the exact period you're researching. And here's a fun fact: The family that lived there may have been the inspiration for the original novel."

No more than an hour later, Jamie was standing in front of the six steps leading up to the museum's front door.

Located on East Fourth Street in the East Village, the Merchant's House Museum was built as a private residence by Joseph Brewster, a hatter, in 1832. The architect, Minard Lafever, designed the redbrick and white marble row house with a late-Federal style exterior and a Greek Revival interior. The five-story building has a ground floor (part of which is below street level), a parlor floor, two bedroom levels, and a "dormer," where the servants lived. There are also a small attic and a cellar.

In 1835 Seabury Tredwell, a prosperous hardware merchant, bought the house for $18,000. It remained the family's home for the next ninety-eight years. And most exciting of all to Jamie: The inside of the house looked almost exactly the same as it did in the 1850s, including all the original furnishings, which were the most elegant for its time. It is the sole surviving home from that period in New York City, which is why it's a National Historic Landmark and has been on the US National Register of Historic Places for more than a decade.

The area in which the house is located was one of the most fashionable districts in the city, known as the Bond Street area, when Tredwell moved from across town with his wife Eliza. They had a large family—six daughters and two sons. Tredwell was a hard man, and a strict disciplinarian. The sons didn't follow into the family business and never made a name for themselves in society. Two of the daughters married well enough, but four were still living at home when their father passed away.

It was the youngest daughter's story that caught Jamie's attention. Gertrude, or Gittie as she was sometimes called when she was a child, was born in an upstairs bedroom in 1904. According to an old wives' tale, she fell hopelessly in love with a medical student named Louis Walton. Gertrude pled with her father to allow them to marry, but the old man adamantly refused. Tredwell believed the young man was beneath the successful businessman's station and was simply after the family fortune. Complicating matters, the boy was Irish while Tredwell was proud of his English heritage. Plus the young man was Catholic, and they were staunch Episcopalians. With her suitor dispatched and no other prospects on the horizon, Gertrude never married. She stayed on with her father, inheriting the family manse after his death.

It was the central plot of *Washington Square,* Jamie marveled—that is, if the story were true. Unfortunately, as he learned from a docent shortly after entering the house, the oft-told tale about Gertrude's young physician has never been verified, and in recently discovered letters Henry James names a British heiress, not Gertrude and her father, as the model for his novel.

Besides, Gertrude's saga had a very different ending than the book. At the time of her father's death in 1865, Gertrude was living there with her mother and four of her sisters. Over time, they passed away one by one. Her sister Phoebe didn't die until 1907 at the age of seventy-eight. But finally there was only Gertrude, living as a recluse. She stayed there long after the neighborhood worsened and despite numerous offers to buy the property. She seldom strayed from the house and, except for a few minor concessions for comfort, never remodeled it. And she threw almost nothing out!

In 1933, when Gertrude died just shy of her ninety-third birthday, the house and everything in it passed into the hands of her mother's grand-nephew, a New York attorney named George Chapman. He immediately recognized the historical importance of the place, and he spent three years readying it as a museum.

Jamie was glad Chapman had opened it to the public. The place was a visual feast! Experiencing the house in three dimensions was infinitely better than checking out old photographs in the library or watching movies featuring other designers' work. Here was the real deal for him to study! The museum held more than three thousand items in its collection, from furniture, fixtures, books, china, draperies, and gas chandeliers to the family's personal possessions, including more than forty of the women's dresses and accessories. He couldn't take it all in.

Jamie wandered into the immense double parlor, immediately noting that it was more than twice the size of the room he'd have to design. (Upon more careful examination, he realized that they were two rooms connected by sliding doors, separating them into a front parlor and a rear sitting room that doubled as the formal dining room.) As Jamie reached the curved landing on the staircase leading up to the second floor, he couldn't help but notice the short, elderly woman wearing a long, light brown taffeta gown at the top of the steps. *She must be a costumed docent,* Jamie thought. Great! Perhaps she could answer a few questions he had about the decor.

As he reached the top step, Jamie caught a glimmer of the woman as she entered one of the front bedrooms. He hastened his step, turned into the room, and—nothing! There was no one there. The room was filled with all the expected furnishings: the canopy bed, the nightstand, the mirror, the curtains. But the mysterious stranger—Gertrude—was gone.

Jamie was not alone in what he encountered. People had been seeing the apparition of a woman at the house, presumed to be Gertrude, even before the museum opened. Perhaps the first sighting was by children who were playing a bit too noisily on the sidewalk outside the building a few days after Gertrude's death. The kids were startled when a petite woman of a certain age abruptly opened the front door to the empty mansion and brusquely shooed them away.

To this day Gertrude's apparition appears by the fireplace in the parlor, on the staircase, and by her bed on the second level. Sometimes visitors don't see her, but they feel a cold spot by the bed or notice a depression in the bedspread as if someone were lying there. The spirit becomes particularly active when any renovation or restoration is taking place in the house. It seems she likes things "just so."

Of course, the hauntings might not always be Gertrude. Staff members report having experienced paranormal activity all over the house, and they are convinced that Gertrude now shares her home with several other spirits.

As they walk through the house, museum guests sometimes have the sensation that an invisible presence is watching them, or they feel a spectre as it passes by. A favorite area for ghostly encounters is the kitchen and throughout the rear of the house. White, wispy shafts of light have been captured on film in the back bedroom on the second floor. For some time in the 1950s, caretakers heard raps coming from inside the wall in one of the other bedrooms. To this day piano music is sometimes heard in the parlor, though no one is ever at the instrument's keyboard. Electrical equipment throughout the place will go on the fritz. The scent of unseen fresh flowers, violet toilet water, and bread baking occasionally wafts in the air. Small objects tend to move or become lost, only to be found later in other parts of the house, and the dining room door sometimes opens on its own. Now and then the footsteps of two or three people— soft as those of small children—are heard running down an empty corridor or on the stairs. Have Gertrude's sisters returned as well? And museum staffers have now begun to see the apparitions of servants, especially since their former living quarters on the fifth floor have been opened to visitors. Seabury Tredwell himself is said to have turned up from time to time.

Still, most of spectral doings are chalked up to Gertrude. After all, she lived there for almost a century. What are a few more years?

# Appendix A
# Ghost Writers

There are hundreds of hauntings occurring all over New York City, and a disproportionate number of sightings take place in Greenwich Village. It's possible to find both the legendary and modern encounters described in detail in books, magazines, and on the Internet. In addition to those sources, there are numerous books about the early years of Manhattan—and Washington Square and the Village in particular. What follows in this appendix is a representative sampling. All of these titles should be available (albeit with a little hunting in some cases), either in a bookshop, on loan from your library, or online.

Throughout my research I've consulted dozens of websites, too numerous to mention, primarily for historical information about the haunted sites and the areas in which they're located. But I include here several metasites that contain directories of haunted locations and provide links to other Internet sites dealing with ghosts, the occult, and the unexplained. Any official sites of individual venues are noted in Appendix B, "Haunted Hangouts."

## BOOKS

Adams III, Charles J. *New York City Ghost Stories*. Reading, PA: Exeter House Books, 1996. Adams is a man of many hats. Hailing from Reading, Pennsylvania, he's a longtime broadcaster on the city's WEEU radio station and is the chief travel writer for the *Reading Eagle* newspaper. He's also authored more than a dozen books on folklore and ghost stories from the Pennsylvania–New Jersey–Delaware region. This book on Manhattan spirits hits all the highlights of Greenwich Village ghostdom.

Bartell, Jan Bryant. *Spindrift: Spray from a Psychic Sea.* Portland, OR: Hawthorne Books, 1974. A memoir by Jan Bartell, published posthumously, about the twelve years of paranormal experiences she and her husband endured while living at the haunted "Mark Twain House" in Greenwich Village.

Beauvoir, Simone de. *America Day by Day.* New York: Grove Press, 1953. Originally published in French as *L'Amérique au jour de jour.* First published in English by G. Duckworth of London. The journal covers the author's observations during her four months of travel in the United States in early 1947.

*Flashmaps! Instant Guide to New York.* Toy Lasker, ed. Chappaqua, NY: Flashmaps Publications, 1969. A pocket-size directory of Manhattan filled with street and subway maps as well as locations of the major tourist sites, theaters, churches, restaurants, schools, and other venues. Includes separate maps of Greenwich Village, Midtown, Lower Manhattan, and other sections of the city.

*Fodor's Flashmaps New York City,* 9th Edition: The Ultimate Map Guide/Find it in a Flash. New York: Random House, 2008. The most recent update of the reliable perennial.

Folpe, Emily Kies. *It Happened on Washington Square.* Baltimore, MD: The Johns Hopkins University Press, 2002. A thorough, eminently readable account of the history and denizens of the Greenwich Village landmark.

Goetz, Ruth and Augustus. *The Heiress*. New York: Dramatists Play Service, 1998. A theatrical adaptation of *Washington Square,* the 1880 Henry James novel. The play had its Broadway premiere at the Biltmore Theatre on September 29, 1947, starring Basil Rathbone as the father, Wendy Hiller as his daughter, and Peter Cookson as her scheming suitor.

Guiley, Rosemary Ellen. *The Encyclopedia of Ghosts and Spirits*. New York: Facts on File, 1992. This enduring one-volume encyclopedia is a "must" in any ghost hunter's collection. Its hundreds of entries, mostly regarding hauntings in America and the United Kingdom, are augmented by articles about central figures in paranormal research and Spiritualism.

Harris, Luther S. *Around Washington Square: An Illustrated History of Greenwich Village*. Baltimore, MD: The Johns Hopkins University Press, 2003. As its name suggests, this chronicle of central Greenwich Village is overflowing with fascinating period photographs of the district.

Hauck, Dennis William. *Haunted Places: The National Directory*. New York: Penguin, 1996.

———. *The International Directory of Haunted Places*. New York: Penguin, 2000. Simply stated, Hauck's national directory and its smaller international companion volume are considered to be essential classics. These invaluable volumes contain almost three thousand haunted locations, plus sites where UFOs and mysterious creatures have been encountered.

Hladik, L'Aura. *Ghosthunting New York City (America's Haunted Road Trip)*. Cincinnati, OH: Clerisy Press, 2010. Part of a new series for both the armchair and the active ghost investigator. Hladik describes her visits to thirty haunted sites scattered throughout New York City that are open to the public. Fifty additional haunted locations are listed.

Holzer, Hans. *Yankee Ghosts: Spine-Tingling Encounters with the Phantoms of New York and New England.* Emmaus, PA: Yankee Books, 1986. The self-proclaimed "Ghost Hunter" and prolific author Hans Holzer describes his paranormal investigations in the Northeast, including the brownstone at 12 Gay Street in Greenwich Village. The author of more than 140 books on ghosts and spirit activity, Holzer died April 26, 2009, at the age of eighty-nine.

—. *Great American Ghost Stories.* New York: Dorset Press, 1990. In this collection Holzer recounts his investigation of 27 Jane Street with medium Ethel Meyers.

—. *America's Haunted Houses: Public and Private.* Stamford, CT: Longmeadow Press, 1991. In one of the tales, Hans Holzer teams up once again with medium Ethel Meyers to examine the ghostly rappings and footsteps in a home at 11 Bank Street.

Horn, Stacy. *Unbelievable: Investigations into Ghosts, Poltergeists, Telepathy, and Other Unseen Phenomena from the Duke Parapsychology Laboratory.* New York: Ecco, 2010. Well-researched study of the ESP and paranormal testing by J. B. Rhine and his colleagues. The book includes a scientific look at some famous hauntings, including the Morris-Jumel Mansion. Horn also investigated the Elizabeth Bullock haunting and detailed her findings in an online article, "My Favorite

Ghost Story That Didn't Make The Book," found at www
.echonyc.com/~horn/unbelievable/?p=491.

Irving, Washington. *A History of New York.* Chicago, IL:
M. A. Donohue, 1910. Originally written under the
pseudonym Diedrich Knickerbocker. Filled with colorful
sketches of life in New Amsterdam and New York from
around 1600 to the time of the American Revolution.

James, Henry. *Washington Square.* New York: Signet
Classics, 2004. First published in 1880, the novel, set
primarily in one of the mansions lining the north
perimeter of Washington Square, tells the story of an
overbearing, disapproving father, his shy daughter, and
her conniving would-be beau.

Lanigan-Schmidt, Therese. *Ghosts of New York City.* Atglen,
PA: Schiffer Publishing, 2003. The author documents
well over a hundred haunted locations in the five
boroughs of New York City, including about two dozen
in Greenwich Village. The book has an extensive
bibliography, including firsthand correspondence and
interviews, as well as a thorough index.

Macken, Lynda Lee. *Ghostly Gotham: New York City's
Haunted History.* Forked River, NJ: Black Cat Press,
2002. Macken collects stories of spirits found all over
Manhattan, from Battery Park to Harlem Heights.

McFarland, Gerald W. *Inside Greenwich Village: A New York
City Neighborhood, 1898–1918.* Amherst: University
of Massachusetts Press, 2005. This book about the
multiethnic nature of the Village concentrates on just
twenty years at the turn of the twentieth century, a
period that includes the Triangle Shirtwaist Factory
fire and Marcel Duchamp's notorious ascent of the
Washington Square Arch.

*Merchant's House Museum Room by Room Tour Booklet.* New York: Merchant's House Museum, 2011. A twenty-eight-page monograph describing the museum's collection. Includes floor plans of the house. Available in the museum gift shop and through its website, located at www.merchantshouse.com.

Millay, Edna St. Vincent. *Renascence and Other Poems.* New York: Dover Publications, 1991. Contains the poem "The Little Ghost," written in 1917.

Miller, Terry. *Greenwich Village and How It Got That Way.* New York: Crown, 1990. This "origin story" of Greenwich Village tells the tale of its first European settlers and why the streets and lanes were laid out in such a seemingly haphazard fashion. The book also attempts to explain the attraction of the Village to artists, musicians, bohemians, and other "free-thinkers."

Norman, Michael, and Beth Scott. *Historic Haunted America.* New York: Tor Books, 2006. True ghost stories from the nation's past, including the spectre of Peter Stuyvesant that haunts St. Mark's in-the-Bowery.

Ogden, Tom. *The Complete Idiot's Guide to Ghosts and Hauntings.* Indianapolis: Alpha Books, 2004. First-person accounts of ghost sightings, many published for the first time, are interspersed among better-known paranormal legends from around the globe. Chapters are delineated by the types of venues the spirits haunt.

_____. *Haunted Theaters.* Guilford, CT: Globe Pequot Press, 2009. Thirty-five hair-raising tales of ghosts who tread the boards in playhouses and opera houses throughout the United States, Canada, and London.

_____. *Haunted Hotels.* Guilford, CT: Globe Pequot Press, 2010. Twenty-five stories of apparitions, paranormal phenomena, and other spooky goings-on at hotels, inns, and rooming houses in America and around the world.

Parks, Tara Leigh. *Ghosts of Manhattan.* Atglen, PA: Schiffer Publishing, 2008. The usual suspects along with a few surprises appear in this collection of ghostly wives' tales, including several spirits that roam the Village.

Piehler, Christopher, in collaboration with Scot Alan Evans. *The Triangle Factory Fire Project.* New York: Dramatists Play Service, 2004. Director Evans helped playwright Piehler shape this drama based on eyewitness accounts, court transcripts, and other firsthand information regarding the tragic fire at the Triangle Shirtwaist Factory on March 25, 1911.

Revai, Cheri. *Haunted New York City: Ghosts and Strange Phenomena of the Big Apple.* Mechanicsburg, PA: Stackpole Books, 2008. A collection of ghost traditions from the five boroughs of New York City.

Revai, Cheri, and Heather Adel Wiggins. *Haunted New York.* Mechanicsburg, PA: Stackpole Books, 2005. In a series of short sketches, the authors profile approximately sixty haunted sites in New York State.

Sante, Luc. *Low Life: Lures and Snares of Old New York.* New York: Vintage Books, 1992. Chronicles the underbelly of New York City's Lower East Side—the criminals, con men, prostitutes, and their ilk—from around 1840 to 1919.

Schoenberg, Dr. Philip Ernest. *Ghosts of Manhattan.* Charleston, SC: Haunted America, 2009. Schoenberg, who offers the Ghosts of New York walking tours (including a comprehensive survey of haunted spots in Greenwich Village), regales readers with lively stories about legendary haunts in the Big Apple.

*Some Say They Never Left: Tales of the Strange and Inexplicable at the Merchant's House Museum.* New York: Merchant's House Museum, 2007. Compiled by Anthony Bellov. A thirty-three-page booklet with black-and-white illustrations, published by the museum and available in its gift shop and through its website at www.merchantshouse.com.

Stonehill, Judith. *Greenwich Village: A Guide to America's Legendary Left Bank.* New York: Universe, 2002. This ninety-six-page book by a longtime president of the Greenwich Village Society for Historic Preservation concentrates on the houses, hangouts, and lives of famous Village artists and writers. It is profusely illustrated and includes four walking tours.

*Streetwise Manhattan Map.* Sarasota, FL: Streetwise Maps, 2011. A laminated, folding, pocket-size city map of Manhattan. Features the location of many city landmarks, indicated by outline drawings of the buildings. Includes bus and subway maps.

Strong, George Templeton. *Diary. Vol. 2. The Turbulent Fifties. 1850–1859.* Edited by Allan Nevins and Halsey Thomas and published in four volumes. New York: Macmillan, 1952. Strong's 2,250-page diary wasn't discovered until the 1930s. Detailed, idiosyncratic entries of the full journal cover events from 1835 to 1875.

Wetzsteon, Ross. *Republic of Dreams: Greenwich Village: The American Bohemia, 1910–1960.* New York: Simon & Schuster, 2003. This monumental 650-page work concentrates on the Village during the first half of the twentieth century as it established itself as a home to bohemians and counterculture. Wetzsteon tells his story largely through chronologically ordered biographies of some of the area's most famous—and sometimes notorious—inhabitants and habitués during that period.

## MEDIA

Berger, Meyer. "Ghostly Coincidences Puzzle Bohemian Couple in 125-Year-Old House in Greenwich Village." *New York Times,* 26 June 1957.

*The Heiress.* Originally produced and directed by William Wyler for Paramount Pictures, 1949. DVD released in 2007 by Universal Studios as part of its Universal Cinema Classics. Screenplay by Ruth and Augustus Goetz, adapted from their 1947 Broadway play. The film stars Ralph Richardson, Olivia de Havilland, and Montgomery Clift in the three central roles.

## WEBSITES

www.hauntedamericatours.com

In addition to the usual directories of haunted places, this website features original articles, top-ten lists, a store, and information about upcoming paranormal conventions. Reader comments and photographs are encouraged. As might be expected, Haunted America Tours can also help you find and book local ghost tours operated in cities across the United States.

www.haunted-places.com

An online directory of US and international hauntings. The site also provides information about books, TV shows, and radio programs devoted to the supernatural. Subscription to a newsletter, the *Haunted-Places Report,* is also available.

www.theshadowlands.net

Founded by Dave Juliano in 1994

Dave Juliano and Tina Carlson, co-directors

The Shadowlands catalogues more than thirteen thousand haunted sites from all over the world, separated by the country, state, and city in which the hauntings occur. There are capsule descriptions—usually a hundred words or less—of each location. The website also provides links to information about other unsolved mysteries, such as UFOs, Bigfoot, and the Loch Ness Monster.

# Haunted Hangouts

Feel like seeing the Greenwich Village ghosts for yourself? Here are all of the names, addresses, and other information you'll need to visit the spirit-inhabited venues in Lower Manhattan mentioned in *Haunted Greenwich Village*. Entry to some sites, such as museums, libraries, theaters, and restaurants, may be limited to those who patronize the services of the business on the premises. Many of the other venues are private residences. Please don't knock and make inquiries of those living inside. There's nothing wrong with walking by the buildings to check them out, however.

Please note that the listings given here refer to the original haunted sites. In some cases, the addresses of the structures currently standing at those locations may differ slightly. (For example, the original Francis House was at 27 Jane Street, but there is no longer a building at that street number. The apartment complex that replaced it has its entrance at 31 Jane Street.)

For those who would like to visit these venues as part of an organized group, there is a commercial walking tour available that passes many of the haunted sites in Greenwich Village.

Ghosts of New York
PO Box 656780
Flushing, NY 11365
(718) 591-4741 or (888) 699-2550
www.ghostsofny.com

Ghosts of New York, founded by Dr. Phil Schoenberg, offers five different ninety-minute walking tours in Manhattan, each of which covers about a mile. Perhaps his most popular is the stroll past the haunted sites in Greenwich Village.

## CHAPTER 1: GHOST CENTRAL STATION

Washington Square Park
Bordered by Waverly Place (also known as Washington Square North), West Fourth Street (Washington Square South), University Place (Washington Square East), and MacDougal Street (Washington Square West)
New York, NY 10012
(212) 639-9675

The unmistakable and monumental Washington Square Arch is found along the north boundary of the park, where Fifth Avenue meets Waverly Place. The old hanging grounds, including the Hangman's Elm, are located in the northwest corner of the park at West Fourth and MacDougal Streets.

## CHAPTER 2: THE SPINDRIFT SPECTRES

The Mark Twain House
14 West Tenth Street
New York, NY 10011
Private residence.

The Mark Twain House & Museum
351 Farmington Avenue
Hartford, CT 06105
(860) 247-0998
www.marktwainhouse.org

Tours times vary. In recent years there have been rumors that the house is haunted.

The Emma Lazarus House
18 West Tenth Street
New York, NY 10011
Private residence.

## CHAPTER 3: THE ASCENSION OF JOHN LAFARGE

Church of the Ascension
Fifth Avenue and West Tenth Street
New York, NY 10003
(212) 254-8620
www.ascensionnyc.org

The Church of the Ascension in New York City is located on the northwest corner of Fifth Avenue and West Tenth Street, but its offices are located in the parish house at 12 West Eleventh Street. In addition to holding regular services, the Episcopal church is open weekdays from noon to 1 p.m. for prayers and meditation and at 6 p.m. for Eucharist. The church has been recognized for its historic importance, first as a New York City Landmark in 1969, then a National Historic Landmark in 1988. This house of worship should not be confused with the Roman Catholic Church of the Ascension located on 107th Street.

The Tenth Street Studio Building
51 West Tenth Street
New York, NY 10003

The original building in which LaFarge had his workspace was razed in 1956. The apartment building that replaced it in 1958 has its entrance at 45 West Tenth Street. The new structure is not thought to be haunted.

## CHAPTER 4: THAT OLD COLLEGE SPIRIT

Brittany Residence Hall
55 East Tenth Street
New York, NY 10003

Brittany Residence Hall is the former Brittany Hotel. Visitation by residents, guests, and those on New York University business only.

## CHAPTER 5: THE TRIANGLE TERROR

Brown Building of Science
23–39 Washington Place
New York, NY 10003

At the time of the fire, the structure was known as the Asch Building. The Triangle Shirtwaist Factory was located on the eighth, ninth, and tenth floors. Visitation on New York University business only.

## CHAPTER 6: THE PHANTOM OF THE FIREHOUSE

The former Fire Patrol No. 2
84 West Third Street
New York, NY 10012

The station house for Fire Patrol No. 2 was sold in September 2009 to newscaster and television personality Anderson

Cooper. The building has undergone a complete renovation and is now a private residence.

The former Edgar Allan Poe House
85 West Third Street
New York, NY 10012

The building that is now on the site of the original Poe House is part of New York University.

Il Buco
47 Bond Street
New York, NY 10012

The source of (and rationale for) the legend connecting Edgar Allan Poe to the ghost haunting the basement of the building is unknown. There have been no recent reports of any activity.

Silver Center for Arts and Sciences
(former site of New York University's Gothic Tower)
100 Washington Square East
New York, NY 10003

Poe, Samuel Morse, and Walt Whitman used to haunt the lecture hall that stood on this site from 1837 to 1894. The current building is not haunted.

Fire Station Engine 33/Ladder 9
42 Great Jones Street
New York, NY 10012

Great Jones Street is another name for the two long blocks of Third Street between Broadway and Bowery.

## Chapter 7: Aaron Burr Returns

D'Agostino Residence Hall
110 West Third Street
New York, NY

At the southeast corner of the intersection with MacDougal Street. One of five residence halls for NYU Law School students. Visitation by residents, guests, and those on New York University business only. Its early nineteenth-century ghost has been seen all along the block of Third Street between MacDougal and Sullivan Streets, especially at the corner of Sullivan and outside the former Cafe Bizarre, which was located at 106 West Third Street. The club, along with other buildings, was torn down to make way for the residence hall.

One If By Land, Two If By Sea
17 Barrow Street
New York, NY 10014
(212) 225-8649
www.oneifbyland.com

The Morris-Jumel Mansion
65 Jumel Terrace
New York, NY 10032
(212) 923-8008
www.morrisjumel.org

The historic landmark is open 10 a.m. to 4 p.m. Wednesday through Sunday; open Monday and Tuesday by appointment. Closed major holidays. There is a nominal admission fee for the self-guided tour. Guided tours are also available.

## Chapter 8: Stage Fright

Cherry Lane Theatre
38 Commerce Street
New York, NY 10014
(212) 989-2020
www.cherrylanetheatre.com

The theater is one block south of Bleecker Street off Seventh Avenue. It houses a 179-seat main stage and a sixty-seat studio space. The Cherry Lane Theatre is New York's oldest continuously operating Off Broadway theater.

Theatre Royal, Drury Lane
Catherine Street
London, England WC2B 5JF
United Kingdom
(44) (870) 890-1109
www.reallyuseful.com/theatres/theatre-royal-drury-lane

There are daily one-hour group tours of the theater, Sunday by special arrangement. The interior visit includes backstage areas. Tickets are available at the box office or through many London ticket agencies.

Provincetown Playhouse
133 MacDougal Street
New York, NY 10012

South of the intersection with West Fourth Street (also known as Washington Square South). New York University acquired the property in the 1980s. The theater has been incorporated into a new building on the site, which is not haunted.

The website www.provincetownplayhouse.com offers historical information for the Provincetown Players and the playhouse in New York. More information is available at www.steinhardt.nyu.edu/music/facilities/provincetown.

Norma Millay Ellis house
(sometimes referred to as the Edna St. Vincent Millay House)
139 Waverly Place
New York, NY 10014
Private residence.

Steepletop
(the home of Edna St. Vincent Millay and Eugen Jan Boissevain)
PO Box 2
436 East Hill Road
Austerlitz, NY 12017
(518) 392-336

Austerlitz is approximately 135 miles north of New York City. Norma and Charlie Ellis lived in and maintained Steepletop after the poet's death. The estate is now administered by the Edna St. Vincent Millay Society, to which Norma bequeathed the grounds after her death. The place is not haunted. For visiting information, please check the tour link on the organization's website at www.millay.org/tour-information.

The former Paul Rudnick apartment
132 Waverly Place
New York, NY 10014

Private residence. There have been no recent claims concerning John Barrymore's ghost.

Little Thimble Theatre
10 Fifth Avenue
New York, NY 10011

As of this writing, a Le Pain Quotidien restaurant is located on the ground floor of the building.

The former Jean Cocteau Repertory Theatre
(located in the former Bouwerie Lane Theatre)
330 Bowery
New York, NY 10012

The building is found at the intersection of Bowery and Bond Street. Adam Gordon purchased it in 2007 for conversion into a private residence with street-level retail space.

## CHAPTER 9: THE GHOST ON GAY

The former Frank Paris residence
12 Gay Street
New York, NY 10014

Since Paris's time there, the house has had other owners and has undergone a complete interior renovation. It is a private residence.

## CHAPTER 10: THE TIMES THAT TRY MEN'S SOULS

Marie's Crisis
59 Grove Street
New York, NY 10014
(212) 243-9323

The piano bar is open daily 5:30 p.m. to 4:00 a.m.

## Chapter 11: Belly Up to the Bar

Chumley's Bar
86 Bedford Street
New York, NY 10014
www.chumleysnyc.com
Currently closed. Future uncertain.

## Chapter 12: 'Twas the Night before Haunting

The Church of Saint Luke in the Fields
487 Hudson Street
New York, NY 10014
(212) 924-0562
www.stlukeinthefields.org

## Chapter 13: Gentle into That Good Night

The White Horse Tavern
567 Hudson Street
New York, NY 10014
(212) 989-3956
www.whitehorsetavernnyc.com

The casual-dress pub is open daily from 11 a.m. to 2 a.m. (until 4 a.m. Friday and Saturday). It serves American cuisine, including classic pub staples.

Hotel Chelsea
222 West Twenty-third Street
New York, NY 10011
(212) 243-3700
www.hotelchelsea.com

Besides the White Horse Tavern, the ghost of Dylan Thomas also is said to haunt the Hotel Chelsea, where the poet was lodging when he died. The hotel is rumored to be home to the spirits of novelist Thomas Wolfe and punk musician Sid Vicious as well.

## CHAPTER 14: A NIGHT TO REMEMBER

The Jane Hotel
113 Jane Street
New York, NY 10014
(212) 924-6700
www.thejanenyc.com

The hotel, completely refurbished in 2008, is the former American Seamen's Friend Society Sailors' Home and Institute. Located at the intersection with West Street, the Neoclassical building stretches from 113–115 Jane Street to 503–507 West Street. It was designated a New York City Landmark in 2000.

## CHAPTER 15: THE FACE ON THE TEN-DOLLAR BILL

The former Francis House
(current site of The Rembrandt apartments)
27 Jane Street
New York, NY 10014

The Rembrandt apartment building, with an entrance at 31 Jane Street, stands on the onetime site of the Francis House.

Trinity Churchyard
74 Trinity Place
New York, NY 10006

The churchyard is open 7 a.m. to 4 p.m. weekdays, 8 a.m. to 3 p.m. on Saturday and holidays, and 7 a.m. to 3 p.m. on Sunday. Alexander Hamilton's grave is in the southern portion of the cemetery in Division 12.

### CHAPTER 16: THE HOUSE ON BANK STREET

The Bank Street House
11 Bank Street
New York, NY 10014
Private residence. The house is no longer haunted.

### CHAPTER 17: THE ACCIDENTAL ARSONIST

The Waverly Inn
16 Bank Street
New York, NY 10014
(917) 828-1154

### CHAPTER 18: THE ASTOR APPARITIONS

The Public Theater
(the former Astor Library)
425 Lafayette Street
New York, NY 10003
(212) 539-8500
www.publictheater.org

Colonnade Row
428–434 Lafayette Street
New York, NY

Most of the interior spaces in the former Colonnade Row houses are private. The Astor Place Theatre, longtime home of Blue Man Group, is located at 434 Lafayette and can be visited during performances.

Sunnyside
9 West Sunnyside Lane
Irvington, NY 10533
(914) 591-8763

Tours are available of the historic Washington Irving home. The house is no longer said to be haunted.

## CHAPTER 19: THE SUBWAY SPECTRE

Astor Place subway station
Lafayette Street and Astor Place
New York, NY 10003

Astor Place is a short street approximately two blocks long that runs from Broadway to Third Avenue and St. Marks Place. The name also refers to the immediate vicinity surrounding the street.

City Hall subway station
New York Transit Museum
Boerum Place and Schermerhorn Street
Brooklyn, NY 11201
(718) 694-1600
www.mta.info/mta/museum

The New York City Transit Authority's main museum is located in Brooklyn Heights. There is also a gallery annex in Grand Central Station, just off the Main Concourse in the Shuttle Passage. In the past, the Transit Museum has given tours of the original City Hall subway station, but they have been infrequent in recent years. Even then they have been for members of the museum only. Check with the Transit Museum tour coordinator for details. Subway riders on the southbound 6 who remain on the car can catch a quick peek of the station before the train loops around for its northbound return. Not haunted.

The Shore Line Trolley Museum
17 River Street  East Haven, CT 06512
(203) 467-6927

What remains of August Belmont Jr.'s private subway car, Mineola, is owned by the Shore Line Trolley Museum. It's in need of massive restoration and is not kept on display.

### Chapter 20: Escape from Beyond

McSorley's Old Ale House
15 East Seventh Street
New York, NY 10003
(212) 478-9148
www.mcsorleysnewyork.com

The former Houdini brownstone
278 West 113th Street
New York, NY 10026

There have been no specific appearances reported, but it has long been thought that Houdini's spirit haunts his old home in the Morningside Heights district of Manhattan. The building is in private hands and may not be visited.

The Houdini mansion
2400 Laurel Canyon Boulevard
Hollywood, CA 90046

The house was on Laurel Canyon just north of the junction with Lookout Mountain Avenue and at the intersection with Willow Glen Road. At the time the Houdinis stayed there, the address for the mansion was 2398 Laurel Canyon Boulevard. The home was owned by R. J. Walker. The Houdinis most likely resided across the street in Walker's guesthouse located at 9435. The guesthouse is long gone. The mansion has been torn down, and the land is private property. Today a tall fence surrounds the lot, making it impossible to view from the road.

Knickerbocker Hotel
(now the Hollywood Knickerbocker Apartments)
1714 Ivar Avenue
Hollywood, CA 90028
(323) 463-0096

The former hotel has been converted into long-term apartments for seniors. There is no access permitted to the rooftop where the annual Houdini séances were held.

Houdini gravesite
Machpelah Cemetery
82–30 Cypress Hills Street
Ridgewood, NY 11385
(718) 366-5959

Houdini's burial site is not purported to be haunted. There are several graves on the Houdini plot, including those of

Houdini himself, his brother Theo, and their mother and father. Although there is a marker for Bess Houdini, she is actually buried at Gate of Heaven Cemetery in Hawthorne, New York.

## CHAPTER 21: THE BOUWERIE BOGEY

St. Mark's Church in-the-Bowery
131 East Tenth Street
New York, NY 10003
(212) 674-6377
www.stmarksbowery.org

Located at the intersection of Tenth Street, Stuyvesant Street, and Second Avenue. Times vary, but part of the churchyard is usually open during weekday business hours when staff members are in the offices. The church is open for services and can also be entered during special arts performances.

## CHAPTER 22: THE BIRD STILL "SINGS"

Tompkins Square Park
Between East Seventh and Tenth Streets and Avenues A and B
New York, NY 10009

Charlie Parker Place
Avenue B between Seventh and Tenth Streets

The former Charlie Parker residence
151 Avenue B
New York, NY 10009
Private residence.

## CHAPTER 23: THE BANSHEES AT THE BOWERY

The Bowery Hotel
335 Bowery
New York, NY 10003
(212) 505-9100
www.theboweryhotel.com

## CHAPTER 24: AS LUCK WOULD HAVE IT

KGB Bar
85 East Fourth Street
New York, NY 10003
(212) 505-3360

The KGB Bar is located on the second floor. EastVille Comedy Club and the Horse Trade Theater Group's two spaces (the Kraine Theater on the first floor and the Red Room upstairs) also operate out of the building. The entire property, especially the stairwell, seems to be haunted.

Hollywood Roosevelt Hotel
7000 Hollywood Boulevard
Hollywood, CA 90028
(323) 466-7000 or (800) 833-3333
www.hollywoodroosevelt.com

The mirror haunted by Marilyn Monroe is no longer on display. The hotel is filled with spirits, however. Among the most notable is Montgomery Clift. He stayed in Room 928 while filming *From Here to Eternity*. His ghost is never seen, but people hear his spirit inside that room playing a bugle (which he learned to do for the movie). His footsteps are also heard pacing the ninth floor. The Blossom Room, a meeting space off the lobby where the first Academy Awards were held, is haunted by a distinct cold spot—a two-story column of cold air—as well as the spectre of a dark male figure. The hotel is for registered guests and does not welcome casual sightseers.

## CHAPTER 25: THE SPINSTER SPIRIT

Merchant's House Museum
(also known as the Old Merchant's House Museum and the Seabury Tredwell House)
29 East Fourth Street
New York, NY 10003
(212) 777-1089
www.merchantshouse.com

The museum is open Thursday through Monday, noon to 5 p.m. There is a fee for admission, with discounts for seniors and students. Guided tours every Friday at 2 p.m., included with regular admission. The museum holds special exhibits as well as the permanent collection. In October the museum offers Candlelight Ghost Tours.

# Appendix C

# Take a Walk on the Wild Side

It can be a daunting task to navigate Greenwich Village. In fact, it's rather easy to get lost in the West Village among the angled side streets and short lanes. On the next several pages you'll find three short suggested walking tours that will take you past the most haunted sites the Village has to offer.

Each walk can be comfortably handled in a half day and covers one of the three main sections of the Village as defined by their traditional borders. The time you take will vary considerably depending upon whether you want to go inside the buildings or if seeing the façades is enough. The length of your walk will also be affected by all of the other stuff there is to do along the way in the Village—shopping, restaurants, and just plain people-watching.

The city subway is open 24/7. Many of the parks, however, have evening curfews. Museums and most churches also have restricted hours. Some of the venues, such as theaters, bars, and restaurants, can only be entered if you patronize the business. Also, visits onto the campus of NYU and entrance into its buildings are subject to university policy. If want to enter any of the facilities, please plan in advance. Check operating hours in Appendix B, on the Internet, by telephone, or at the site's box office. Finally, many of the houses on these tours are private residences and are not open to the public.

All of the recommended walks begin and end at Greenwich Village's most notable landmark, the Arch in Washington Square Park. That way, if you wish to combine two or more of the routes in a single day, you can do so without much backtracking. Naturally, you can start your walk at any place that strikes your fancy. For the most part, the order of the sites on the walk follows the sequence in which they were first mentioned in the book.

Accompanying each map on the following pages is a list of the haunted places. For each location, the numbered line gives the site's name, followed by the chapter in this book that tells its story. The second line is its address, and the third line of each listing gives a short description of the reported ghostly activity at that venue.

Please remember that these are all places where ghost or other paranormal activity has been reported in the past. There's no guarantee the sites are currently haunted.

In fact, some of the original venues may no longer be standing, and the street numbers of the buildings currently at those locations may be slightly different. Since the publication of this book, buildings may have been demolished, and businesses may have relocated. Although every effort has been made to be as precise as possible to pinpoint the sites' locations on the maps, they are necessarily approximate.

Let's start walking!

## THE CENTRAL VILLAGE

Before setting out on this route, please note that, except for services, the interior of the Church of the Ascension can only be visited for prayers on weekdays from noon to 1:00 p.m.

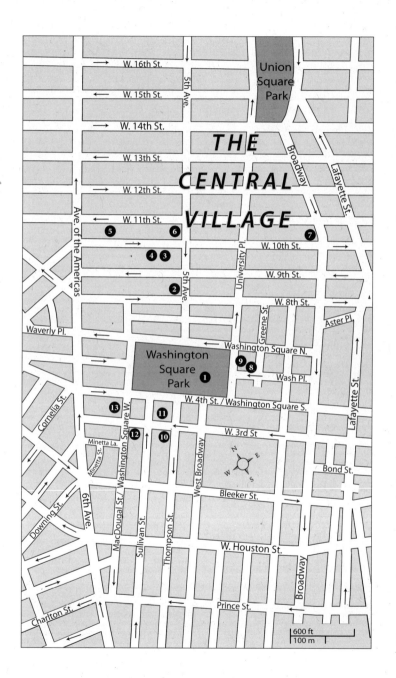

**THE CENTRAL VILLAGE**

W. 16th St.

W. 15th St.

5th Ave.

Union Square Park

W. 14th St.

W. 13th St.

Broadway

Lafayette St.

W. 12th St.

W. 11th St.

**⑤** **⑥**

**⑦**

W. 10th St.

**④③**

University Pl.

W. 9th St.

**②**

5th Ave.

W. 8th St.

Ave. of the Americas

Aster Pl.

Waverly Pl.

Greene St.

Washington Square N.

Washington Square Park

**①**

**⑨⑧**

Wash Pl.

Cornelia St.

**⑬**

Washington Square W.

**⑪**

W. 4th St. / Washington Square S.

Minetta La.

**⑫**

**⑩**

W. 3rd St

Minetta St.

N

W E

S

Bond St.

6th Ave.

Downing St.

MacDougal St. / Washington Square W.

Sullivan St.

Thompson St.

West Broadway

Bleeker St.

Lafayette St.

Broadway

W. Houston St.

Prince St.

Charlton St.

600 ft
100 m

**[1]** Washington Square Park (Chapter 1)

(Waverly Place, West Fourth Street, University Place, and MacDougal Street) Ghosts of original Native American inhabitants; people buried under square; innocent execution victims at Hangman's Elm; Marcel Duchamp, John Sloan, Gertrude Drick, and three companions atop the Arch; Edgar Allan Poe; Woody Guthrie; Eleanor and Franklin Roosevelt's Scottish terrier, Fala

**[2]** Little Thimble Theatre (Chapter 17)
10 Fifth Avenue

Items shift on tables and unexplained music in basement caused by unseen spirit

**[3]** The Mark Twain House (Chapter 2)
14 West Tenth Street

Mark Twain; up to twenty-two unidentified spirits

**[4]** The Emma Lazarus House (Chapter 2)
18 West Tenth Street

Emma Lazarus

**[5]** The Tenth Street Studio Building (Chapter 3)
51 West Tenth Street

John LaFarge; Margaret Perry LaFarge

**[6]** Church of the Ascension (Chapter 3)
Fifth Avenue and West Tenth Street

Presence felt of John LaFarge; accidents caused by his spirit

[7]The Brittany Residence Hall (Chapter 4)
55 East Tenth Street

Footsteps heard; presence felt of Molly, a former student

[8]Brown Building of Science (Chapter 5)
23–39 Washington Place

Urge to flee building; union picketers on sidewalk out front

[9]Silver Center for Arts and Sciences (Chapter 6)
(former site of NYU's Gothic Tower)
100 Washington Square East

Edgar Allan Poe; Samuel Morse; Walt Whitman

[10]The former Fire Patrol No. 2 (Chapter 6)
84 West Third Street

Schwartz, a fire patrolman from the 1930s

[11]The former Edgar Allan Poe House (Chapter 6)
85 West Third Street

Thumps and babbling voice in attic from spirit of madwoman
held captive there

[12]D'Agostino Residence Hall (Chapter 7)
110 West Third Street

Aaron Burr, alone or sometimes in phantom horse and carriage

[13]Provincetown Playhouse (Chapter 17)
133 MacDougal Street

Dark form on staircases; temperature drops; unexplained noises

## THE WEST VILLAGE

Walk begins at the northwest corner of Washington Square Park, heading west on Waverly Place.

[1]The former Paul Rudnick apartment (Chapter 8)
132 Waverly Place

John Barrymore in top floor apartment

[2]Norma Millay Ellis house (Chapter 8)
139 Waverly Place

Possible apparition of little girl in garden behind house

[3]The former Frank Paris residence (Chapter 9)
12 Gay Street

Footsteps and shadows on staircase; footsteps throughout house; man in tuxedo and cape; man in suit outside on pavement and doorstep; Paris's pet dog; scent of violets; odor of onions frying

[4]Marie's Crisis (Chapter 10)
59 Grove Street

Thomas Paine

[5]One If By Land Two If By Sea restaurant (Chapter 7)
17 Barrow Street

Aaron Burr; Theodosia Burr

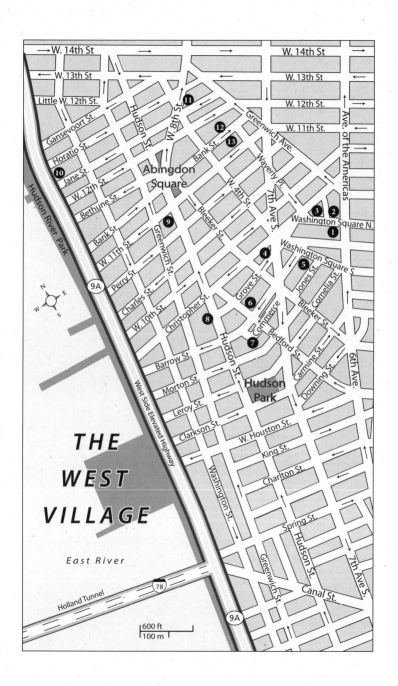

# THE WEST VILLAGE

W. 14th St
W. 13th St
Little W. 12th St.
Gansevoort St.
Horatio St.
Jane St.
W. 12th St.
Bethune St.
Bank St.
W. 11th St.
Perry St.
Charles St.
W. 10th St.
Barrow St.
Morton St.
Leroy St.
Clarkson St.

Hudson St.
W. 8th St.
Bank St.
Greenwich Ave.
W. 12th St.
W. 11th St.
Abingdon Square
Greenwich St.
Bleeker St.
W. 4th St.
Waverly Pl.
Christopher St.
Hudson St.
Grove St.
Commerce
Bedford St.
Hudson Park
W. Houston St.
King St.
Charlton St.
Washington St.
Spring St.
Greenwich St.
Hudson St.
Canal St.

W. 14th St
W. 13th St
W. 12th St.
W. 11th St.
Ave. of the Americas
7th Ave. S.
Washington Square N.
Washington Square S.
Jones St.
Cornelia St.
Bleecker St.
Carmine St.
Downing St.
6th Ave.
7th Ave. S.

Hudson River Park
9A
West Side Elevated Highway

East River

78
Holland Tunnel
9A

N E W S

600 ft
100 m

**1** **2** **3** **4** **5** **6** **7** **8** **9** **10** **11** **12** **13**

**[6]** Chumley's Bar (Chapter 11)
86 Bedford Street

Henrietta Chumley; Leland Chumley; breaking glasses; unexplained jazz music; erratic jukebox

**[7]** Cherry Lane Theatre (Chapter 8)
38 Commerce Street

Male phantom in white at top of lobby staircase and male ghost in hallway near dressing room, thought by some to be Aaron Burr, Thomas Paine, or Washington Irving

**[8]** The Church of Saint Luke in the Fields (Chapter 12)
487 Hudson Street

Clement C. Moore

**[9]** The White Horse Tavern (Chapter 13)
567 Hudson Street

Dylan Thomas; dark figure in cape; unknown traveler and the Native American servant who prepared his remains for burial

**[10]** Hotel Jane (Chapter 14)
113 Jane Street

Moaning sounds from spectral survivors of the *Titanic* crew; cold spots; erratic elevator

**[11]** The former Francis House (Chapter 15)
27 Jane Street

Alexander Hamilton

[12]The Bank Street House (Chapter 16)
11 Bank Street

Disembodied footsteps caused by hidden cremated ashes of Elizabeth Bullock

[13]The Waverly Inn (Chapter 17)
16 Bank Street

Phantom dressed in nineteenth-century waistcoat and top hat who plays with fire

## THE EAST VILLAGE

Walk begins at the northeast corner of Washington Square Park, heading east on Waverly Place.

[1]Colonnade Row (Chapter 18)
428–434 Lafayette Street

Washington Irving

[2]The Public Theater (Chapter 18)
(the former Astor Library)
425 Lafayette Street

Austin L. Sands; Washington Irving; Joseph Papp; Jewish immigrants from HIAS period

[3]Astor Place subway station (Chapter 19)
Lafayette Street and Astor Place

The Mineola (August Belmont Jr.'s private subway car)

**[4]** McSorley's Old Ale House (Chapter 20)
15 East Seventh Street

Harry Houdini; phantom black cat

**[5]** St. Mark's Church in-the-Bowery (Chapter 21)
131 East Tenth Street

Peter Stuyvesant; three or four unidentified female phantoms, one of which may be Matilda Hoffman

**[6]** The former Charlie Parker residence (Chapter 22)
151 Avenue B

Charlie "Bird" Parker

**[7]** Charlie Parker Place (Chapter 22)
Avenue B between Seventh and Tenth Streets

Charlie "Bird" Parker

**[8]** Tompkins Square Park (Chapter 22)
Bordered by East Seventh and Tenth Streets and Avenues A and B

Charlie "Bird" Parker

**[9]** Il Buco (Chapter 6)
47 Bond Street

Spirit thought to be Edgar Allan Poe that empties bottles in the cellar

**[10]** The former Jean Cocteau Repertory Theatre (Chapter 17)
330 Bowery

Presence felt of former troupe member

**[11]**The Bowery Hotel (Chapter 23)
335 Bowery

Unidentified female spirit in white on second floor; electrical disturbances; erratic elevator

**[12]** Fire Station Engine 33, Ladder 9 (Chapter 6)
42 Great Jones Street

An unidentified former fireman at the station

**[13]**KGB Bar (Chapter 24)
85 East Fourth Street

Frank Conroy; an unidentified figure on the staircase; a headless man; a dark figure's reflection in a mirror on the second landing; Charles "Lucky" Luciano

**[14]**Merchant's House Museum (Chapter 25)
29 East Fourth Street

Gertrude Tredwell; Seabury Tredwell; servants; moving objects; scent of flowers, violet toilet water, and baking bread; rappings; piano that plays itself; children's footsteps

# About the Author

**Tom Ogden** is one of America's most celebrated magicians. He has performed professionally for more than thirty-five years, from the tinsel and sawdust of the circus ring to the glitter and sequins of Las Vegas, Atlantic City, and Lake Tahoe. He has opened for such acts as Robin Williams, Billy Crystal, and the Osmonds.
His work has taken him to more than a hundred countries and all seven continents.

Ogden's television work has included appearances on NBC's *The World's Greatest Magic II* and FOX's *The Great Magic of Las Vegas,* as well as numerous commercials. He has twice been voted "Parlour Magician of the Year" at the famed Magic Castle in Hollywood and has received a dozen additional nominations in other categories.

Ogden's books include *200 Years of the American Circus* (which was named a Best Reference Work by both the American Library Association and the New York Public Library), *Wizards and Sorcerers, The Complete Idiot's Guide to Magic Tricks, The Complete Idiot's Guide to Ghosts and Hauntings, The Complete Idiot's Guide to Street Magic,* and five books in Globe Pequot Press's "Haunted" series. He has also been profiled in *Writer's Market.*

Ogden resides in Los Angeles.